Praise for *The Digital Marketing Handbook*

The Digital Marketing Handbook stands right next to my copy
of *The Copywriter's Handbook* and will soon be a classic in the
online marketer's world. Bly walks his talk and knows from
firsthand experience the type of websites that can work for your
business. The chapter on funnels is vital for building trust with
your customers! Don't just read this book—use Bly's strategies
daily to reap real profits in the virtual world!

—PETER FOGEL, AUTHOR AND COPYWRITER WWW.PUBLICSPEAKLIKEAPRO.COM
PUBLIC SPEAK LIKE A PRO

Bob Bly's *The Digital Marketing Handbook* is a must-read for
anyone thinking about starting a website that sells. Bob leaves
nothing on the table . . . you get the full benefit of his almost
four decades of marketing and copywriting experience in this
step-by-step guide for becoming a successful digital marketer.

—KATIE YEAKLE, EXECUTIVE DIRECTOR OF AWAI

Anyone can create an ecommerce website, but Bob Bly cuts through
the fog of how to make it into a profit center. Featuring actual
websites, specific examples, and clear step-by-step
instructions, this guide should be on the desk of
every ecommerce entrepreneur.

—STEVE FANTASIA, BRIGHT SOURCE MEDIA, INC.

The Digital Handbook stands beside a half dozen books on my
credenza. I've read it and intend to read again. In this case, it's
because a single reading is not enough to absorb more than
a fraction of the valuable insights, strategies and tips
contained inside this valuable compendium of
current marketing knowhow.

—MARK FORD, AUTHOR, ENTREPRENEUR, PUBLIS
CREATING WEALTH AND WEALTH BUILD

Bob has done it again! Every book he writes is not only filled with useful, actionable advice but he is able to explain it in a way that everyone understands. And his latest book, *The Digital Marketing Handbook*, is no exception. Bob virtually takes you by the hand and tells you exactly what you need to do to create a website that sells. If you want to increase your online bottom line this year, READ THIS BOOK!

—MARYELLEN TRIBBY, FOUNDER AND CEO OF WORKINGMOMSONLY.COM, AUTHOR OF *REINVENTING THE ENTREPRENEUR*

Bob Bly's focus on the various online revenue models, and thorough explanation of each type, provides thoughtful and invaluable insight that can greatly help an internet entrepreneur decide which direction to take. I particularly enjoyed the sections explaining the Agora model as well as the discussion on potential AdSense revenue streams. This book is rich in actionable strategies by an author who enjoys helping others develop multiple streams of both passive and active income.

—RON JASPER, CEO OF CONATIVE INFORMATION TECHNOLOGY

By far, one of the most comprehensive A to Z guides for online marketers. Every entry-level or mid-level marketer would benefit from this resource as part of their library.

—CAROLYN HINSON, EXECUTIVE MARKETING DIRECTOR OF WELLNESS RESEARCH AND CONSULTING

The Digital Marketing Handbook is an excellent tool. It takes what can seem to be a difficult cycle of creating an ecommerce solution that makes steady sales to a simple concept that anyone can do successfully. I found it very enlightening. Whether you have a website now or want to build one, you should start by reading this book.

—KIMBERLY CATALANO, SENIOR VICE PRESIDENT MARKETING AND SALES OF GALAXY PRESS

THE **DIGITAL MARKETING** HANDBOOK

A STEP-BY-STEP GUIDE

TO CREATING WEBSITES

THAT SELL

ROBERT W. BLY

AUTHOR OF *THE MARKETING PLAN HANDBOOK*

Entrepreneur
PRESS

Entrepreneur Press, Publisher
Cover Design: Andrew Welyczko
Production and Composition: Eliot House Productions

This publication is designed to provide accurate and authoritative information
in regard to the subject matter covered. It is sold with the understanding that
the publisher is not engaged in rendering legal, accounting or other professional
services. If legal advice or other expert assistance is required, the services of a
competent professional person should be sought.

Library of Congress Cataloging-in-Publication Data
  Names: Bly, Robert W., author.
  Title: The digital marketing handbook: a step-by-step guide to creating
      websites that sell / by Robert W. Bly.
  Description: Irvine, California : Entrepreneur Media, Inc., [2018]
  Identifiers: LCCN 2017050089| ISBN 978-1-59918-621-4 (alk. paper)
      | ISBN 1-59918-621-7 (alk. paper)
  Subjects: LCSH: Internet marketing. | Electronic commerce.
  Classification: LCC HF5415.1265 .B579 2018 | DDC 658.8/72—dc23
  LC record available at https://lccn.loc.gov/2017050089

Printed in the United States of America

22 21 20 19 18   10 9 8 7 6 5 4 3 2 1

To Dr. Ryan Subrati

CONTENTS

ACKNOWLEDGMENTS

As always, thanks to my literary agent, Bob Diforio, for finding a home for this book. I am grateful to my editors, Jennifer Dorsey, Vanessa Campos, Corbin Collins, and Karen Billipp, for having me write the book for Entrepreneur Press and making it much better than it was when the manuscript first crossed their desks. Thanks to Jennifer Holmes, Kim Stacey, Aimee Beck, Marilyn Pincus, and Justin Cassata for their invaluable editorial and research assistance. And to Craig Murphy of ALTAgency.co.uk for his insight into the psychology of web marketing.

I owe a debt of gratitude to Daniel Dumanig, my web master, and Jodi Van Valkenburg, my internet marketing manager, for helping me run my little online information products business, CTC Publishing. Finally, thanks to all of my clients, colleagues, and others who either increased my knowledge of making money on the web or provided information, ideas, tips, or samples of their work.

A few sections of the book appeared, in slightly different form, in articles published in *Target Marketing, Early to Rise, The Direct Response Letter, Mequoda Daily,* and *DM News.*

INTRODUCTION

In the early days of the internet, the first websites were known as "billboard sites." They displayed static pages, often with relatively dry and straightforward sales copy about the company, its products, and its services. At that point, businesses just wanted to establish a web presence with their sites and to provide product information online—not to turn a profit directly from the site.

Today, websites are increasingly morphing from pretty pictures and repositories of product information into something much more valuable: business-building assets that not only support branding and feed prospects' information needs, but also build a relationship with customers and function as highly profitable cash-flow machines—digital assets that generate more inquiries, leads, prospects, customers, orders, and sales *directly from the site*.

In short, web marketing is evolving from a cost center into a profit center—which is good news for you! In this book, I'll show you how to make that transition, converting your website from pretty pictures on a static page into a powerful ancillary (or even primary) revenue producer for your business—one that can make you and your company a lot more money.

If your websites are already making money, I'll show you how to take them to the next level so they generate even more revenues— potentially much more. That's possible because websites have transformed from a general advertising medium into a direct-response channel. And when you're doing direct response, no matter how well your marketing is performing, you can almost always do better.

If you want your websites to produce more immediate results for your existing brick-and-mortar store, service business, or other traditional business, I'll show you how to upgrade your digital marketing with online business models, calls to action, lead magnets, inquiry generators, traffic drivers, and other tools that will multiply the return on investment (ROI) from your website and related web marketing as never before—mainly by adapting proven direct-response marketing methods to your web activities.

Why do I say your business's digital marketing should embrace direct response? Here are three quick examples to give you a taste of what I mean, with dozens more to come throughout this book, along with full explanations and instructions for implementation:

- ◆ *You send an email inviting prospects to download a free white paper.* They click on a link, go to a landing page, fill in their information, click Submit, and get the free white paper— and you have captured a name, email address, and sales lead to follow up and convert to a customer. That's classic lead-generating direct marketing—not branding or image advertising.
- ◆ *You put together a webinar.* You send out emails driving prospects to a registration page, and people register. Your audience hears your message, and you make special offers to them during and after the event via email follow-up. This is typical direct-response seminar marketing, only electronic instead of with a newspaper ad or mailed paper brochure.

◆ *You run online ads in various enewsletters and banners on websites.* You also rent elists and send those prospects email marketing messages. In response, people click to a web page promoting a product, part, or other item. A percentage of visitors go to your shopping cart and pay with credit card or PayPal. You make direct sales—what we in the pre-digital age called "mail order marketing"—or one-step direct marketing.

With direct response as your driving force and primary objective, your websites can do better. A lot better. That means more traffic, conversions, leads, customers, orders, sales, and profits. By combining proven direct-response methods with the technological capabilities inherent in all your digital marketing—websites, landing pages, online ads, email marketing, social media, blogs, and more—you can take your business to the next level. Be your company's marketing hero. Help your business make more money than ever before. And in doing so, see your own compensation, income, and wealth rise to unprecedented levels.

On the off chance that your business does not even have a website, this book is your opportunity to launch your site on the right track. Read Chapter 1, choose the right online business model from the get-go, and you'll be light years ahead of competitors who haven't got a clue about how to monetize their sites.

And yes, you do need a website, whether you are an industrial distributor or a neighborhood thrift shop. In the internet age, your organization's digital presence is paramount to success: according to a survey from *Enterprise Innovation*, 86 percent of respondents look to the internet first when searching for information or recommendations.

I have been in marketing since the late 1970s. Like many of those in my generation, I have profitably adapted our proven direct-marketing and -selling techniques to websites and other digital marketing channels, including email, online ads, landing pages, content marketing, and even social media.

Now, in *The Digital Marketing Handbook: A Step-by-Step Guide to Creating Websites That Sell,* I want to share with you tested direct-response methods that can increase your online revenues 50 percent, 100 percent, even 200 percent or more. How much more? With direct response, the sky is the limit. So get ready for the ride of your life as you make your internet sales soar to the stratosphere.

I do have a favor to ask. If you have found a digital marketing medium or technique that works like gangbusters for you, please let me know so I can share it with readers of the next edition of this book. You can reach me here:

Bob Bly
Copywriter and Internet Marketing Strategist
www.bly.com

Here's to happy—and profitable—reading. I fully believe the strategies in this book can totally transform your business—as they have for me, my clients, and my colleagues.

CHAPTER 1

CHOOSING YOUR ONLINE BUSINESS MODEL

Today, it is easier than ever to create a website. Anyone can do it. And if you go online, it seems as if almost everyone has: more than a billion websites occupy the internet today.

But how many of those billion-plus sites actually make money directly? A small minority. For instance, *Forbes* reports that there are only 102,728 ecommerce retailers in the U.S. generating sales of $12,000 a year or more each—a tiny fraction of the total online retail sites. As for non-ecommerce websites, an astounding number of these marketers don't even know how much or whether their site is contributing to the bottom line.

A big reason why so many sites just sit there on a server instead of making money is that most businesses have not figured out how to monetize the web, meaning use their site to make more sales. This book is primarily about how to turn your website from a mere online presence into a profit center that can make thousands or even millions for you and your company.

Having even a small slice of the online-sales pie can make you rich beyond the dreams of avarice. According to eMarketer Daily (12.6.2017), 3.47 billion people use the internet regularly. What's more, Akamai's report "The State of Online Retail Performance" says that total ecommerce sales in 2016 exceeded $350 billion, up 15.6 percent over the previous year. The revenues generated by websites of conventional brick-and-mortar businesses—which typically use the web mainly for branding, conveying product information, and lead generation—are more difficult to measure.

The first step in making more money from your websites is not to just have a bunch of pages with content but to build your websites using one of several online business models proven to generate web revenue.

In addition to being the first step, picking the right online business model is also the most important step in making more money from your websites for two reasons: first, without the right model, you may get plenty of traffic, clicks, impressions, page views, downloads, and even opt-ins. But you won't make much money if any at all. Second, once you build a site and program it, changing to a different model is tremendously difficult, time consuming, and costly. So if you can, choose the right model first, and then build the site. Obviously, for your existing sites, you will have to retool them to follow a proven business model. More labor for you? A bit, yes. But I'll give you shortcuts to help you do it better and faster.

Today, there are a number of website models, and associated internet marketing campaigns built around them, proven to generate significant revenues. In this chapter, I'll show you the major models, how they work, and the pros and cons of each.

Your homework will be to pick one. And keep this in mind: choosing the right model is a critical step in monetizing your web presence—the foundation upon which your profits are built. So pick wisely.

Central vs. Hub-and-Spoke Model

Information marketer Fred Gleeck once said to me, "If you want to make $500,000 a year online, it's easier to have 10 sites producing

$50,000 each, or 50 sites generating $10,000 each, than to build one site and build its revenue to the half-million-dollar mark."

So one decision is whether you want to build one central high-profit site, such as Amazon, or build your digital marketing presence with the hub-and-spoke model of a group of microsites, as both Fred Gleeck and I do (see Figure 1–1).

As a rule of thumb, larger businesses tend to gravitate toward the central site model because they have the resources to create and manage them. For a small operator on a limited budget, the

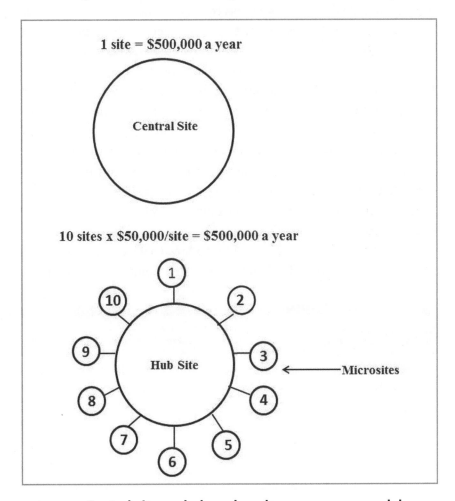

FIGURE 1–1. **Central site vs. hub-and-spoke ecommerce model.**

hub-and-spoke model is easier to start and build. Also, merchandise and service businesses favor the central site model, while information marketers gravitate toward a hub-and-spoke model.

Most businesses that have microsites also have a central site from which all microsites can be reached via hyperlinks. The central site is the hub, and the microsites are the spokes.

If you choose the hub-and-spoke model, use a hosting service that hosts an unlimited number of sites for a fixed monthly fee. For instance, if you operate a hundred microsites and pay $49 a month for hosting, which I do, your cost is less than half a dollar per site a month.

Also, choose a shopping cart system, such as 1ShoppingCart or Infusionsoft, that reports activity both by microsite and total. Figure 1–2 shows the total revenue from all my sites for a given week. Note that if you can average $10,000 a week from your collection of microsites, that comes out to gross revenues of half a million dollars in sales a year.

For the microsites' domain names, you can either make them an extension of your main domain or create a unique domain for each. For instance, my enewsletter subscription page is www.bly.com/reports. You can have a virtually unlimited number of pages with such extensions on your main domain.

On the other hand, my microsite on how to write and sell ebooks is at www.myveryfirstebook.com. Dedicated domains for microsites

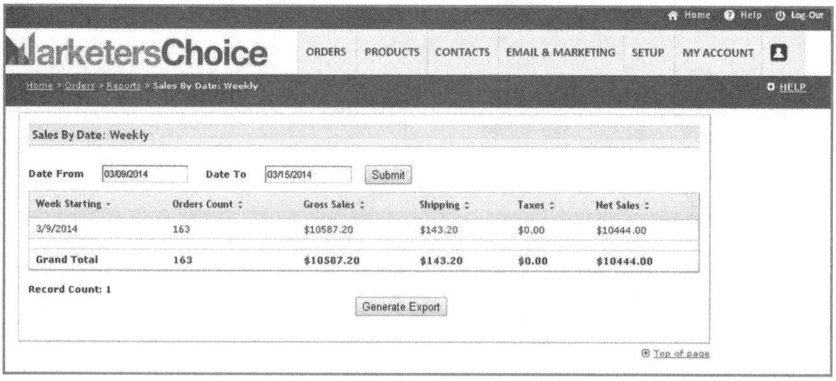

FIGURE 1–2. **Sales report for one week of sales in my online business.**

should be short and easy to remember. That way, when you are speaking to someone and want to send them to your microsite, you can easily remember the domain.

Is having many separate domains expensive? No. It's cheap. It costs about $8 or $9 a year for the domain name fee, and about 50 cents a month for hosting. A domain and site constitute the real estate of the internet, and it's a lot less expensive than physical real estate. Yet it can make you as much or more money.

Traditional Central Site

The central sites for thousands of traditional companies, from small and medium-size to Fortune 500, use a traditional website layout and design, as shown in Figure 1–3 on page 6. These conventionally de-signed websites have a homepage, which is the page you come to when you click on the site URL, and secondary pages each devoted to a different topic; e.g., a specific product, a single service, overview of capabilities, applications, company history, and whatever additional topics the marketer wants to cover and the website visitors are interested in.

These single-topic secondary pages are reached by clicking buttons in the menus displayed in the top, side, and bottom margins of the main homepage—sections B, D, and E in Figure 1–3. The button has a description or name of the page (e.g., About Us) and a hyperlink to that page.

The homepage should immediately and on its own tell visitors what is being sold, who it is for, and why they should be interested. The secondary pages taken together should cover two things: 1) what the marketer wants visitors to know and 2) what visitors coming to the site want to know and are looking for.

For instance, on www.bly.com, I have a page titled Clients, because potential copywriting clients always ask, "What companies have you written copy for?" It is something they want to know. I also have a page titled Case Studies, which are short success stories about work I have done for clients. People don't ask me for case studies, but I know that showing them, even though unasked for, helps close many sales.

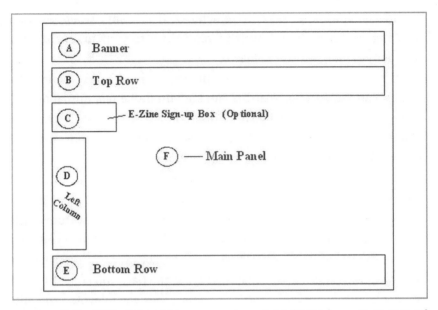

FIGURE 1–3. **Traditional non-ecommerce central site layout; B, D, and E are hyperlink menu buttons to secondary site pages.**

My main site, www.bly.com, is a traditional central site. The web-monitoring site StatShow.com reports that this site has a global rank of number 88,732, putting it in the top 100,000 most popular websites worldwide. Online for more than two decades, bly.com reaches roughly 161,340 users and gets 354,960 page views each month.

In Chapter 10, I take you through www.bly.com so you can see the page-by-page design and organization of a standard central site. For my information product sales, I have a dedicated microsite for each product, as described in the hub and spoke model; you can see these sites by going to the menu at the bottom of the www.bly.com homepage and clicking on Products.

Ecommerce Central Site

Bigger online retailers use central sites that are traditional ecommerce online stores. "The writing on the wall is clear," says Ryan Deiss, CEO of DigitalMarketer. "If you sell products to consumers, you need a high-converting ecommerce store."

Amazon is the 800-pound gorilla in this space, with Alibaba closing in. Amazon sells around 350 million different products online, making it a giant web department store of sorts, the equivalent of a digital Walmart or Target.

More common than the big multiproduct ecommerce sites are smaller ecommerce stores selling a single line of products. A good example is Blue Nile, which specializes in diamond jewelry, or Pro Flowers for flowers.

Open up the Blue Nile site www.bluenile.com as you read this section. It's really a model for how to create a single-product-line ecommerce site vs. a multiproduct online store such as Amazon.

The Blue Nile homepage is cleanly and clearly laid out; in fact, it's almost too stark; though they were obviously going for an understates and elegant look to match the brand image.

At the top is a banner with the Blue Nile logo and the tag line, "Love Is Brilliant." It's a relevant play on words because diamonds are valued for their brilliance.

The copy, or text, under the banner positions the site more effectively: "You'll only *look* like you spent a million." From there, the homepage has pictures of jewelry and product descriptions that are hyperlinked to pages showing and describing those products. Simple, basic, and sensible.

But the site is not just product display, description, and selling. There is a menu button at top right called Education. When you click on it, you get a rich library of useful information on diamonds and how to shop for, judge, and buy them.

The mission of the website—to help the consumer shop for and buy a diamond or other jewelry online—is crystal clear. The entire site is designed to make the transaction as easy and painless as possible.

Most of the hyperlinks on the homepage go to specific products, so you can see what stones and jewelry are available. These pages are augmented by a useful but not overwhelming choice of helpful content and functionality—mainly tips on buying diamonds, product searches, and interactive jewelry design.

It's fun and easy to shop for jewelry on Blue Nile. You can easily find what you are looking for, the shopping cart works well, and links let you drill down for more product detail and consumer information, whether it's a close-up photograph of a ring or a schematic diagram showing how a certain setting holds the stone in place.

On an ecommerce site, the major tasks the user wants to complete include a) shopping for and finding products, b) learning more details about products, c) completing a purchase, and d) handling customer service-related activities such as reporting a problem with delivery or canceling or returning an order. The Blue Nile site gets an A+ for the first three tasks and an A for the fourth.

The page layouts are nearly perfect. Adequate use of white space creates a clean, uncluttered look and makes the images—jewelry photos—stand out. You never feel overwhelmed by the text or graphics and so are inclined to spend more time browsing and shopping: a very pleasant experience.

One way to increase orders on your ecommerce websites is to offer a strong money-back guarantee of satisfaction. Blue Nile's policy reads: "Our 30-day money-back guarantee gives you time to make sure your purchase is perfect. If you need to return it for any reason, we'll happily provide you with an exchange or full refund." Figure 1–4 shows a guarantee I use on some of my microsites.

FIGURE 1–4. **Money-back guarantee for a website.**

Single-Topic Content-Rich Site for Enthusiasts

Blue Nile is not for geologists, jewelry designers, or rock or gem collectors; it is a consumer product site for anyone who wants to buy diamond jewelry.

On the other hand, an "enthusiast" website is one designed for people who are highly interested or even have an obsession with a topic, activity, sport, hobby, or field of knowledge. Figure 1–5 on page 10 shows a site for World War II enthusiasts, Figure 1–6 on page 11 is the homepage for a site on chemistry, and Figure 1–7 on page 12 is my site for aquarium hobbyists.

Enthusiast sites attract an audience by offering lots of free content for visitors on the site's main topic. They make money in several ways: selling advertising on the site; selling merchandise on the site that the site owner buys from manufacturers and wholesalers at a discount; and running Google AdSense. When you sign up for Google AdSense, Google automatically places ads on your site for products the Google algorithm has determined your visitors might buy.

You get paid by pay-per-click (PPC) actions from visitors on your website (also microsites, blogs, and social media channels). You must reach $100 by the 20th of each month before AdSense will send you your payment unless you have a hold on your account, which could be for any number of reasons. You need to have the hold cleared before the 20th of each month to still get paid that month or wait until the next month to get your money. Go here to learn more: www.google.com/adsense/start/how-it-works/#/.

While you can add Google AdSense to some social media venues, you can also use Google Ad Exchange, which offers some added capabilities such as anonymous or semi-transparent brand inventory (shows up to the side of a Google search result with product pictures but no brand); provision for fixed CPMs (cost per thousand impressions) in Preferred Deals; and Private Auctions and Multiple Buyers. Other perks include advertiser blocking (so competitors don't advertise on your site), ad technologies blocking, and cookie and data usage blocking, per the DoubleClick Ad Exchange Seller forum. You can find out more about the differences

FIGURE 1–5. **Website for World War II enthusiasts offering books, DVDs, merchandise, and free content.**

FIGURE 1–6. **Chemistry website offering free content, chemistry sets, chemicals, and lab equipment.**

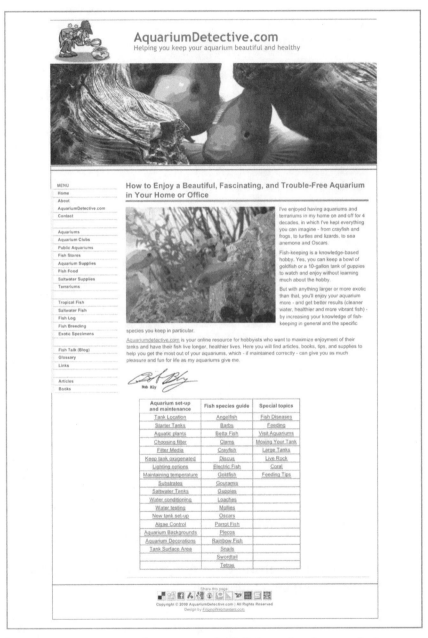

FIGURE 1–7. **Homepage for my tropical fish enthusiast website; I still need to add affiliate links to sites selling fish tanks and supplies.**

between AdSense and Ad Exchange here: https://support.google.com/adxseller/answer/4599464?hl=en.

Aside from selling products and services from your website or your blog, AdSense is the one way to make money without having to do much else after you get it all set up. You can also use other ad networks, such as www.Sharethrough.com, www.Content.ad, www.Kixer.com (ads on mobile apps), Adsterra Network (https://adsterra.com), Ad Maven (www.ad-maven.com), www.Adbuff.com, www.AdBlade.com, and others. Always check with your hosting provider to make sure you can do this first.

The Agora Model

The Agora Model (Figure 1–8) is a widely used business model for on-line information marketing but now is also used to sell merchandise. It was pioneered by financial, travel, and health newsletter publisher Agora.

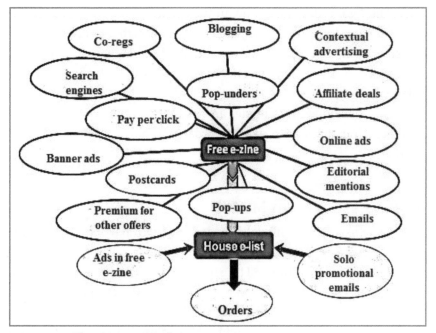

FIGURE 1–8. **The Agora Model.**

The ovals with arrows pointing to the rectangle labeled "Free ezine" are various methods of driving web traffic. They include online ads, email marketing, affiliate deals, postcards, search engines, blog posts, and other traffic drivers explained throughout the book. The goal of a traffic driver is to get the user to click on a symbol or word that is hyperlinked to a web page or form.

In the Agora Model, you use the traffic drivers to send people not to your homepage or a product microsite, but to a page specifically designed for getting people to opt in to your list by subscribing to a free online newsletter. By doing so, you build your opt-in elist of people who have given you their email address and, more important, permission to send them emails. You own and control the list—unlike, say, your Facebook or LinkedIn group, which Facebook or LinkedIn can shut down on a whim.

In online marketing, two of the most valuable assets you can own are a well-optimized website that ranks on the first screen of the Google search engine results page (SERP) and a large and responsive elist. The Agora Model is based on the latter.

As you build your elist, you market to subscribers in two primary ways: ads in your enewsletter and standalone email marketing messages sent to the list. The latter generate the bulk of your online sales.

Agora developed this model and used it to build an information marketing business with sales approaching half a billion dollars a year.

Needs Assessment Model

The needs assessment model invites visitors to participate in a free online needs assessment or evaluation in the topic of the site, such as weight loss with eDiets. The site recommends products you can purchase based on your answers to the assessment questions. You are sold a low-price or "front end" product to start, then upsold to a more expensive "back end" product after purchasing the entry-level product.

Over a decade ago, when I first clicked onto the www.ediets.
com homepage, the main graphic featured a picture of actress Victoria
Principal. As the site evolved, ediets.com eventually switched to
a photo of a woman who looks more like the visitor and is not a
celebrity.

The homepage is what I call "tabloid style"—lots of interesting
little items to choose from. I don't love tabloid-style homepages
because there's no single point of focus and no unifying positioning
copy to tie it all together or define the site's brand. But they work,
which is what matters most.

Your eye might be drawn to the call to action (CTA) for the meal
plan to the left of the woman's photo or the Free Diet Profile under
it. You enter your height, weight, and age and then click through a
series of screens asking you more questions. EDiets can then design
a customized weight loss plan for you, for which they charge a
monthly fee. Along the way, you are offered a number of free ezine
subscriptions and information on advertised products.

On my first visit to the site, I completed the Diet Profile but did not
purchase the recommended diet plan. When I returned to the profile
a month later to update it, I was immediately served a page that said,
"Welcome back, Bob. We've saved all your information. Click here to
view it now. Click here for a special offer for return visitors!"

The eDiets site helps users choose which information program
is best for them. Choices include diets, meal plans, exercise
programs, and support. The site then communicates with you daily
and automatically with emails containing timely, personalized
information and inspiration.

Much of the advice is customized based on your answers to online
questionnaires. Interaction with the site is personalized, and the
content you receive is tailored based on your age, weight, body mass
index, eating habits, exercise routines, and other relevant personal
data. After all, how can you give me exercise advice if you don't know
how lean or heavy I am or what kind of shape I am in?

All the terms and information on the site are written in plain
English aimed at a lay audience: weight, exercise, diet, meal plans,

recipes, fitness, and personal trainer. There's no nutritional or medical jargon of any kind.

The pages are relatively clean and easy to read. In some instances, however, too many options and items are jammed onto the screen, creating a slightly cluttered look.

The site is sensibly organized into sections, and you can choose from using the buttons at the top of the screen or boxes and sidebars below.

Funnels

The sales funnel is an online business model you can use in tandem with a central website or the hub-and-spoke model.

For a B2B website, the sales funnel converts traffic to sales in stages: capturing the prospect's contact information; qualifying the lead; nurturing the lead throughout the sales cycle; helping prospects explore the products; engaging potential customers and clients; and finally closing the sale.

For an information marketing business, the funnel captures the name and email address to build the list, upsells to an inexpensive front-end product, and then cross-sells and upsells additional product.

The methods for constructing sales funnels for both consumer and B2B products and services are so vital to maximizing website ROI that I cover them in more detail in Chapters 3, 4, and 5.

Launches

The product launch formula (PLF) is an internet marketing tactic or model pioneered by Jeff Walker and described by him in his book *Launch* (Morgan James 2014).

The formula has four steps, each a sequence of emails and in some cases other promotions as well:

1. *Pre-Prelaunch.* You use this to start building anticipation among your most loyal fans. The pre-prelaunch is also used to judge how receptive the market will be to your offer.

2. *Prelaunch*. This is where you gradually romance your market with three pieces of high-value prelaunch content, while also answering the objections of your market, over a period of 5 to 12 days.

3. *Launch*. Your launch sequence starts with the email that says, "We're open, you can finally buy now," and continues for a finite amount of time, usually anywhere from 24 hours to 7 days, until you finally shut it down.

4. *Post-Launch*. This is the cleanup sequence, where you follow up with your new clients as well as the prospects who didn't buy from you.

Used primarily for information products, the launch can generate massive sales of a single product within a relatively short time period.

Membership Sites

Membership sites have long been a popular model for entrepreneurial internet marketers selling information products, advice, coaching, and consulting. More recently, businesses selling merchandise and services have begun creating membership sites to generate ancillary passive income—anything that makes money without direct labor— as an adjunct to their core business.

Generating passive income is one of the great things about a membership site. Passive income streams generate positive cash flow for you on Sundays, holidays, vacations, and even while you sleep. With active income streams, you get paid only when you are working.

The tradeoff with a passive income stream site, specifically a membership site, is this: with any passive income generator online, there is a lot of work upfront, with minimal revenue until the site is established and running. But from then on, it can generate a nice monthly revenue stream with little or no additional work on your part.

By comparison, you can ramp up an active income stream, particularly for a service business, fairly rapidly and start generating revenue right away without a huge investment in infrastructure. But then you have to continually work and perform the service to make money; it never lets up. Figure 1–9 compares the revenue of passive vs. active income.

With a membership site generating passive income, you can supplement your core business income with a second cash flow stream. For this reason, I often advise solopreneurs and SOHO (small office, home office) businesses to develop at least two income streams, one active and one passive, and to build each to annual six-figure revenues. That way, if you can't or don't want to work anymore, you can live nicely on the passive income with little or no effort on

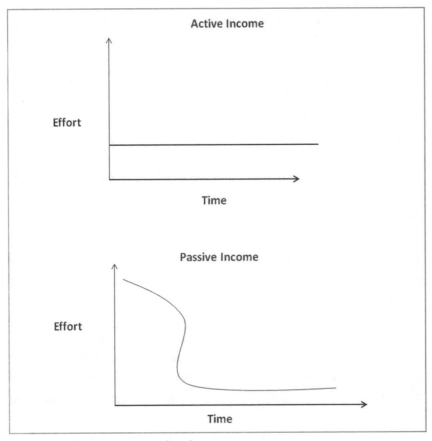

FIGURE 1–9. **Active vs. passive income.**

your part. Membership sites are covered in greater detail in Chapter 15. You can see the homepage of my membership site in Figure 1–10.

FIGURE 1–10. **My membership site's homepage, produced in partnership with Fred Gleeck.**

CHAPTER 2

PROFITS EQUAL SALES MINUS EXPENSES

The formula for website profitability is: $P = S - E$. That stands for profits equal sales minus expenses.

Most digital marketers concentrate on maximizing sales. That's essential in building your business.

But you can also achieve higher profitability by reducing expenses. Many businesses do things too expensively online. As a result, the ROI from the website is smaller than it could be.

This is not a trivial point. I am an engineer by education, and in school we were taught, "An engineer is somebody who can do with one dollar what any idiot can do with a hundred dollars." In pure science, getting the result is all that counts. In business, it is $P = S - E$, and the trick is to maximize sales at minimal expense. If E is greater than S, you may be making sales, but you are not making any money.

In this chapter, you'll learn how to maximize profits by minimizing expenses. The rest of the book focuses mainly on improving sales, though there are some tips in this chapter for boosting sales, too.

The Web Helps Level the Playing Field

One of the great things about the web is that while it doesn't totally level the playing field between small businesses on a minuscule marketing budget and giant corporations with deep pockets, it at least gets them in the same ballpark.

For instance, a Fortune 500 company can afford $1 million for an ad campaign or however many millions building a sparkling corporate headquarters. But real estate on the web is cheaper and within everyone's reach. You pay the same $10 for a domain name whether you are Larry Ellison or Bob Bly. And if I grab a great domain name first, too bad for Larry. Also, while Oracle can afford prime-time TV spots and I can't, I can put up a homepage every bit as attractive as his for a few hundred dollars.

My ex-boss at Koch Engineering, a manufacturer of process equipment, left to start an industrial firm selling mixers for chemical plants and other applications. He said, "As a small business, I could never afford full-page print ads in trade magazines, which takes deep pockets. But now with the web so much more affordable, I can easily compete with industrial firms many times our size. The web is the great equalizer between small and large companies."

You can put up an entire website for as little as $1,000 and start making some money from it right away. If you can raise $5,000 to start your online business, even better: you can afford additional digital marketing that can accelerate your sales curve.

There are two ways you can reduce expenses:

1. Slash overhead costs to as low as you can.
2. Be frugal and smart about your marketing and operating budget.

To keep overhead low, solopreneurs and self-employed professionals work either at home or at affordable facilities they rent or lease in industrial sections of town. By avoiding the fancy business districts, they significantly reduce their monthly rent. Those who work in a home office can get the home office tax deduction.

If you sell physical products, you can store inventory at an outside fulfillment house, which also can ship products to your customers. This avoids the cost of building or leasing a warehouse.

You don't need much equipment and software to start:

- a PC and a high-speed internet connection
- an integrated shopping cart software package
- merchant accounts to take credit card and PayPal payments online

For your team, start with freelancers and virtual assistants who have their own equipment and office space. Then, consider staff employees. Your virtual team should include a website designer, a certified public accountant (CPA), a bookkeeper, an attorney, and a graphic artist.

Finding Affordable Help for Your Online Business

You can save money outsourcing many of your needs on sites such as www.fiverr.com and www.upwork.com where you can find content writers, web designers, programmers, video producers, and other vendors your ecommerce business might need who work at relatively low cost. The vendors who bid on jobs at these sites price low because they primarily service smaller internet businesses, which have more limited budgets than big companies.

As you grow your business, your workload may require heavier reliance on, and more hours for, your virtual assistants (VAs). If the time your VA spends on your work approaches 30 or more hours a week, to the point where you are the VA's only client, ask your CPA whether you must now for tax purposes treat the VA as an employee and not an independent contractor.

Regarding bookkeeping, accounting, cash flow management, and sales tax for an internet business, you must pay sales tax in those states where you have "nexus"—a physical presence. Many shopping cart software packages can track the sales you make by location. I use 1ShoppingCart software to manage my online business. It collects and tracks sales tax automatically, making it a breeze to report as income.

By reducing operating, administrative, and marketing expenses, your fledgling ecommerce business can be profitable shortly after startup, even with modest sales.

Corporate Status and Health Insurance

Many insurance companies make it difficult for entrepreneurs, especially when just starting out, to get adequate health insurance. It can be particularly challenging when two spouses run a small business. They say you are not a real business and do not quality for business rates and therefore want to charge you more expensive personal rates.

You can prevent this in two ways. First, switch to becoming an S Corporation. Second, make sure you and your spouse are equal partners so insurance companies see you as a true business.

You do not want to be one of the millions of Americans who aren't covered by insurance.

Avoid This Expensive Error in Media Buying

When a media buying company offers to sell you ad campaigns in digital media, they offer a reduced fee per ad if you commit to running half a dozen or more campaigns.

I advise digital marketers to buy only a single ad in an untested medium, even though the cost is higher than buying in volume. Reason: if that ad does poorly in the first insertion, it will only do even worse in the next insertions. Solution: test your ad at the one-time rate. If it is profitable, then commit to another three or at most six insertions.

Health insurance is increasingly a problem in small business: with the cost so high, small companies often no longer cover all the premiums and expect workers to contribute 20 percent or so to the coverage cost.

Remember, I am not a CPA, so consult insurance and tax professionals for advice before taking action.

Download Speed

There is an old saying in business, "Money loves speed." Although it wasn't intended to apply to the speed of your website, in fact it does!

The slower the site downloads, the more people abandon your site before the page appears, and as a result, the lower your conversion rates. Ideally the page should load in three seconds or less.

Here is a free website optimizer tool you can use to measure the time a given web page takes to download simply by entering the page's URL on www.websiteoptimization.com/services/analyze/. The site almost immediately displays how long it takes the page at the URL to download.

Here are a few tips to make your pages download faster, from consulting firm Mequoda:

◆ Eliminate as many nonessential images as possible.
◆ Web pages should be at a lower resolution than print; 72 pixels per inch makes the page look good on the screen.
◆ Reduce the size of the initial site page; the fewer lines of HTML code you have, the faster the page loads.
◆ If your page connects to a database, select only the fields you need to show data from, not the whole database.
◆ Avoid putting Java applets on HTML pages because they can cause the page not to work on some browsers and platforms.

Online Payments

In the P = S − E formula, the S, which is sales or revenues, goes way down on sites where the online payment systems do not work correctly. Many customers who encounter a problem paying online simply abandon the shopping cart and do not make the purchase rather than persist. For this reason, if you want to sell products and services on your website, then making it easy for consumers to pay online is essential. You'll have to make sure the operation is seamless, secure, and efficient.

Yes, you pay a small percentage of each sale to the credit card merchant or PayPal on each order. But you get paid immediately, and that's more profitable than waiting 60 days or more for a check or having to dun later payers on past-due invoices.

Your customers need to know and trust that your system will keep all their personal information private and safe from internet thieves who specialize in trying every which way to hack sites for people's financial information.

The obvious benefits of setting up your website to accept payments are that you will sell more often, payments are faster and seamless, and your store is open 24/7 so you can make money while you sleep. Having the ability to accept credit card payments online adds a more professional appearance to your business image and will also encourage more sales, especially if customers are ordering software, ebooks, or white papers, which they can immediately download.

There are a number of possibilities for accepting credit card payments, one of which is PayPal.com, one of the most well-known third-party merchant credit card and debit card processors. At the time of this writing, PayPal announced its intention to expand from taking just online payments to retail as well.

There are no contracts or cancellation fees with PayPal. Many consumers prefer to pay with PayPal because the credit card information is hidden as part of the transaction process, so it is a good idea to have a merchant account with one or more credit card companies; Visa is perhaps the easiest to start with.

Your first step is to review what your company or website plans to sell, whether it is a catalog of many different products or only a few products and services. Also, consider the possibilities for future business expansion because you don't want to have to change providers once you set everything up.

If you are selling just a few items on your site, then a business PayPal account is your best solution for now. However, if you plan to sell many products, then look into the PayPal Express Checkout system, which can integrate with many popular shopping cart systems such as Yahoo! Small Business, ASecureCart, 3dcart, and a host of others. PayPal provides a listing of pre-integrated shopping cart systems on its website under the Merchants tab.

What if you are a coach, consultant, creative designer, or other type of professional who needs to receive down payments before starting work? One easy way is billing by email from your business PayPal account through their customizable invoicing process.

You are offered a basic design, which you can then redesign, add your logo, and also add other information which can act as the contract-on-the-go. When using the invoicing route, the fees currently are $3.20 on a $100 sale, or 2.9 percent plus $0.30 per transaction. Always check first on the website for up-to-date information on fees under the Merchants/Pricing tab.

If you are selling many different products and services on your website, then you will need a web store system that provides shopping carts, a gateway to your merchant account, and an autoresponder system tied to the shopping cart and payments system to send order confirmations via email. You can find some of these resources in Appendix B.

The autoresponder system can also help with suggesting other products that tie in with what a customer is buying, and if the customer is interested, that offer will get added on to the same purchase. One company who specializes in this type of package is 1ShoppingCart, which gives you a variety of options to utilize for your sales system.

As you research which type of online payment system you want to use, be sure to ask about fees and services associated with the following: monthly fees, contract severance fees, processing fees, time span from customer payment to availability of funds in your merchant account, setup fees, discounting fees, transaction fees, payout schedules, and security deposits.

When you use PayPal, the funds go directly into your account, which you can access immediately with your PayPal business debit card. Other companies have different payout timelines which occasionally can be difficult.

Amazon's fee-based sellers program has different ways you can advertise and sell your products on their website, but payments collected are automatically transferred every two weeks.

The Amazon sellers program is different from the Kindle Direct Publishing (KDP) section where you can sell the books you write. Those payments from KDP, however, are transferred every two months, and there must be a positive balance of $10. Basically, all sales are handled for you under both arrangements, so you don't need a merchant account for processing cards.

If you are looking for a merchant account provider other than PayPal, check with your bank first to see what they can offer. If you've been there a while as a loyal customer, they may be able to work out a good deal for you.

Make a list of each company as you do your research, based on your needs, and compare the pricing for each of the categories listed above, as well as any extra services the company might provide. Sometimes, based on what you want, the benefits provided by a company may outweigh its slightly higher transaction fees.

Clickbank.com is another third-party merchant that works for digital download products such as ebooks, subscription newsletters, music and games, software, and documents such as white papers.

Its advantages are a quick startup, no monthly or cancellation fees, and customers can buy with a variety of payment types, including credit cards and PayPal. ClickBank provides detailed sales reporting and weekly payments including direct deposit to your bank account.

Additionally, ClickBank has a huge network of affiliates who can sell your products, and affiliate payments to them are automatically deducted from your ClickBank account. Check on current fees for transactions, discounts, dormant account fees, chargeback fees, and if requesting payouts by check, what those fees might be. As with any business, fees can change over time, so it is important to know the right questions and get the answers upfront.

A shopping cart system may also be essential based on how many products you may choose to sell directly from your site. This allows your customer to purchase one or more products within the same shopping experience and then pay for everything in one transaction at the end of the shopping session.

If you are selling large amounts of products, then a web store— an ecommerce site selling a wide range of items; e.g. Amazon, Alibaba—may be the best way to go as you can build a catalog containing photographs and descriptions of each product which allows customers to browse through and purchase more products at the same time.

There will also be a segment of your customers who do not use credit cards or PayPal and would prefer to pay by electronic check (e-check). This payment option is handy to have when you have international buyers as well. The processing and conversion to your money system is easy and less expensive than with credit cards and is handled through the National Automated Clearing House Association (NACHA).

Avoiding Shopping Cart Abandonment

When you are running an online business selling products, the last thing you want to see is a full shopping cart that a customer did not take through to purchase completion. This is called shopping cart abandonment.

Here are a few quick tips for recovering potential sales. First, always encourage customers to sign up for an account and newsletter when first landing on the homepage. This is a way to gather preliminary customer information, including an email address, where notifications of discounts and new products can be sent.

When designing the shopping cart infrastructure, set up the email address function for an automated reminder of what is waiting in the shopping cart for purchase if the customer leaves early. Only send these once or twice. This is important if the customer does not empty the cart before leaving, meaning there is still purchasing interest.

Send a discount notification, particularly if this is a first-time buyer. Time-limited purchasing and shipping bonuses also provide an incentive to help persuade the customer to complete the purchase.

Incorporating a product wish list option provides a method of selecting products for purchase either the same day or in the future. This tracks customers' interests and provides insights into what people like most, which can be used for email marketing blasts.

The Proceed to Checkout button should be clearly visible, as should the button for Return to Shopping. This makes it easier for the customer to continue shopping after checking the shopping cart contents and price, including shipping.

Incorporate all key online payment methods, which are basically the credit cards you accept plus PayPal. Show trusted security protocols displaying Verisign coverage on your shopping cart purchase page. Use these tips to make shopping online fun and safe for your customers.

Don't Overspend

One growing internet company spent a small fortune moving to a more upscale office, which they decorated with top-of-the-line office furniture, including ornate mahogany desks and leather chairs. The problem: as a strictly web company, the office got virtually no visitors. So the fancy facilities never impressed anyone and was largely a waste of money.

Likewise, hold off on the new Jaguar or Mercedes. I knew one guy who bought a Jag he could not afford in anticipation of a big raise in salary, stock options, and a bonus, which never materialized. Now, he can't make the monthly car payments and is barely keeping his head above water.

The best advice I got in this regard came from a Florida writer who said, "Live below your means." Spend less than you make so you can invest and build your net worth.

Start saving for retirement early. With compound interest, you can build your net worth to a large sum within a few decades. If you start saving only as you reach retirement age, you'll have a much more difficult time, unless you own your own business and can sell it for seven figures. See a financial or investment advisor for more advice as I am not licensed to guide you here.

Constantly Be Learning

If you are an employee, keeping your skills up-to-date—whether in IT, marketing, or whatever your specialty is—makes you more valuable to the business. It also makes you more marketable should you want to change jobs and companies.

If you are a business owner, staying conversant in core skill sets such as web design, programming, and digital marketing enables you to better manage your staff because you understand what they are doing.

CHAPTER 3

MARKETING FUNNELS FOR CONSUMER PRODUCTS

Marketing funnels of consumer products are the various paths on which potential customers travel to reach their destination: the purchase of a product. Each potential customer enters onto a path from a different point of product awareness, such as a social media marketing channel or an online advertisement, and then continues along the path, intersecting with other paths of potential customers.

Along the way, on each of these paths through the funnel, you create marketing actions for your customers to engage and drive them to the next step, such as signing up to receive a weekly email that offers entertaining information related to the product or signing up for a free white paper or brochure. This is the first point of capturing leads that can be nurtured further with targeted messages.

Each path, or channel, into the funnel may need a different set of steps to engage the customer depending on how they first entered the path. As customers take the next step, they move down into the neck of the funnel toward the purchase of the product.

Some will get to the goal sooner than others depending on the urgency of their needs. Regardless of whether the purchase happens at once or if customers continue to show interest but do not buy, continuing to tag customers in some way is an essential part of keeping them on the path through the funnel—no matter how slow the journey.

Figure 3–1 on page 35 shows the funnel for selling information products to consumers. The marketer gets people to enter the top of the funnel with a free content offer such as a free enewsletter or special report.

Once people opt into the marketer's elist to get the free information, they are at the top of the funnel. The next step is to convert the prospects into first-time customers by selling them a product.

Next, as you move them through the funnel, you sell them increasingly more expensive products as well as additional products in the lower price range. A customer who buys a second product is called a "multibuyer."

The 90/90 rule of online marketing says that 90 percent of online subscribers who buy a product do so within 90 days of joining your list. Therefore, it pays to convert prospects into buyers as quickly as possible.

As consumers move down the funnel, they are upsold to increasingly more expensive products as well as cross-sold on other related items in the same price range as the initial purchase.

The AIDA Funnel

A classic funnel for persuasion is AIDA, which stands for Attention, Interest, Desire, and Action. Let's take a closer look at each of those elements and dive into what they mean for you.

Attention

Your layout for a product-based marketing funnel starts with the awareness process, by which you get the prospect's attention, let her

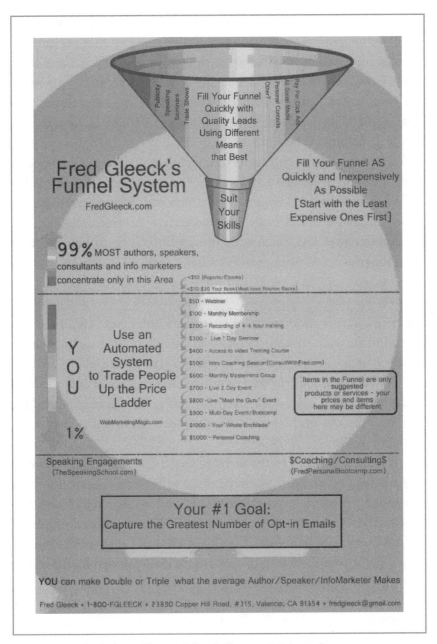

FIGURE 3–1. **Marketing funnel for information products.**

know you exist, and sell a product she might like. One of the ways to
first garner attention after setting up your website, blog, and several

business accounts on social media is to use Google AdWords to build small online advertisements. Customers who use similar keywords in their search strings to those you use in your advertisement will see these ads. There is also search engine optimization (SEO), where using your researched keywords on your website pages increases your chances of being discovered when customers are looking for what you sell (e.g., collars for large dogs).

You can also create advertisements using the social media platforms where you have a presence. This way, your product reaches far more potential customers than if you were simply posting from your business account page. Once potential customers click on any call-to-action (CTA) buttons or links you include in your posting, then the process of gaining and retaining their attention begins.

Interest

Once you have aware potential customers, your next step is to give them information that interests them enough to want to know more about your products. You can have them sign up for emails that focus on your product, or you can give them a free white paper. A white paper is not an advertisement but gives information on the product, the reason for its existence, and what it is designed to do for customers.

Your blog can add to the website's value by talking about one of the product features or applications, a customer success story, or news about product improvements. Or your email can include a link to a video that shows existing customers discussing how the product helped them. After watching the video, potential customers can click on a CTA button or link to find out more about the product and buy it if they are ready at this point.

Desire

Potential customers who see how this product can help them may now have a desire to try it out for themselves. Or they may want to know more or compare your product to others in the marketplace for pricing and features.

If you have researched your competitors, then you can offer something unique to your prospects that competitors don't have. Continue to engage with your potential customers to keep them focused and excited about your product so they take the final step. One excellent tool for increasing desire is a webinar where viewers can see the product in action.

Action

Send out emails that include your CTA button, and if you consider giving a time limit to make the purchase before the product price goes up. Create a sense of urgency by giving a short time span to buy or by telling customers there are only a few books or software packages left. You can also add perks like a 60-day money-back guarantee, an appointment with your interested customer for a product demo, if applicable, or a free phone consultation.

This section has given you a basic view of what a marketing funnel is and what it should do while using the four AIDA components of customer engagement. The rest of this chapter looks at several case studies of companies using marketing funnels to bring in customers from multiple marketing channels.

Amazon Funnel

One of the great examples of an online superstore that records what customers view while visiting the website—and turns that information into sales—is Amazon. The Amazon website installs cookies onto a customer's computer browser, ensuring that Amazon remembers what the customer looked at and makes suggestions about products based on those bought in the past or other comparable or complementary products. This process guides customers through a funnel by cross-marketing (and selling) other products that they may prefer, or persuading them to buy two or more items instead.

If a customer buys Korean noodles, for instance, pictures and hyperlinks to kimchi, dumplings, and other Korean foods are lined up underneath the product they are buying.

From this point, the customer receives reminders about buying more Korean and perhaps other Asian foods while on Amazon. Not only will she get notifications while on the Amazon website, but those suggestions will also follow her across other platforms, such as Facebook and browser homepages and anywhere else targeted advertisements appear.

Walmart works the same way, offering daily emails, reminding customers of the items they had looked at the day before. If there is a sale, then that is promoted as well. Both companies rely heavily on cookies—small bits of code that enable website owners to track customers who have visited so merchants can better understand what their customers are looking for and want. The merchants can then use cookie information to guide customers to similar products of interest.

Even at the point of purchase, the journey does not end for connecting with the customer. There are also upsell promotions where a customer who is buying, say, a software package is offered an add-on software program before checking out with the shopping cart.

Cross-sell promotions also occur at the checkout point, although they are equally effective just after the purchase is verified. A customer receives a thank-you email but also a notice that there are other products they can buy to enhance and complement the original purchase.

If a business is selling a bag of flowering seeds, for example, they might send a notice about starter seed pod containers at the shopping cart checkout point. You'd tell your customer they could plant seeds inside each pod instead of risking putting them in the ground, where they could be destroyed by bad weather or pesky animals. You might also offer plant food to give the plants a solid nutritional foundation for growing stronger right from the early sprouting stage.

Veterinarian Funnel

In a recent posting by content marketer Raghav Haran for www. SingleGrain.com, a digital marketing agency, a funnel case study example showed how a veterinarian could expand her business using a joint marketing/sales funnel system. The funnel consisted of two campaigns: one for owners with healthy pets that covered how to keep pets disease-free, and the other for those with sick or aging pets. It started with a video sales letter reflecting how owners can give their sick and aging pets a better life.

The video's opening frame shows the veterinarian standing at her kitchen counter with raw vegetables, pet medications (maybe vitamins, too), and raw meat laid out and ready to be cooked in a roaster oven. This visual message implied that cooking healthy, fresh food for one's pets, as opposed to canned or packaged foods that might contain suspect sources, may lead them to have a healthier life.

Both campaigns led to blog postings offering further advice on pet care. Customer leads were captured here, as well as from another funnel from Facebook advertisements. As an incentive, potential customers could view an informative video if they first agreed to receive emails.

Next in the marketing funnel, emails gave important advice, told stories about pet issues, talked about what pet brands were safe to use, and gave away little gifts from time to time. Interested pet owners could sign up for the website's membership to receive more in-depth information and buy products.

This system helped the veterinarian get leads from anywhere on the internet, with members from all over the country. While only local pet owners would bring in their pets for examinations, the veterinarian expanded her financial base with her advice and products, thus increasing the streams of added income.

The result of the marketing funnel system implementation, according to Haran, was that the veterinarian boosted her ecommerce platform by 50 percent with 541 new email subscribers ($950 spent on ads), garnered 23 recurring subscription members ($730 a month), earned $3,568 in initial sales, and generated $15,000 total revenue from other promotions in one month. Sumer Copywriting created the funnel design, along with the video sales letter and email content.

This case study is an excellent example of how a small business can expand its platform and visibility exponentially by adding a well-tuned marketing channel with creative content that leads to recurring sales in membership fees and product sales. The basis of her successful marketing channel is content that emotionally affects customers' desires to keep their pets healthy and alive much longer than might ordinarily be expected as well as products that aid that goal.

Email content is also considered a conversion funnel as speaking knowledgeably about things that matter to pet owners builds trust in her advice and products. Another positive outcome: she will get referrals from her membership site as well as from local customers who bring in their pets for their examinations.

1-800-Flowers Funnel

1-800-Flowers.com received the Gold Award from www.TopTenReviews.com in May 2017 for best deliveries. The company came out on top in every service category. When looking at the funnels it uses, one big plus is its mobile app, which allows customers to order flowers on the go. Many other florists do not offer this service, including FTD Florists, the second-place winner in the Silver Award. Customers interested in using the mobile app create their account online first, save their contact and credit card information, and then download the 1-800-Flowers app to access their account.

Many of the florist companies listed have partnerships with other supporting companies, but 1-800-Flowers lists them across the top of the homepage when customers sign in. This allows buyers to expand their gift-giving adventure, although another account sign-up is needed. Designer products are also offered as well as gourmet food and beverage gifts.

A nice touch that 1-800-Flowers offers is a "sympathy advisor" customers can reach by phone for help with ordering flowers for a funeral. None of the other ten reviewed florists offer that. Customer service is available by chat on the website, although most of the other listed florists also offer that.

As part of 1-800-Flowers' marketing/sales funnel, anyone a customer sends flowers to for a special occasion (such as a birthday or anniversary) stays in the customer's account database. The customer then receives reminders in advance of that person's birthday or anniversary prompting the buyer to order again.

One notable social media application that 1-800-Flowers has capitalized on is the new improved Facebook Messenger bot system, which handles basic transactions online and helps boost a company's bottom line. Just a few months after creating its own bot, 1-800-Flowers noticed 70 percent of its new customers came from Facebook.

With the Messenger bot system, advertisers use Facebook's targeting parameters to decide which population segment they want to reach. When a person clicks on an ad in their feed, there is now a CTA button available that says "send message" that goes to any link the company wants it to. For instance, the click could take the visitor to a page where she can immediately order the product being advertised (Mashable.com, "Here's How Bots Work on Facebook Messenger").

Any company like 1-800-Flowers, Walmart, or Amazon that receives the customer's response can now connect with that customer using content messages, until otherwise notified. The company can complete transactions, based on the bot used, or direct customers to the right landing page for more information or to buy a product.

Once customers engage with these companies, such as by creating an account, they receive a cookie or other tag that brings up advertisements of products they have looked at wherever they go on the internet. That way, should they decide to look again at something they were interested in previously, they can now simply click on the link. Even if the customer does not buy just yet for whatever reason, the company is nurturing the customer with its funnel by bringing the product to their attention.

Groupon Funnel

Most everyone has heard of Groupon, which offers coupons and discounts on services and products. First awareness in Groupon's marketing/sales funnel comes from advertisements, referrals, direct search, and from signing up for the email list. When customers sign up, they get a coupon code for a discount on the first order. Once customers have created the account, Groupon begins learning their preferences and wishes, based on search terms, and tailors its offers to those things that interest them most, according to Matt Ackerson of online sales funnel company www.Autogrow.co.

Groupon's focus is to connect consumers with many different merchants by sending out emails with product and service offerings in the subscribers' local area. Customers must sign up and create an account with contact information to access Groupon's offerings.

For example, a 60-minute deep tissue massage normally costs $65; but it only costs $39 with a Groupon coupon. Coupon deals for products and services, including restaurants and various shops in a given local area, can range from 50 to 90 percent off, giving subscribers significant deals. In Groupon's case, funnel conversion and nurturing takes place inside the customer's account through daily coupon offerings.

Once the customer signs in and is directed to local deals, he gets a list of top-selling deals in all categories. To look for a specific service or product category, the user can make a category choice from the list on the left side of the page. It is simple and direct.

Netflix Funnel

Netflix is one of the most popular and successful streaming video services in the United States, along with its partnering service of DVD rentals. Customers can sign up for a month's free trial period and then start the subscription, which they can cancel anytime.

Potential customers can access Netflix from multiple channels, such as Facebook, where Netflix posts its latest movies and video series.

The advertising video on Facebook starts out with a screen message asking, "Are you the kind of person that cannot watch a movie about animals unless you know whether or not they survive?" Then, it invites the viewer to keep watching if they want to know more, unless the viewer does not like spoiler alerts, in which case, viewers should leave—now. Each Netflix movie and video series, promoted on Facebook, offers a teaser video to entice viewers to sign up for a Netflix account.

On Twitter, where Netflix posts information about its latest offerings, it also highlights business and financial news statements, along with links to the news articles and TV reports. This shows that Netflix is responsive to the social media platform it is on, including who is more likely to be viewing Netflix on Twitter.

Netflix, now at 104 million subscribers, attributes its growth to its original show creations and access to top movies almost as soon as they leave the movie theater. As of the end of 2017, Netflix has accrued 41 million fans on Facebook, 4 million on Twitter, and nearly 6 million on its U.S. Instagram account.

Netflix has a very short marketing funnel: once consumers reach the entry point of awareness on social media sites, there is little else to do other than click on the link to go to the Netflix website. If viewers are not already subscribers, then they just need to sign up for the free trial and start watching whatever movie brought them there in the first place.

Burberry Funnel

Burberry is a luxury clothing line originally started in Britain in 1856. The Burberry trench coat was the first piece of outdoor clothing to become a Burberry trademark.

In 1879, Thomas Burberry invented the weatherproof fabric gabardine to make trench coats, which were later used by some polar explorers and military forces. Over subsequent decades, the Burberry clothing line has evolved to become a top luxury brand for men, women, and children and is sold in many luxury stores.

As with many other luxury brands, such as Louis Vuitton, Prada, and Chanel, Burberry closely guards how it presents its brand and reputation to consumers, particularly as it also has serviced many members of the British royalty. Burberry was one of the first to move wholeheartedly into the digital world, using its website to deliver a special personal experience of high quality and authenticity for its products and service that its customers expect.

It is even more critical now for luxury item producers to form and keep customer relationships as part of their retention strategy, which means that luxury brand marketing channels must engage with customers on a more personal and emotional level than Amazon or Walmart would. Luxury item buyers, who tend to be loyal fans of their chosen brands, buy because of their lifestyle preferences rather than looking for price bargains. Purchases are also peer-driven, particularly with younger luxury consumers.

As part of Burberry's marketing funnels strategy, the website connects to users through videos, stories about the history of the trench coat, and a music platform called Burberry Acoustic, which supports local artists.

Burberry, which has more than 10 million followers on Instagram and more than eight million followers on Twitter, launched five successful digital campaigns between 2004 to 2014, accounting for its tremendous online growth to date.

Burberry's success is based on communicating emotionally with the customer on each of its channels, listening to what customers want in their personal styles, and creating desire for the Burberry offerings. This gives the Burberry customer a top-level enjoyable experience, which leads to online sales.

The company also uses the "Burberry love" theme, whereby customers interact with the company by leaving messages about how much they love various products and clicking on heart icons placed next to each product and the new local musical artists shown on Burberry Acoustic.

Consequently, these luxury customers tell their friends, who in turn come to experience what their friends are experiencing on the

Burberry marketing channels. They then become part of the Burberry story.

The Burberry example shows that marketing channels and their funnels must match up to the customers that an online business wants to attract. While the standards of constructing such channels and funnels are relatively the same (for now), content and customer interaction principles change to meet what a business sees as the customers it wants to attract to the final goal—the landing site, where the purchase is made. If you do not have the right customers coming to your channels, then you will have little success in getting them further on down the funnel to your final goal.

Theme-Based Content

What is theme-based content? The Burberry example goes to great lengths to give an experience that only Burberry can offer because of its luxury line of clothing and how it communicates with its customers. It is more about the experience for customers engaging with Burberry, who are exposed to well-crafted professional video content such as runway shows, that also makes it enjoyable to watch (and listen) at the very least.

Alternatively, if you are a company that offers survival gear, then you are marketing to customers looking for the best products to help them survive while out camping in the wilderness. It is a very different mindset from the luxury retail consumer, yet professional videos showing how to use these products are a very good strategy in helping to sell these items. If you could show your customer how a uniquely designed tent was unpacked and then constructed, it would make it easier for them to follow the printed instructions once the time came to do it.

How you want your customers to view you should be uppermost in your mind as you create your marketing channels, which lead into the funnels and finally the purchasing goal. This means creating content that speaks to that experience you want them to have, hitting on the emotions that are most applicable to the product being sold.

In the tent example, one emotion might be fear of not knowing how to use the product and suffering in the middle of nowhere without it functioning properly.

In addition to offering the CTA links and buttons to go to the landing page, offer content in emails, or even videos on social media sites, that show exactly what customers must do under certain circumstances. Selling a product is a main goal, but how you get that sale is more important, and that happens by educating the customer first so they understand the product. Then, they are more likely to understand that they need this product and will buy it.

One online company, www.Survivallife.com, is offering tons of information on how to survive in many different situations. It has a collections-based store where you can buy from categories such as knives, clothing, tools, camping, and so on. You can also get a membership subscription to the Family Protection Association (FPA) on a monthly or annual basis.

The sister site of Survival Life is www.Survivallife.com, which also offers information and links to blog-reviewed products that are sold on Amazon.com. Both sites are primarily content based and have a presence on top social media sites such as Facebook and Twitter as well as others.

Conversion Content Timing

It is important that you do not offer all, or most, of your content at the top of the funnel entrance point. As you acquire potential customers, you can use a drip method of giving content, which is part of a conversion process along the path to the goal. The drip method helps to build a stronger customer relationship over time because your customers receive information that helps them understand whether this product will meet their needs.

You may attract customers at the starting point (lip of the funnel) by offering infographics (see Appendix C) on Pinterest or showing a specially crafted video that creates awareness and interest to know more. As you move into the conversion section, you build your blog posts to provide relevant information, maybe offer a free small ebook, show an interview with an expert in the same venue as the product, or build a report based on recent data. You must decide how your product should be represented, and that determines the content provided.

In a nurturing capacity, you might then offer a webinar on your product showing all its features in action and some of its benefits. Supporting emails on one or two topics offered in the webinar can enhance the nurturing process further.

At each step of the way, you might offer a landing page link or CTA so that if the customer is ready to buy, they can do so right away. If they have not yet bought, then at the final conversion/nurturing stage, you can build a specific landing page outlining information presented along the funnel path and adding in new information, along with the CTA to make the purchase.

The most important part of creating your marketing funnel is to plan it first, review and analyze each section objectively, and then begin the implementation process.

A/B Testing the Funnel Content

As you build your funnel content, you can test the content for each stage of the path from awareness to interest, desire, and the final point of action. Always review your analytics to see how customers are engaging your content, such as emails; what they do when they go to view videos; what kind of responses you get with webinars; how many pick up your free ebook; and what your customer unsubscribe rates are, if any. You can then adjust accordingly.

You may decide, for example, that you want to switch around when customers will get a video from the first level of attention to the final nurturing step. One checkpoint you may want to review is whether your keywords are making enough of an impact in the first awareness level to bring in customers from marketing channels. Or you may want to change when certain email content goes out, such as at the end stage instead of the conversion level. You can also decide whether to dedicate a blog topic to a feature that has not been explained well enough and put a link to that post in the nurturing section.

Customer vs. Product Focus

You may also need to analyze your content and decide whether it focuses too much on the product and not enough on the customer. The product is for the customer; that is why it exists. Therefore, the customer must be part of the content focus, such as offering examples of when they would need the product to help them.

When you review the content, also decide if you are asking potential customers to do something too soon. Do not be too eager to get the sale. Your customers will catch on to you and may begin unsubscribing from your emails.

That is why following your opt-out rates (discussed in Chapter 12) will tell you a lot about what is happening, such as when people unsubscribed to your emails. What email did they get, or where did you take them to view content, such as a video, that may have caused them to take this action? Was the content too much, too soon in the funnel?

The marketing/sales funnel can be one of the trickiest parts of your marketing strategy. And while you may make mistakes when you first start out, keeping on top of what your customers are showing you based on their actions allows you to fix the problems and achieve better success. Always create the best content you can, look for new ways to present content that your readers may not have seen before, be original, and remember to align all your content with your product, in relationship to your customers' needs and desires.

CHAPTER 4

MARKETING FUNNELS FOR B2B PRODUCTS

In the consumer marketing funnel, we convert a lead to a first order, then upgrade the new customer to more products as well as higher-priced products. We in essence nurture the customer and the sale to maximize lifetime customer value (LCV).

In a B2B website for big-ticket products, our funnel's goal is to generate a qualified lead. At or near the bottom of the funnel, a salesperson gets involved and is ultimately responsible for closing the sale.

As shown in Figure 4–1 on page 50, we use the same traffic drivers in B2B as we do in other funnels such as the Agora Model (see Chapter 1) and consumer products funnels (see Chapter 3). The steps are:

1. Capture the prospect's name, company, and email address.
2. Qualify the prospect. Do they have the money, authority, and desire to buy our solution to their problem? Is our solution a good fit for them?

3. Nurture the lead with steady contact delivering a mix of persuasive sales messages, offers (e.g., a free demo or free trial), and helpful content on the application, the technology, and the method of solving the problem.

4. Explore by having the salesperson contact the lead to see whether the fit is indeed good and to gauge the readiness of the prospect to move forward, as well as answer questions and objections.

5. Engage by giving the prospect an estimate, quotation, or proposal asking for a decision.

6. Get the prospect to sign the estimate, proposal, or contract and make the sale.

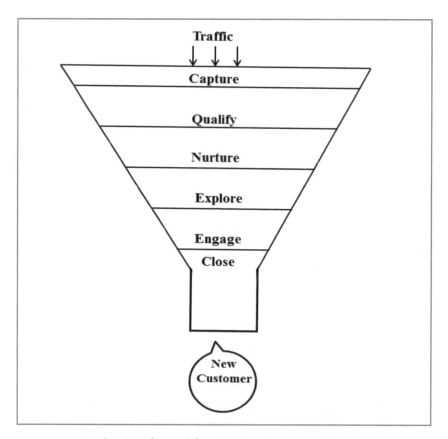

FIGURE 4–1. **Marketing funnel for B2B lead generation campaign.**

So, if you sell B2B products online, how do you generate leads and sales? What process does your customer go through from "Never heard of 'em" to "We want that product now"? Sales trainer David Hoffeld uses data from neuroscience, behavioral psychology, and social psychology, among other disciplines, to answer that question on a foundational level. He claims to have discovered customers' natural buying motives and processes. In *The Science of Selling* (TarcherPerigree 2016), he explains that people buy in predictable ways and that the buying process (and thus the selling process) consists of a series of specific commitments, together with a positive emotional state.

Accordingly, your marketing funnel is a visual or verbal representation of that process—from first awareness of your product or company to purchases, cross-sells, and upsells. The series of steps that constitute the buying process should be outlined in advance and represented pictorially and verbally. Believe it or not, many marketers do not know where their customers come from and haven't created a detailed plan for converting prospects to customers. Without a plan, marketers can neither optimize their efforts nor measure their progress at the various steps of the buying process. Moreover, knowing *where* your prospect is in that process is imperative for understanding your objective at any given step of the buying process and for making the sale.

In this chapter, I will highlight a number of B2B companies and their marketing funnels. These companies sell online primarily by generating sales leads and secondarily through direct sales from their sites. By taking a look at these companies' marketing funnels, you'll be able to generate some ideas about how to craft and refine your own marketing funnel.

Innovative Information Solutions

Innovative Information Solutions (IIS) is a B2B technology solutions company in the areas of application performance, business continuity, security, and IT infrastructure. IIS is also an IBM Gold Business Partner and sells IBM power servers.

As you can imagine, these are difficult sales. No company purchases any of these solutions or products impulsively. Prospects require a lot of information to make such a purchase—and typically have established buying requirements that include budgetary and time restrictions.

So how does a company successfully sell something as complex as a power server? Could these IBM power servers be sold directly from the website? They could. But the problem is that the conversion rate—the rate at which prospects order—would be extremely low. The conversion rate would be low because complex purchases such as these require much more deliberation on the part of the buyer than the average purchase.

Instead, the company sells these IBM power servers by offering prospects (via a landing page on their website) a free performance assessment of their current power server. The prospect simply fills out an information form with their name, phone number, company, and company email to request their free performance assessment. As IIS states on the landing page, this performance assessment is valuable to prospects because it helps them optimize their system's performance, save money on their next upgrade, identify and solve performance problems, and plan for growth.

This strategy of offering something of value for free in exchange for contact information is known as lead generation—also known as two-stepping since the offer is not the product itself (the power server) but a free thing of value (an assessment of the prospect's current power server). Lead generation is a soft-sell approach that inspires trust and reciprocity. When done right, lead generation also provides a steady flow of qualified prospects for the product offered. From this flow of prospects, merchants can qualify further and develop a relationship more likely to result in a sale.

When prospects sign up to receive the free power assessment, they're contacted by a company representative to schedule their assessment. At the point of the assessment, trust is established, and the prospect is more likely to purchase an IBM power server if needed. Plus, since the company has offered a free assessment and gained information about the prospect's needs, the company can better position the IBM power server as the answer to those needs.

Innovative Information Solutions' marketing funnel looks roughly like this:

1. Drive traffic to the website;
2. offer a free assessment;
3. deliver the free assessment;
4. position the IBM server as the prospect's power server of choice based on their needs; and
5. make the sale.

Here's another example of the IIS funnel: the website offers a free white paper, "Why IBM I on Power," for a detailed description of the system's features and benefits. This free white paper—again, offered in exchange for the prospect's contact information—achieves a number of objectives in the marketing funnel. It:

◆ identifies and qualifies interested prospects.
◆ gathers their contact information for follow-up.
◆ helps position the merchant's solution as the best solution for the prospect's needs.

Offering a free white paper or report that positions your product as ideal is a powerful technique. You can undercut your competitors and steer prospects toward your offering without trashing those competitors.

Here's an example: let's say you sell malpractice insurance to attorneys. You could write a special report such as "Ten Things You Must Consider When Purchasing Malpractice Insurance." The document is informational in nature, but you can frame the information in a way that favors your offering over your competitor's.

Perhaps you are the only company in your industry that focuses exclusively on legal malpractice insurance, as opposed to malpractice insurance for a number of industries. Then in your special report, you would point out how important it is to choose a provider who focuses exclusively on legal malpractice insurance—which, of course, positions you uniquely as the ideal provider. IIS likely does this with its white paper.

By publishing a free white paper, IIS also positions itself as an expert, which engenders trust. Lastly, even if prospects don't buy right away, IIS will be able to follow up with prospects as many times as the company's funnel dictates. So there are many good reasons for offering something of value for free in exchange for prospects' contact information.

As you may have noticed, the company needs to drive traffic to the landing page in the first place—so part of the marketing funnel consists of traffic generation. Driving awareness and traffic comprises the first part of their marketing funnel; it's where prospects first enter.

To drive traffic, B2B companies such as this typically advertise— with trade show displays and events, banner ads, direct mail (postal letters and postcards to lists of relevant purchasing agents), specialty newspapers, and industry journals, among other means. These companies also usually have telemarketing forces that generate leads and follow up with leads generated on their websites.

Traffic generation is a major part of any marketing funnel for a B2B company that operates online. I will talk about traffic generation more in depth later in this book, but for now, here are some other possible traffic sources:

- *Google AdWords*—when people search for your optimized keyword, they see the ad above or below the search results. Advertisers pay per click—thus the term "pay per click" (PPC) advertising
- *Facebook advertising*—this is mostly for business-to-consumer (B2C) advertising; but Facebook ads can work for some B2B advertising, particularly the business opportunity field. This is also a form of PPC advertising.
- *LinkedIn advertising*—LinkedIn is more appropriate than Facebook for most B2B advertising, though the effectiveness of LinkedIn advertising is still an open debate.

- ◆ *Twitter advertising*—another example of PPC advertising, but the targeting of Twitter ads isn't as specific as that of Facebook and LinkedIn ads.
- ◆ *Search engine optimization (SEO)*—publishing a lot of content optimized by keyword is one of the best ways of generating traffic since, these days, most of your prospects are using Google to find products and services. People also use Google and other search engines to discover information about something that could solve their problem or answer a question. I'll be talking more about this "inbound" marketing later in this chapter.

D&B Hoovers

Here's another example of a B2B marketing funnel. Let's say I sell to B2B companies, and I'm looking for companies I can send my sales letter to. If I enter "business to business marketers" into Google, I'll likely see an ad like this: "Unlimited Company Lists—Database of 85 Million Businesses. Build Lists with Contact Info" from www. Hoovers.com.

Since I'm looking to build a list with contact info, this ad's message is extremely attractive to me. So I click on it. I'm then brought to a landing page that offers me a free trial of their database. D&B Hoovers' page lists a number of features and benefits of the product and why I'd want to use it. All I have to do is put in my contact information, and I can try it out for free.

This example from D&B Hoovers is another example of lead generation. The company isn't selling its database of B2B companies immediately right from the page; it's offering a freebie first—in this case, a free trial. A free trial is an effective offer because before buying access to a database such as this, wouldn't you first want to try it out? Trying out the database minimizes the risk involved in a purchase like this.

Also, when visiting the landing page, a live chat window appears on the screen asking me if I want a price for a custom D&B Hoovers subscription. So there really are two offers: 1) the offer for a free trial and 2) the offer for a free quote for a custom subscription. The offer for a free trial is a "softer" sell—it's less pressure. I get to try it out and see if I like it. If I don't, no biggie; I'll just cancel.

Now maybe I don't trust that the deal will be honored and that I'll actually be able to cancel, but the offer itself is relatively low pressure. The offer for a free quote for a custom subscription, however, is more pressure, isn't it? If I request a quote for a custom subscription, I'm decidedly more committed than if I merely tried out the database.

But in relation to this, let's consider one of IIS' offers from earlier. Its offer of a free download of a white paper is definitely less pressure than a free trial, don't you think? Downloading a document informational in nature is less committal than actually trying out the product or service itself. So the pressure of the offer is relative to the committal required on the part of the prospect. And remember, the marketing funnel is a representation of the commitments we're taking our prospect through on the way to a sale.

Now, let's say I like D&B Hoovers' database and want to continue using it beyond the trial period. D&B Hoovers has probably taken my credit card information during my application for the free trial and will simply bill me if I continue beyond the trial period.

So here is D&B Hoovers' marketing funnel, from the vantage point of the buyer:

1. I see the company's Google AdWords ad, which has been optimized for particular keywords (such as "business-to-business marketers").
2. I click on that ad and am brought to the landing page, where D&B Hoovers makes me a couple of offers.
3. One of the offers is a free trial of the database.
4. The second offer is a free quote for a custom subscription.
5. I can take one or perhaps both of these offers.
6. I purchase one or both of the products.

Is this D&B Hoovers' complete marketing funnel? Certainly not. There are, I'm sure, many more ways that D&B Hoovers converts prospects to customers—likely through direct mail and the other ways I mentioned. Yet outlined here is one aspect of their funnel that wins them a lot of customers.

Grainger

Let's take a look at an example of a company that does things a bit differently. Grainger is a Fortune 500 industrial supply company that sells motors and other industrial tools and equipment. It is one of the most successful B2B ecommerce sites on the net. In 2016, sales from their website accounted for about 47 percent, or about $4.7 billion, of total worldwide net sales of $10.14 billion.

Grainger's website is essentially a shopping cart. There, I can search for the right product by motor number, part number, horsepower, voltage, speed, and more. The filtering system on the site enables the visitor to search by a number of different criteria. I can also browse if I don't know exactly what I want. And I can buy these products directly from the site using my credit card. Grainger isn't "two-stepping"; it's making direct sales.

What accounts for the difference in approach between the way Grainger does it (direct sales) and the way these other B2B companies sell (lead generation)?

One of the reasons has to do with the fact that people visiting Grainger's website often already know what they want. Grainger drives much of its traffic through Google AdWords and SEO. People looking for specific industrial keywords will likely see Grainger advertised or through organic search results. When prospects click on the link, they are brought to the specific page of the site that features that product or part. And they can buy right from the site if they choose.

Another reason for the difference in approach between one-stepping and two-stepping is the tangibility of products vs. the intangible nature of services and products that require demonstration (such as D&B Hoovers' database). Grainger's industrial motors, for instance, are sold for the most part simply by stating the features of the product—the brand, the frame, motor thermal protection, voltage, and so forth.

Generally speaking, a service is a more complex sale than a product, since a product is tangible and can be seen. A service, on the other hand, is intangible and often requires demonstration. I don't know exactly how the service will turn out until I'm rendered the service—and by then, it may be too late to change my mind. Some products are intangible as well, such as D&B Hoovers' database. The less I'm aware of the outcome of a purchase, the higher the risk.

This element of risk is why D&B Hoovers attempts to offer a free trial—to reduce the risk involved in an intangible product such as a database. In the case of buying a motor or other piece of industrial equipment, I see the product itself listed on the company website. And I've likely used one or more of the brands sold through the website, so there's trust established.

Grainger offers a 30-day money-back warranty. If I'm dissatisfied for any reason, I can return the product. As for the database, I don't know whether the information will be up-to-date and useful to me, as I don't have access to it prior to trying it out. For all these reasons, a B2B database is a harder sell than a motor and should be sold via lead generation.

One of the criteria you can use to determine whether you should sell directly from your website or simply generate leads is the degree of risk involved with buying your product or service—and this usually involves tangibility. The more tangible the end results for the buyer, the more you can sell directly. The less tangible, the more you'll want to engage in lead generation as opposed to direct selling. It's invariably easier to demonstrate outcomes with a tangible product.

Also, when selling to markets with restrictive buying requirements (for instance, where buying windows are fixed), you may opt to do lead generation since the prospects may want what you're selling but are not currently in the predetermined buying window. By receiving their contact information, you can stay in front of them until their buying window opens up again.

You can also make multiple offers at the same time—both a lead generation offer and a straight-up sales offer ("hard" offer). This captures prospects ready to buy now and also captures prospects not ready to buy—whether due to timing, budget, or trust issues. For instance, you could sell your product directly and offer, in addition, the option of more information.

I make multiple offers when prospects sign up for my *Business-to-Business Marketing Handbook* available on my site. They have the option to receive a) just the handbook; b) an estimate in addition to the handbook; or c) a Copywriter Information Kit with more information that will sell my copywriting and consulting services. These offers cover the full spectrum: both those ready to buy now and those who need more information to make a purchase.

The question arises: will people fail to buy your main offering because there's a soft offer as well? On the contrary, the more options you give, the more you'll include people in your funnel and the more sales you will ultimately make.

Ferguson

Ferguson is a plumbing supply company that sells kitchen and bath fixtures, HVAC, lighting, and many other building supplies. Like Grainger, Ferguson operates one of the most successful ecommerce sites on the web.

And like Grainger, Ferguson sells directly from its website. But Ferguson's website is sleeker and more attractive than Grainger's. There's more content. And the company is B2C in addition to B2B, as they sell to both contractors and homeowners. Ferguson generates traffic in much the same way as Grainger, such as through optimized keywords.

HubSpot

Now, let's take a look at a B2B company whose marketing funnel looks much different from those of the companies we've seen in this chapter thus far. HubSpot is a B2B company that specializes in inbound marketing, offering Customer Relationship Management (CRM) software and other software for marketers and salespeople. They also offer marketing and sales training. HubSpot describes inbound marketing as follows:

> *Inbound marketing is an approach focused on attracting customers through content and interactions that are relevant and helpful—not interruptive. With inbound marketing, potential customers find you through channels like blogs, search engines, and social media.*

HubSpot generates much or even most of its traffic through social media and SEO.

Let's say I'm looking for the best way to use social media to attract customers and I search for "social media marketing" in Google. A blog post from HubSpot will likely appear high in the search engine rankings since the company has spent a lot of time and money producing an almost endless array of content on its blog and optimizing these blog posts for keywords. Thus the prospect tends to enter HubSpot's marketing funnel by reading one of its blog posts—or perhaps by reading one of its Facebook posts shared by a friend or advertised by the company.

Inbound marketing is the opposite of outbound marketing. In outbound marketing, the intention is to interrupt your prospect and try to grab their attention away from something else. Perhaps the easiest way to see the difference between the two is to look at the different media they use. Here are some examples of inbound marketing and outbound marketing.

Inbound marketing:

◆ SEO
◆ Organic shares
◆ Viral marketing
◆ YouTube videos
◆ Blog posts
◆ Podcasts

- White papers
- Infographics
- Social media

Outbound marketing:

- TV commercials
- Direct mail
- Billboards
- Banner ads
- Magazine and newspaper ads
- Radio ads
- Cold-calling

What about social media advertising? Is it inbound or outbound marketing? This depends on the nature of the advertisement. The placement by itself doesn't determine whether it's inbound or outbound. The question really is: is the advertisement valuable content, such as an advertisement for a white paper or free ebook? If so, it is an example of inbound marketing, since the advertiser is not seeking to push product but is rather trying to engage and inform.

In truth, the distinction between inbound and outbound approaches in a funnel is not always clear cut. For example, what about direct mail that promotes a free book on investing? This seems to be mainly outbound marketing. The offer is for valuable content that the prospect is attracted to. A social media ad with a free offer exhibits the same phenomenon. So don't get too caught up on the terminology here. Instead of restricting yourself to one, focus instead on producing a balance of inbound and outbound marketing methods.

The advantages of inbound marketing approaches in your funnel are numerous. However, the disadvantage of this approach is that it takes a lot of time to build enough content to dominate SEO as companies like HubSpot do. Inbound marketing also takes a lot of money since inbound marketers such as HubSpot pay writers to write quality blog posts and other content.

Inbound marketing strategies are important considerations for the long term, but they will not produce much revenue in the short term. To produce revenue in the short term, you'll need to establish robust outbound marketing strategies in your funnel that attract customers now.

GKIC

GKIC is a B2B company founded by author and speaker Dan Kennedy. It specializes in marketing for small businesses, offering various information products and coaching that help small-business owners sell more of their products and services. Let's take a look at GKIC's marketing funnel.

GKIC uses lead generation to attract customers. Where do customers enter the funnel? From various sources, but here are a couple examples: GKIC attracts many customers through Facebook advertising. For some time, GKIC ran an ad offering Dan Kennedy's book on direct marketing for just one dollar. People who bought the book were introduced to GKIC's many products and services through web addresses and offers featured in the book.

Their marketing funnel looks something like this:

1. I see the ad on Facebook for Dan Kennedy's direct-marketing book for just a dollar.
2. I click on the ad and am brought to GKIC's landing page, where I leave my contact information in exchange for ordering the book at the discount.
3. I receive the book and am exposed to the many offers and website references in the text.
4. I may purchase more books from the company or some of its higher-level products and seminars.
5. I'm told about even higher-level services such as Kennedy's consulting, copywriting services, and conferences.

This kind of funnel moves upward, doesn't it? The prospect begins at the bottom and ascends to progressively more expensive products and services as the prospect perceives more of the value and trusts the merchant more. Some of the other marketing funnels we've been looking at have been more linear, oriented toward one primary product or service. GKIC's marketing funnel is based on entry-level products that introduce the customer to its various higher-level products. GKIC's funnel teaches the lesson that a business should always have something else to sell—and preferably, something even more expensive.

Because of this upward focus, GKIC's marketing funnel employs email marketing much more than the other companies highlighted thus far. Since GKIC requires "lead nurturing," a process in which leads are cultivated through systematic bonding and trust-building, it's more important for GKIC to stay in front of customers. The company stays in front of its customers and prospects with a regular enewsletter, which links to blog posts and content that regularly get customers returning to the website and buying more products. I'll talk about enewsletters more in depth in Chapter 11.

GKIC's marketing funnel doesn't always begin at the bottom, however. Many customers discover GKIC through seminars and conventions put on by GKIC or other companies, such as American Writers and Artists Inc. (AWAI). Still other customers discover GKIC through Infusionsoft marketing software. GKIC fills the pipeline with customers in a number of ways. There are multiple entry points in the funnel. All of GKIC's products and services are available directly via its website; like Grainger, the website is a shopping cart model.

GKIC also uses a recurring revenue model. People can gain access to the GKIC Membership Site and receive a number of products for free, including boot camp tickets and information products. By selling business owners and marketers member subscriptions, GKIC receives recurring revenue from these members.

Membership sites obviously have the advantage of ongoing, predictable revenue. GKIC employs a recurring revenue model as opposed to depending just on one-stop shopping. It does sell many products and services on a one-time, flat-fee basis—but much of its revenue stems from month-to-month memberships. Stan Dahl's company Marketing Rebel likewise uses a recurring revenue model. It sells membership subscriptions as well as discrete products and services.

MarketingProfs

MarketingProfs is another B2B marketing company. Some of its premium services include corporate marketing training and courses. MarketingProfs does an admirable job of providing a number of entrances into its marketing funnel, through both outbound and inbound means. It offers a library of over 200 ten-minute tutorials as well as an enormous collection of blog posts, online seminars, and forums. Like HubSpot, MarketingProfs is SEO-heavy.

And like GKIC, MarketingProfs' funnel moves upward. Someone may discover MarketingProfs through a free blog post via a search engine search and end up enrolling in a marketing boot camp or attending one of their events. Instead of a membership site, as with GKIC, MarketingProfs offers corporate training and online university courses.

MarketingProfs University features courses and workshops open to the public in SEO, writing, email marketing, social media marketing, and more. The courses are taught by instructors, and the graduate receives a certificate of completion. Marketers sign up for these courses directly from the website.

MarketingProfs sells its corporate training, on the other hand, via lead generation. Prospects are encouraged to watch an online demo and email the company for more information. Its target audiences are typically marketing directors and VPs of organizations who organize this training for their employees, similar to how sales managers order sales training for their salespeople.

MarketingProfs corporate training occurs through lead generation rather than direct sales because a trained salesman from MarketingProfs is required to identify the problems and needs of the prospect's organization. This way, the training can be positioned according to the organization's purposes and needs.

Additionally, for the same reasons I stated above, MarketingProfs engages in lead generation because of corporate training's high-price points. Their university courses are lower-priced, with real online instructors, course materials, and a certificate of completion. We pretty much understand what we're getting when we enroll in an online course. But corporate training is quite different. We don't know what to expect. So the company uses an online demo and asks prospects to email for more information.

MarketingProfs also hosts a large marketing forum annually with keynote speakers and networking opportunities. Like GKIC, many people enter the marketing funnel simply through their events or events associated with the company. And like GKIC, MarketingProfs is an aggressive email marketer.

Both MarketingProfs and GKIC show the advantage of creatively fusing informative, valuable content with sales offers in one's marketing funnel. And both are fundamentally information marketing companies, though with the addition of offering communities in which that information is disseminated, shared, and taught. If inbound marketing is defined by the mechanism of attracting customers through educating and entertaining content, then GKIC and Marketing Profs are expert inbound marketers.

Agencies, Freelancers, and Consultants

Agencies, freelancers, and consultants are different entities altogether. Yet, like the companies we've seen thus far, many of these businesses—whether website design companies, copywriters, or business consultants—generate a great deal of their leads and sales straight from their website. According to Hubstaff, freelancers with websites earn up to 65 percent more than those who don't.

I'm a freelance copywriter and consultant, and I generate many leads through my website since my page shows up high in the search engine rankings for the keyword "direct response copywriter." On my website, I include several lead generation devices. One is a graphic link for those ready to buy now (Figure 4–2 on page 66) in the upper right corner of my homepage, www. bly.com.

When prospects click on that link, they're brought to a contact form with qualifying information for them to fill out. They can use this form to get in touch with me about a project need.

Some of my other lead generation devices are free offers, designed
to add people to my elist, as in
Figure 4–3.

These are softer offers. Prospects
have their choice between several
different free offers: the *Business-
to-Business Marketing Handbook*,
reports on how to sell information
products, and the enewsletter. They
can also choose the free "Marketing
Rules of Thumb," which is a PDF

FIGURE 4–2. **Call to action (CTA)**

document that doesn't even require them to enter an email address.

Why do I offer this content for free? First, because I want to
inform and educate and second, because I want to add interested
prospects to my elist. I will talk more about building an elist in
Chapter 9. The enewsletter that I send out regularly to my elist lets
me stay in front of thousands of prospects and positions my services
and information products.

Your marketing funnel should not be left to chance. Be absolutely
clear on how you want to generate customers. What are the specific
steps and commitments they will have to go through to convert from
prospect to customer? Plan them out. You won't be able to map out all
the details of your marketing funnel, but you do want to have a plan.

FREE B2B MARKETING HANDBOOK

Sign up today to receive Bob Bly's FREE E-newsletter

Free Marketing Rules of Thumb

FREE Report: How To Sell Info Products

Find all of Bob Bly's information products HERE!

Bob Bly Copywriter
Copywriter/Consultant
31 Cheyenne Dr.
Montville, NJ 07045
Phone 973-263-0562
www.bly.com
e-mail: rwbly@bly.com

FIGURE 4–3. **More calls to action**

CHAPTER 5

WEBSITES AND MARKETING FUNNELS FOR SERVICE FIRMS

You may think the web is better suited to merchants who sell physical products like books, CDs, home decor, furniture, clothing, toys, and the like. But a well-designed website and accompanying multichannel marketing campaign can also sell professional services such as copywriting, coaching, book cover design, plumbing, interior design, and dozens of others.

What if you are a plumber or or contractor, or want to offer job search coaching, resume writing, or tutoring to people only in your local area? Is a website, which can reach people globally, the best idea for you? The short answer is: absolutely. People use the web to find local businesses more than they use the Yellow Pages. According to search engine marketing company Hang Ten SEO:

- ◆ 46 percent of all searches on Google are local.
- ◆ 18 percent of local searches lead to a sale.
- ◆ 50 percent of consumers who performed local searches on their smartphones visited a store within one day.

◆ 34 percent of consumers who performed local searches on their computer or tablet visited a store within one day.
◆ 50 percent of mobile searches are looking for a business name, address, phone number, or service information.

The bottom line is, it pays to have an effective website for your service business even when you serve clientele limited to your region, state, or town.

Whether you are selling local or nationwide services, you need a website that will find and qualify prospects for you and weed out everyone else. It doesn't matter if your site is getting thousands of hits a month if none of those hits turn into likely prospects for your services. You are getting traffic for nothing. So let's examine the ingredients that go into an effective service-selling website.

You need a sales funnel so that when potential clients come to your site, you can take them through the service-selling process: generate an inquiry, qualify the prospect, fulfill the lead, follow up, give a cost estimate or proposal, and close the sale (see Figure 5-1 on page 69).

In the service-selling funnel, you offer some free information to people who respond to your marketing. For instance, you send them an email that drives them to your website to download a free information kit on your services, a free special report, or both.

For the people on the email list you rented who did not respond, you can keep marketing to them; each time, more will reply.

For those prospects who do respond, you fulfill their request and deliver the information they asked for. These leads are then put into a follow-up email sequence that can include emails, phone calls, and other contacts. Liz Lorge of Leadpages writes, "You need a plan that includes a follow-up sequence so your leads don't get cold. Integrate an email marketing automation tool with your landing page tool. With email automation, you can set rules that trigger entire multi-email campaigns when someone submits a landing page."

Some prospects ask for an estimate, approve your proposal, and hire you. Others do not buy your services. The nonbuyers are put

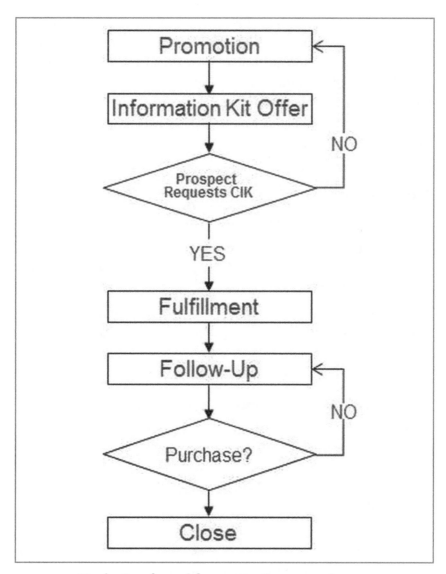

FIGURE 5–1. **Marketing funnel for promoting a service.**

into an email sequence or other follow-up marketing system and are contacted periodically. About 5 to 10 percent or more of those who did not buy your original proposal will be converted to clients over the course of this follow-up.

How much should you follow up with nonresponders? One approach is to continue to follow up until they tell you to stop. If you publish a monthly enewsletter (see Chapter 11) and add all prospects to the subscriber list, they will automatically hear from you at least once a month, creating a top-of-mind awareness that turns more of these leads into clients. See Figure 5-1 on page 69 for an overview of the service marketing funnel.

The Anatomy of a Service Business Website

Website content is of two basic types:

1. Information your prospects need to know to buy from you.
2. Information you know that will persuade prospects to buy from you.

The content you include on your website should do one of these two things. If not, it might look nice, but it is simply a waste of your and your reader's time.

Examples of "need to know" information include:

◆ An overview of your services (your homepage)
◆ Examples of your work
◆ Pages devoted to each of your major services (consulting, coaching, and so on)
◆ An About You page highlighting your relevant background and credentials
◆ A client list

The stuff that helps convince prospects that you're the person they should hire, even if they are not looking for it, includes:

◆ Client testimonials
◆ Case studies
◆ Publications (e.g., books, articles)
◆ Speaking engagements
◆ Media coverage
◆ Videos

- ◆ Podcasts
- ◆ Radio and TV appearances
- ◆ Webinars
- ◆ Blogs
- ◆ Enewsletters

You may already have some of the elements above in place, and if not, that's OK. As you move forward in your business, you will get the opportunity to create some of these things, like webinars, and get to write for professional publications in your field. But what do you need in the meantime? Let's go over the basics of a successful service business website.

Homepage

This is the main page of your site. It is the first thing your visitors will see, so you need to make that first impression count. Briefly explain your background, highlight your relevant experience, and tell visitors why you are the one they should hire. Focus your copy on them and their needs instead of you and your accomplishments. This is not the place to brag but to show prospects why your services are the solution to their problems.

Blog

Short for "weblog," a blog is a page on your website where you post regular updates, usually in a more informal, conversational style. You can post articles, case studies, client testimonials, and important news about you or your industry on your blog. Blogging offers five major advantages to the service-based business:

- ◆ Boosts your website's search engine ranking
- ◆ Encourages repeat web visitors
- ◆ Establishes you as an expert in your field
- ◆ Extends your reach
- ◆ Highlights your value

Blogging is especially valuable for service businesses that offer professional services (such as software development) as it gives them a regular forum for educating the market on their methodologies and ideas. It's also good for companies selling trade services (such as home remodeling) because the blog acts as a vehicle for disseminating how-to tips, which help convince prospects of your expertise.

Contact Page

Your website won't do you much good if your visitors can't get in touch with you. Your contact page should include all the ways you want people to reach you, such as your email address or contact form, your various social media, and even your phone number and physical address if appropriate for your business. For local businesses with a storefront, give driving directions and hours of store operation. Make it easy for them to find you (e.g., "we're on the corner of Fifth and Main next to the gas station").

Portfolio of Work

A portfolio—images of your work—is a must if you are a copywriter, graphic designer, interior decorator, house painter, landscape service, or you work in some other creative field where prospects want to see examples of your handiwork. Include only the best examples of the types of work that you currently offer your clients.

Online Newsletter

A free online newsletter is a great way to stay in touch with website visitors who have shown an interest in hiring you or might in the future. A newsletter's main advantage is it gives you a list of customers and prospective customers that you control—not someone else. Compare that to marketing on Facebook, where a simple algorithm change could ensure your marketing message is only seen by three people in Guam who aren't in the market for your services. An elist of potential clients can be one of your biggest marketing assets, especially since it enables you to keep in regular touch so when a need arises, the client calls you first.

Online newsletter articles are also ideal for showcasing your expertise and knowledge with technical tips, how-to advice, recommendations, new ideas, and so on.

Testimonials

Testimonials are short, positive reviews of your service from satisfied customers. They help prove your value by showing your new website visitors that you have helped people just like them in similar situations.

How do you get testimonials? It's simple. First, do a good job with each and every client, and then ask them to give you one. Satisfied clients are more than happy to share their positive experience with others. Just make sure you ask their permission to use their testimonial on your website as well as in any other marketing you do.

Case Studies

In marketing parlance, case studies are short documents that explain in detail how you helped a client solve a problem. Case studies are written in a simple problem-solution format and use real numbers and specific details when applicable. Like the testimonial, they show how you have solved similar problems for clients just like your prospects. Unlike testimonials, they go into much more detail about what the problem was, why the client chose your firm to solve it, what you did, and the results.

Service Pages

You might offer more than one related service or have more than one specialty or market segment. In this case you might want to create a page on your site for each of those services or specialties. If you're a book editor, for example, you might offer basic copyediting as well as developmental editing (two very different components of one thing: editing). On these pages, briefly outline what the service entails, who it is for, and how prospects can hire you.

Frequently Asked Questions

The Frequently Asked Questions, or FAQ, page is a great place to include anything else your prospective clients might need to know that doesn't fit in elsewhere. How long have you been in business? What certifications do you have? Have you done XYZ work before? How do clients order from you? Try to anticipate any questions your web visitors might have, and then answer them here.

Call to Action (CTA)

This is more of a necessary component of your website rather than a specific page, but it is one of the most important pieces of an effective service-based website.

What do you want people to do when they visit your site? Do you want them to sign up for your free newsletter? Request a free consultation? Share your content with others? Whatever it is you want them to do, ask them to do it. The best place to include this CTA is at the bottom of your homepage.

My CTA invites people interested in hiring me to click over to a contact page where they can tell me more about their business and their copywriting needs. From there, they can either request more information or get a free estimate.

To write an effective CTA for your own website, follow these tips:

- ◆ *Create urgency*. Use phrases such as "click now" or "request your free consultation today."
- ◆ *Be specific*. To be effective, your CTA must be as specific as possible. Tell your web visitors exactly what you want them to do and how. Use clear, specific action words like "click," "sign up," or "contact us." Tell them exactly what they are getting when they take the action. If you are offering a free report or free consultation, make sure you tell them that in the CTA.
- ◆ *Be aware of positioning*. According to HubSpot, calls to action "above the fold"—visible on a page without scrolling down—do very well. CTAs in a sidebar of a web page don't perform as well as those in the page's main content area.

Now that we've covered the basics of what should be included in your website, let's look at how to use that site to market your service-based business.

Content Marketing

Content marketing should definitely be one of the arrows in your services marketing quiver. Content marketing has become a major component of the marketing world. According to a study conducted by the Content Marketing Institute, 88 percent of marketers have added content marketing to their plans this year. But what exactly is content marketing, and how can you use it to market your services online?

Content marketing is a type of marketing that involves the creation and sharing of online material such as videos, blogs, articles, and social media posts. It differs from other types of marketing, such as direct response and brand marketing, in that it does not explicitly promote a brand but is intended instead to stimulate interest in a product or service by creating helpful, informative content designed to highlight your expertise and solve a problem.

This content can include blog articles, social media posts, white papers, case studies, videos, infographics, and more.

Why is content marketing so effective for selling services online? Because content marketing:

- *Tells a story.* In content marketing, telling is selling. In this case, you are telling your brand's story in an authentic, not overly salesy way that answers your target audience's questions and demonstrates to them that you and your service are the answer to their prayers.
- *Builds your expert reputation.* As people respond positively to your content marketing pieces, trust in you and your brand grows. Over time, people begin to see you as an expert in your field or specialty. You become a valuable resource, and a significant number of your followers will become your clients.
- *Creates engagement.* Timely, relevant pieces that interest and engage your readers are the main ingredients of content

marketing. When someone responds to a question you posed on Twitter, replies to your blog post, or answers an emailed question, the prospective customer has made the decision to reach out to you. This gives you the opportunity to deepen your relationship with them and ultimately, hopefully, get the sale.

Let's look at some ways you can use content marketing on your website to grow your service business.

Content that Solves a Problem

Content marketing requires a softer touch than other forms of marketing. You can still sell, but your message needs to be more helpful than salesy. Why do people request your service? Because they have a problem that only you can solve. You're not a provider of X, Y, or Z service; you're a problem solver.

What if you offer a resume-writing service, for example? What problem do you solve? You're not just selling resumes. You're selling a brand-new life for someone who wants to move up in the world or transition into a new career. Their problem is they're tired of being passed over for jobs for which they would be a perfect fit. Their problem is they need more money to survive.

Think about the problems you solve with the services you are offering, and craft content that does just that. This shows prospects that you are the best person for the job. Ideally, you want prospects to think, "If he gives away this much great information for free, imagine what I'd get if I paid him."

Content Marketing Is Viral Marketing

Content marketing is in large part about sharing. Create helpful, interesting, and informative content that your viewers will want to share with their friends. Well-written blog posts, insightful infographics, and how-to videos that solve a problem your website visitors have is a great way to encourage sharing behavior. Ask your visitors to share the content with their friends, and make it easy to do so by including share buttons for sites like Facebook and Twitter. In this way, your marketing messages get much wider distribution beyond their original audience.

Content Is More than Just the Written Word

People share valuable content with friends and colleagues even more readily than they do product or service information. So content is a very viral type of marketing and gets passed along more often than pure sales messages.

Not all content has to be an article, book, or blog post. If you have the means and the technical know-how, you can also create how-to videos, host a podcast, conduct a webinar, or create infographics that highlight your expertise.

Posting regular, dynamic content like this will not only make your website "sticky" by encouraging return visits, but it will be shareable and highly popular. In fact, visual content is 40 times more likely to get shared on social media than other types of content, according to social media management firm Buffer. And infographics are actively shared by users on social media (https://blog.hubspot.com/marketing/science-behind-popular-infographics).

Video Marketing for Service Businesses

One of the most effective content marketing strategies is the use of video. Let's take a look at how you can use video on your website to market your services.

Thanks to faster internet speeds, online video has exploded. The video sharing site YouTube now has over a billion users, or almost one-third of all people on the internet. According to venture capital firm KPCB.com, online video now accounts for 74 percent of all online traffic. MWP Digital Media says that 55 percent of website visitors watch videos online every day, and 59 percent of executives agree that if both text and video are available on the same topic, they are more likely to choose video.

The reason for video's popularity is simple. It reaches out to different learning styles. Some people learn better by reading something, yet others by seeing something demonstrated or hearing about it. Video combines all these distinct and separate learning styles into one shareable package. Video also lets your viewers see you; it shows them there is a real person behind the business and encourages them to get to know, like, and trust you.

Suppose you are an interior decorator, baker, resume writer, or book cover designer. You could produce and share how-to videos featuring design tips, a tasty gluten-free recipe, or how to make a book cover using PowerPoint. This would highlight your expertise and get people to know, like, and trust you. Such videos also feature helpful content, which encourages sharing via social media.

The best part is that you don't even have to appear in these videos. Using voice recorder and screen capture software on your computer, you can simply record your voice as you walk through the steps of writing an effective resume, or guide viewers in how to make an attractive book cover.

Another popular video type is the video log, or vlog, which is a lot like a written blog post but done as a short video instead. Almost anything you would talk about in a written blog post is also ideal fodder for a vlog, as long as they are short.

That's just a small sampling of the types of videos you can do, depending on the service you are offering. Now, let's look at some effective ways you can use video to market your service-based site:

◆ *Offer value.* Every video you create should provide something of value to your prospective clients, such as a tip or a how-to demonstration. Never create videos just for the sake of having videos on your site.

◆ *Include a CTA.* What action do you want prospective clients to take after viewing your video? Do you want them to sign up for your newsletter? Share your video with their friends? Visit your website? Whatever it is, ask them to do it. Never assume your viewers will automatically know the next step they should take in their relationship with you and your business. If your video is focused on how you can help them—in other words, what's in it for them—they'll do it.

◆ *Tag your videos.* Add relevant keywords to your video titles and descriptions when you upload them to sites like YouTube so users can find them easily in searches. Give your videos a descriptive file name rather than a bizarre designation generated by your computer.

◆ *Include your URL.* Make sure every video you produce has the URL directing people to your website. This can easily be done with most video editing software.

◆ *Upload the videos to your site.* After uploading your video to YouTube, make sure you also post it to your website. This makes it easier for your prospects to find and gives them a good reason to check your site often. Once your video is uploaded, click on the Share button beneath your video and copy and paste the provided link onto your site. If you have a blog on your website, post the video there as well as on a specialized page on your site designated just for video.

◆ *Keep it short and sweet.* People who aren't familiar with you or your work will not sit through a long-winded video about you. Keep your videos short and to the point. Tell your prospects who you are, what you do, and what's in it for them. And do it in under two minutes. For videos that are educational, instructional, or how-to tutorials, these can run five to ten minutes or even longer.

◆ *Share.* Share your videos far and wide. Post them on Facebook and Twitter, and encourage others to share them. Include share buttons for the various social media platforms to make sharing your content that much easier.

Constantly Promote Your Service Business

Marketing is not a one-and-done selling solution, so don't expect to have tons of clients after writing and publishing only one or two blog posts. Marketing takes patience and dedication. In the beginning, you are going to post content and send online newsletters that will get little to no interaction, and you're going to feel like you are shouting into a void where no one can hear you.

There are other forms of marketing, like pay-per-click (PPC) advertising and direct mail, that you should also do. But don't stop sharing content just because you aren't seeing results right away. If your content is well-produced and informative, you will build an audience in time, and that audience will buy from you.

Focus on the quality of your content and keep pushing stuff out there, especially in the beginning. I started writing articles for trade publications in my field of direct marketing nearly four decades ago. I am still at it today, and the payoff has been huge for me—a six-figure annual income and seven-figure net worth, all from selling my services.

Repurpose and Test Your Content

Don't forget to leverage your content in different ways. An article you wrote for a publication can become a blog post later; a series of articles can be turned into a print book or ebook; and a podcast interview you did can be added to a static image and uploaded to YouTube. Always be thinking of ways one type of content can be turned into something else. This will save you time and money and help you get content out faster to different types of learners.

You should always be testing your marketing, and content marketing is no different. True, you may not be able to track things like direct sales that came as a result of some piece of content, but you can track other things, like shares, downloads, Facebook likes, and requests for more information.

So come up with some content marketing metrics that you want to track. Do you want more followers? Do you want a particular piece of content to be shared a bunch of times? Whatever that number is, can you increase it? Does your audience respond better to videos than blog posts? Knowing answers to these questions will tell you how effective your marketing is and help you improve your results. It will also make your audience happy, and they'll be even more likely to secure your services.

Email Marketing for Service Businesses

While important, content marketing is not the only form of marketing you should be using. Email marketing is also highly effective at driving traffic to your website and converting those visitors into loyal clients.

To build a profitable elist, post your newsletter sign-up form on your website, Facebook page, Twitter account, and even add a link to it in your email signature—anywhere your prospective customers are.

Keep your required fields to a minimum. Just ask for the prospect's first name and email address. Ask for much more than that, and your sign-ups will drop off significantly.

Tell people who opt into your elist exactly what you are going to send them and how often. Give them as much information as possible on your sign-up form so they can easily decide whether or not they want to be on your list. Don't break this promise to them. Send them only what you told them you would send at the frequency you promised to send it.

As soon as they opt into the list, send them an email welcoming them to the list and reminding them why they signed up. If you have a freebie or other special bonus, provide the link to it here as well. This can easily be done with an autoresponder so you don't have to send these emails manually every time someone signs up for your list.

Offer something specific to you and your business to people who subscribe. Some people try to get a ton of sign-ups by giving away something general that a lot of people will want, such as a drawing for a free Kindle, but these seldom work. They only attract freebie hunters who will unsubscribe from your list as soon as they do—or don't—get the prize. Offer something relevant to your audience instead. If you're an estate planner, offer a free estate planning guide.

If you're a book cover designer, offer them a report detailing *Ten Secrets of Dynamite Book Covers*. You get the idea.

People are busy. They don't have time to read a long email full of closely arranged text. Break up long blocks of text into short paragraphs. Include images and subheadings to make it easier for your readers to scan the article.

You can also include "read more" links that send your readers over to your blog to read the whole article or tip when it's more convenient for them. Make sure your subject line is short, to the point, and easy to digest.

The end of your email should include a CTA. Remember when we talked about these earlier? You can implore your readers to request more information, check out a relevant case study, or take the next step in building a relationship with your service business.

But don't send an email unless you have something relevant that will help your readers. Have you written a new article? Published a book in your field? Created a new webinar? These are all legitimate reasons for sending out a newsletter. Don't send something just because it's been a while, just to sell something, or to gloat about being added to some conference.

Email list software includes detailed reports that help you track important marketing metrics like open rates, link clicks, and more. Paying attention to these metrics will help you craft better emails and improve your marketing all the way around. If you are getting a large number of unsubscribes, or low interaction on your links, then you'll need to try something different the next time you send out another email.

By building an effective website and combining it with content marketing and email, you can successfully market your services online.

CHAPTER 6

DRIVING TRAFFIC TO YOUR WEBSITE WITH ONLINE MARKETING

It's not enough to have a website; people have to be able to find it. And not just a few people. To be successful as an online marketer, you need hundreds of people visiting your site every single day. We're talking about website traffic.

Web traffic is a quantifiable term, determined by the number of visitors to your site and the number of pages they visit while there. But generating traffic isn't the only goal of an online marketing strategy; your website also has to demonstrate a high conversion rate.

The conversion rate is the percentage of users who respond to a CTA. They might request more information, sign up for your enewsletter, register for a webinar, or make a purchase.

Online marketing success, then, is all about doing two things: generating traffic and converting visitors into buyers. This chapter presents online marketing strategies you can use to drive traffic to your website, blog, landing pages, and order pages.

The Seven Basic Types of Traffic Drivers

Most promotions designed to drive web traffic fall into one of these seven categories:

- *Direct.* Traffic that comes from people typing your URL into a browser
- *Organic.* Traffic from people finding you through a search engine
- *Referral.* Traffic from people clicking on a link on another website
- *Paid.* Traffic coming from PPC or other paid advertisements
- *Email.* Traffic coming from a link within an email you sent
- *Social.* Traffic coming from a social media platform
- *Other.* Traffic coming from unknown sources

Another thing to consider when developing your online marketing plan is the amazing impact of mobile devices on internet marketing.

According to the Global Web Index, we've surpassed the mobile tipping point: as of 2016, some 87 percent of internet users now have a smartphone (a fact which is fast reinventing the connection between companies and their customers). For this reason, always look at how you can drive traffic on mobile platforms.

Your overriding goal is to increase the volume of any one traffic source while maintaining consistent traffic from other channels. Never depend on only one or two channels. Justin Bridegan of MarketingSherpa writes: "It's always best to have a variety of traffic sources. This minimizes the risk of your website being decimated if your main traffic source dries up." With that in mind, let's dig into the first way to drive traffic to your site: affiliate marketing.

Affiliate Marketing

This section isn't just about becoming an Amazon Associate or Click-Bank affiliate and using that status to drive traffic to your independently owned website. It's also about starting your own affiliate program, where you partner up with people who will promote your product or service—generating revenue for both of you and building your email list in the process.

Here's how it works. You give your personalized affiliate links to select products, which they will use either on their website or in email marketing messages. In return, you'll provide the affiliate with a percentage of the profits that you make on the sales they help to create via their promotional efforts. It's really a win-win situation: you're not only making money from your affiliate's work, but also you're getting lots of web traffic (and—if your offer is compelling— lots of new subscribers) from their referrals.

There are pros and cons to using affiliate marketing to drive traffic to your website, as shown in Figure 6-1.

How exactly do you go about finding an affiliate and convincing them to promote your product? All you need to do is set up a page on your website that explains the benefits of promoting your product.

In addition to detailing what's in it for them financially (how big of a cut they will get from each sale), you'll also explain how they'll benefit from being associated with your brand. Include a sign-up form to make it simple for them to contact you. Then, promote the page to individuals and a wider audience in a targeted niche. For inspiration and a template you can use, visit www.becomeablyaffiliate.com.

Pros	Cons
Fast outreach: Affiliate marketing is a fast way to gain new leads and customers, especially when you're not the one doing the promoting— your affiliate is.	Potential use of unethical tactics: Some affiliates will break the rules because the revenue generated by your product's sale is more important to them than ethics.
High traffic: Product sales will bring a lot of new visitors to your website. Affordable cost: Especially when compared to PPC advertising.	Low level of control: You won't have any control over how your affiliates promote your product and what message they provide to their audience.

FIGURE 6–1. **Driving traffic with affiliate marketing.**

Banner Ads

Web banner advertising has been around since 1994—almost as long as the internet itself. One of the first banner ads linked directly to an AT&T promotional page. It had just ten words: "Have you ever clicked your mouse right here? You will."

Today, you can create a banner advertising campaign with any display network, such as Adsterra, Ad Maven, or Adbuff. And, like everything else in the digital age, banner advertising has evolved: now you can also create ads using social media sites like Facebook Banners, Instagram Sponsored Ads, and Snapchat.

There are two types of banner ads: static and animated. The static banner ad is an image similar to a small print ad, but in the digital world, it leads (with the click of a mouse) to a website or landing page. As you'd expect, the animated banner ad attracts prospects through eye-catching motion.

Banner ads worked for a long time, but today, user behavior has changed, creating two issues for advertisers. First, more than 25 percent of U.S. internet users now block online ads—and the number of ad blockers is expected to grow by another 24 percent in the next year.

The second issue plaguing online advertisers: across all ad formats and placements, the clickthrough rate is low—less than 1 percent, according to one source. Today, only 16 percent of users click on banner ads (http://adage.com/article/digital/online-measurement-16-web-clicking-display-ads/139367/). Yet you can still achieve a positive ROI with a well-designed and written banner. Standard banner dimensions are shown in Figures 6–2 and 6–3 on page 87.

When it comes to banner advertising on mobile devices, ad dimension isn't the only concern; for one, you've got to consider what types of devices will display your ad. Consult the Interactive Advertising Bureau's "Mobile Phone Creative Guidelines" (Figure 6-4 on page 88) for device-related specifics.

Banner ads are just one type of mobile advertising. Exit ads appear when the user exits an app using the Back button. Interstitial

Style	Size
Full Banner	468 x 60
Leaderboard	728 x 90
Square	336 x 280
Square	300 x 250
Square	250 x 250
Skyscraper	160 x 600
Skyscraper	120 x 600
Small Skyscraper	120 x 240
Fat Skyscraper	240 x 400
Half Banner	234 x 60
Rectangle	180 x 150
Square Button	125 x 125
Button	120 x 90
Button	120 x 60
Small Button	88 x 31

FIGURE 6–2. **Standard banner ad sizes (dimensions are in pixels).**

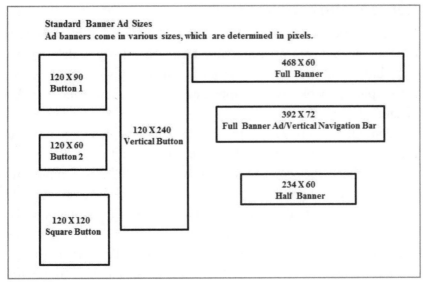

FIGURE 6–3. **Banner ad sizes.**

Ad Type	Dimensions
Static Standard Banner	300 x 50
Static Wide Banner	320 x 50
Rich Banner/Expandable	300 x 50

FIGURE 6–4. **Mobile banner ad sizes for smartphones (in pixels).**

ads are flexible full screen ads which appear whenever the advertiser wishes. Splash ads appear specifically when an app is loading. Sliders are animated banner ads. And native ads match the look and feel of an app by blending the ad into the app itself.

In addition, consider that more and more of your video ads and website videos will be displayed on mobile devices. By 2019, video will account for 80 percent of global internet traffic and 85 percent in the United States. Add to that the fact that over half of video content is viewed on mobile devices, and you've got two compelling reasons to give mobile video marketing a try.

Content Marketing

Content marketing gives you dozens, if not hundreds, of creative ways to focus on the core problem your business—or a product—solves. It includes online articles, blog posts (including guest blog posts), infographics, ebooks, white papers, case studies, and audio or video productions.

Content marketing is effective. In fact, it generates three times as many leads as traditional outbound marketing but costs 62 percent less. So what's the secret to content marketing? That's simple: add value to everything you create. If you're not sure how you can add value through content marketing, ask your existing customers or list members what kind of content would be helpful to them. Social sites like Facebook or LinkedIn are also good sources of content ideas.

A core requirement of content marketing is to publish frequently and consistently. If you cover one topic, publish at least once a week.

If you cover two topics, publish at least twice a week. If possible, publish every day on the content categories that will attract the right audience.

The key to content marketing success, according to Jim Yu, the CEO of content marketing firm BrightEdge, "is to present the right content to the users at the time they need it in an engaging manner, across all channels they visit." That's an enormous task. Fortunately, there are lots of helpful online resources from sites like the Content Marketing Institute and Quick Sprout, which can help you become a master content marketer.

In truth, publishing high-quality content—and lots of it—is not only fundamental to the concept of "content marketing," but it's also essential to each of the other 17 traffic generation strategies we're discussing here. So much so, famed marketer and bestselling author Seth Godin says, "Content marketing is all the marketing that's left."

Co-Registration

This traffic generation strategy has to do with online advertising. It's a process for collecting subscribers by co-advertising along with other site owners or companies collecting opt-in subscribers. Here's how it works: when the user opts in to receive an offer from the other participant(s), they are given the option to subscribe to your information as well.

You've probably seen co-registration in action. Let's say a web publisher runs a contest; as a co-registration partner, the publisher would include a check box on the form for registrants to accept email from a contest sponsor. Co-registration usually gives the subscriber two or more opt-in mailing lists they could join.

Co-registration allows you to target a specific demographic or customer subset. Depending on whom you partner with, co-registration can be less expensive than other types of marketing. Also, with co-registration, building your email list doesn't depend on the amount of web traffic you're able to generate.

There are two major players in co-registration: Opt-Intelligence and CoregMedia, and many choose to work with them. But there are also smaller companies worth looking at, such as AfterOffers and BirdDogMedia.

Temper your expectations with co-registration; the number of subscribers you receive may disappoint you. That's why experts recommend you demand short-term contracts. This way, you're not locked into a co-registration relationship that isn't working.

What can go wrong with co-registration? First, you can fail to capture the interest of the viewer with boring copy—which means fewer co-registrations. Second, you can fail to track your results, leaving you in the dark about the success of your efforts.

Email

Email marketing involves sending commercial messages, typically to a list of people who have given you permission to send email messages ("opted in"). Just a few years ago, the average ROI for email campaigns was 4,300 percent. That fact alone should inspire you to focus attention on email marketing.

Because 56 percent of customers are more likely to buy with a personalized experience, you want to personalize your email marketing messages. As if that's not reason enough, here's another fact about the power of personalization: the average open rate for emails with a personalized message was 18.8 percent, as compared to 13.1 percent without any personalization, in 2016.

Before you get started with email, you need to find the best email service provider (ESP) for your needs. There are lots of ESPs to choose from; some are fee-based, like AWeber and Constant Contact, while others, like MailChimp, are free to use if your subscriber base is small.

Once you select an email provider, you'll put things in place to begin building an opt-in list of interested individuals. Because the average online spending of a repeat customer is twice that of new customers, you'll want to focus a lot of attention on the email channel to stay in touch with existing customers.

The goal of email marketing is to convert an interested customer into a paying customer by driving traffic to sales pages. You can increase clickthrough and conversion rates by making sure the email and the sales page it hyperlinks to are promoting the same offer.

Enewsletters

Without doubt, the enewsletter is a powerful marketing and communication tool. When done well, it can build strong relationships with your subscribers. The problem is, writing a monthly enewsletter can take a lot of time.

Another problem with email newsletters is that they're often cluttered and unfocused because they're supporting every aspect of your business. That's why you should focus on one topic in each issue and include only one clearly worded and persuasive CTA.

Your enewsletter content should be balanced: 80 percent educational and 20 percent promotional. This balance promotes your three overriding goals: drive traffic to your website, build community and reinforce your brand with readers, and make money through the promotions.

Because over a third of email subscribers read their newsletters exclusively on mobile devices, you'll need to keep mobile in mind when designing your enewsletter.

How can you get the word out about your enewsletter? Here are three ideas:

◆ Include your newsletter in directories of other websites or newsletters related to your topics (see Appendix A).
◆ Advertise with a contest or prize drawing, linking back to your newsletter subscription form to be entered to win. Readers who enter the contest will then get your newsletter automatically and will be compelled to visit your website to see contest results.
◆ Promote your newsletter on all your social networks.

Email newsletters drive sales, but they do far more than that. You can boost your social media following by using social sharing buttons. You can connect with your customers and build stronger relationships with them by providing them with valuable content.

Google and Bing Pay-per-Click Advertising

Pay-per-click advertising (PPC) is a model of internet marketing in which advertisers pay a fee each time one of their ads is clicked. Essentially, PPC gives you a way of "buying" visits to your site, instead of earning those visits organically.

Search engine advertising through Google or Bing is one of the most popular forms of PPC advertising. You'll bid for ad placement in a search engine's sponsored links when someone searches on a keyword that is related to the advertised offering. PPC success is achievable if you focus on:

◆ *Keyword relevance.* Develop PPC keyword lists of terms relevant to your audience. Use these lists to write keyword-driven ad text.

◆ *Landing page quality.* If you're sending people to a landing page, you'll need to optimize it with persuasive, relevant content and a clear CTA, tailored to specific search queries.

◆ *Quality score.* Both Bing and Google offer quality scores, which rate the quality and relevance of your keywords, landing pages, and PPC campaigns. Advertisers with better quality scores get more ad clicks at lower costs.

PPC advertising can be expensive. Still, there are three good reasons to try it out:

◆ Businesses make an average of $2 in income for every $1 they spend in AdWords.

◆ PPC visitors are 50 percent more likely to purchase something than organic visitors.

◆ Search ads can increase brand awareness by 80 percent.

To get started with PPC, create an advertiser account on Google AdWords (https://adwords.google.com/home). Bing (https://advertise.

bingads.microsoft.com/en-us) is a cheaper alternative to AdWords, so you may also want to explore its PPC program as well.

Influencer Marketing Campaigns

What is influencer marketing? It's marketing that focuses on using key leaders to drive your brand's message to the larger market. Rather than marketing directly to a large group of consumers, you instead inspire, hire, or pay influencers to get out the word for you.

Why choose this strategy? It's effective for over 80 percent of marketers who have tried it using social media influencers. Also, interest in influencer marketing campaigns has increased more than 90 percent since 2013.

Influencer marketing is a form of word-of-mouth (WOM) marketing. Customers acquired through this channel are retained at a 37 percent higher rate than those acquired through other means.

That's all well and good, but how can you find influencers? There are free tools, such as followerwonk from Moz. It focuses exclusively on Twitter research and analytics and is a handy search engine for influencer discovery as well as provider of tools for competitive comparisons, tracking, and data visualizations. A social authority filter allows you to sort influencers, and you can save reports for future reference.

BuzzSumo is another free research tool which provides insights into the most popular content and the influencers sharing it. You can search by topic or specific website to find the most popular content sorted by total social shares. Search the Influencers option and you'll see results from Twitter data. All results can be filtered for refinement and exported for further analysis.

Fee-based research tools are available, such as Kred, Klout, PeerIndex, GroupHigh, Little Bird, and Keyhole.

Some argue influencer marketing is the wave of the future for online entrepreneurs and big corporations alike. "Influence will lead marketing efforts by 2020," says Ted Coiné of TalentCulture. "It's the most effective form of 'advertising' there is, and when coupled with a solid content strategy, no TV or Facebook ad buy can even compare."

Infographics

Information graphics, or infographics, are visual representations of information, data, or knowledge intended to present information quickly and clearly. The graphic presentation enhances our ability to see patterns and trends. Infographics are very popular right now; in fact, infographics are liked and shared on social media three times more than other any other type of content. See Appendix C for a sample infographic.

Infographics (see Appendix C) are generally long, vertical images that include statistics, charts, graphs, and other information. For more examples, check out Creative Bloq's "60 Best Infographics" or "The Infographics Blog."

Infographics can be especially effective in generating social media shares. You can get a professionally designed infographic by hiring a contractor on an outsourcing site like Upwork, or design your own using a free online tool from Mind the Graph, Canva, or Easel.ly.

Creating an infographic is just part of this strategy; you've also got to promote it.

Start by writing a blog post to accompany your infographic, which expands on the concept presented in the infographic. Now that the infographic and article are on your site, promote them on social media, ensuring that all links come back to your site.

You can then reach out to niche influencers who might find the content in your infographic useful and interesting. Write guest blog posts for websites with high domain authority, sharing your infographic and linking back to your original article as a search engine optimization strategy.

Finally, submit your infographic to infographic archive sites, where others can find and promote them on your behalf: Visual.ly, Visualistan, the Infographics Archive, Cool Infographics, and the Infographic Journal. Post your infographic on Pinterest and Instagram. And always include a hyperlink back to one of your websites or landing pages.

IP-Specific Online Advertising with Geo-Targeting

What we're really talking about with IP-specific advertising is geo-targeting: the method of determining the geolocation of a website visitor and delivering different content to that visitor based on his or her current location, such as country, region or state, city, or metro code or zip code; organization; IP address; internet service provider (ISP); or other criteria.

You can use geo-targeting to increase engagement and conversion rates of new marketing campaigns. Geo-targeting allows for measurement and personalization at a more complex level than possible with traditional media. Here are a few good starting points for using location-based targeting:

◆ Offer incentives (sales, discounts, promotions) to visitors in a specific geographic area.

◆ Target messaging to visitors based on proximity to a store, physical office location, or competitor's location.

◆ Share marketing messages that are specific to local advertising media markets.

◆ Customize the language for a specific geographical location.

Geo-targeting gives new meaning to the time-worn phrase "location, location, location." In online marketing today, you need to pay attention to the location of the consumer and tailor your marketing message accordingly.

Lead Magnets

A lead magnet is a free content offer—an ebook, white paper, case study, e-course, or checklist. The lead magnet should be so relevant to your prospect's needs or problems that they can't help but exchange their contact information to get it.

We'll look closely at the list-building power of lead magnets in Chapter 9. Suffice it to say, the greater the value you give your prospects, the more they will trust you when they give you their email address.

Of all the possible offers—ebooks, white papers, you name it—
which are the most effective lead magnets? Here are five:

1. *The cheat sheet.* The problem-based specificity of the cheat
   sheet, also called a tip sheet, makes it very appealing to prospects (and it's fairly easy to create).
2. *Free templates.* These are extremely popular and generate lots
   of leads, but make sure the template doesn't replace your service or product offering. Templates can be in Word, Excel, or
   any other common program.
3. *Free training videos, workbooks, or a combination of the two,
   delivered through daily emails.* Think about problems that
   require multiple steps for your customers to solve. These
   can make ideal step-by-step training products for your lead
   magnet.
4. *The swipe file.* This is a collection of tested and proven
   copywriting elements (such as headlines and email subject
   lines) or creative ideas the recipient can use to simplify a
   project.
5. *Tool kits.* These can be a little more complex to create, but
   because they are filled with resources, they can make excellent lead magnets. You can use existing resources, blog posts,
   and other content to complete your tool kit. Common tool kits
   include a variety of content types, such as ebooks, worksheets,
   checklists, and video.

Podcasts

Podcasting involves using the internet to make digital recordings of
broadcasts that users can download to a computer or mobile device.
For lots of folks, podcasting is a natural extension of blogging. And
because it's relatively easy and inexpensive, podcasting is considered
the low-hanging fruit of online marketing.

A podcast gives you visibility in a completely different world—
primarily iTunes, but there are other sites where people congregate
to listen in, such as Blog Talk Radio, Libsyn (one of the first podcast

hosting sites), PodBean, Buzzsprout, SoundCloud, Archive.org, and Podomatic.

Podcasting can be a lot of fun, but there is one thing you must do before you start podcasting: you must commit to the channel, just as you would with anything that takes time and effort to do.

Podcasts have the potential to drive lots of traffic to your website. Not only can you direct listeners there at the close of each episode, but every podcast directory in which you list your production (including iTunes) provides listeners with a link back to your website. Other podcast directories include Buzzsprout's Definitive Podcast Directory, Learn Out Loud's podcast directory, and the iPodder directory.

QR Codes

Quick response (QR) codes provide another way to gather contacts for your email marketing efforts. QR codes act like bar codes and provide a smartphone or tablet user with immediate access to a given web page where the user can read the message and take the next step. You could say the QR code is your invitation to a user to begin an offline-to-online transition.

Marketing with QR codes is one of the easiest mobile marketing strategies to get started with, according to Jamie Turner, co-author of *Go Mobile* (Wiley 2012). It does, however, require you to have a mobile website (in addition to a standard version) to direct smartphone users with a QR code.

Before the QR code comes the plan: where are you going to send users and what do you want them to do when they get there? You've got to know the answers to those questions before you start a QR code marketing campaign. Scott Stratten of UnMarketing says it clearly: "Think before you do."

- ◆ The QR code needs to be big and clear enough that even low-quality phones can scan it.
- ◆ There should be a clear indication of which types of mobile devices can use the QR code. If it's for Android only, iPhone

users will be irritated if they try to scan it and get poor results.

Given you've got a mobile website and a solid plan of action, you're now ready to create the QR code you'll use, which is perhaps the easiest step in the process. And it won't cost you anything because there are free QR code generators online, such as QR Stuff and Kaywa QR Code.

What are some ways you can use QR codes? You'll find plenty of good ideas online, including:

- ◆ Add a QR code to the Contact page on your website so visitors can download your contact information to their smartphones.
- ◆ Add a QR code to your business card so people can instantly download your contact information (or respond to a lead-generating offer).
- ◆ Include a QR code, or codes, as part of a webinar presentation for audience engagement.
- ◆ Add a QR code to your LinkedIn and Facebook pages to pull people into your website.

You can also use QR codes on direct-mail pieces to help you gain useful information from your campaigns. The scans can tell you which offers are working best and which geographical areas are responding the most. This knowledge can guide you in refining your next campaign.

Search Engine Optimization

Search engine optimization (SEO) is the process of getting site traffic from the free, organic, editorial, and natural search results on search engines like Google, Bing, Yahoo!, and Ask.com. Without proper site optimization, you can spend every penny you have on a website, but it won't amount to anything if no one can find it easily.

The critical importance of SEO is underlined by these statistics:

- ◆ 89 percent of consumers use search engines for purchase decisions.

◆ 71 percent of business purchase decisions are started with a search engine.

◆ 70 percent of users click on organic results.

◆ 53 percent of organic search clicks go to the first link.

◆ 75 percent of users never click past the first page.

◆ SEO leads have a 14.6 percent close rate, while print or direct-mail ads have 1.7 percent

It is easy to see from those numbers that search provides the most efficient and inexpensive way for you to find leads, so much so that Brandon Pindulic of GrowthHackers says, "Organic leads convert better, come cheaper, and stay longer than leads generated from advertising."

When beginning the optimization of your website, remember there are two SEO arenas: off-page and on-page optimization.

On-page SEO search ranking factors are largely within your control, though of course the Google search algorithm is not. For each web page, you need to identify one keyword phrase and use it in the site's meta tags. Meta tags are words or phrases within the HTML code used to create websites.

To see a site's meta tags, choose View from your browser's tool bar. Then click on Source. A window will open with the site's HTML code. Here are the meta tags that should contain keywords to optimize your site's ranking on Google:

◆ *Title Tag.* After content, the title tag is the most important on-page factor for SEO. The title is what your visitors see at the top of their browser windows when they visit your site.

◆ *Domain Name/URL.* I picked myveryfirstebook.com for my microsite on ebook writing because the keyword "ebook" is in the URL.

◆ *Heading Tags.* (H1, H2, etc.) H1 tags are the page's main head-line. H2 tags are the subheads under the headline that divide the body text into sections.

◆ *Image File Names and Alt Text.* When you send an HTML email with photos to someone who cannot see the images in his email reader, he sees the alt text behind it, which describes the picture he can't view.

◆ *Description Tag.* This is used to provide text in search results and appears under the title tag. When you search on Google, this is the descriptive text you see on the search engine results page (SERP).

◆ *Keyword Tags.* This is a section of the HTML code where you put a list of the keywords prospects are most likely to use when searching for what you sell. You should also incorporate the major keywords at the beginning of your homepage copy.

◆ *Links.* Use internal links to other pages on your site as well as external links to pages on other sites.

Search engines use several off-page SEO factors, some of which you're not fully in control of, including:

◆ Links to your web pages from other websites

◆ Your social presence: content posts are in your purview, but the interactions these posts provoke are out of your control.

◆ Customer reviews from Google, Yelp, Amazon, and the Better Business Bureau

Not all search engines produce conversions to the same degree. Figure 6–5 on page 101 presents recent ecommerce website conversion rates for primary search and social media channels.

SEO can't be ignored. Duane Forrester, former senior product manager of Microsoft's Bing, reinforced this thought when he said, "On a broad scale, I see SEO becoming a normalized marketing tactic, the same way TV, radio, and print are traditionally thought of as marketing tactics."

Social Media

Some online marketers will tell you: the future of business is social. In 2015, some 93 percent of shoppers' buying decisions were influenced by social media.

Channel	Conversion Percentage
AOL Search	4.48%
Bing	3.03%
Yahoo!	2.56%
Ask Search	2.32%
Google	1.71%
Facebook	1.08%
Pinterest	0.36%
Twitter	0.22%
LinkedIn	0.04%
StumbleUpon	0.02%

FIGURE 6–5. **Conversion rates by marketing channel.**

While Facebook is the most widely used social platform in the U.S., with 79 percent of American internet users onboard, other platforms are worth exploring, too. Instagram attracts 32 percent of internet users, Pinterest comes in a close third with 31 percent, and LinkedIn and Twitter lure 29 percent and 24 percent, respectively.

Social media can drive traffic to your website by engaging viewers and offering them useful, relevant content. It can help you to get feedback—by holding surveys, asking questions, and connecting with your audience. The feedback you get can help you adjust your online marketing strategy.

Social media can go a long way in helping you gain the trust of your audience and build your credibility. And your social media account affects your SEO score as well, affecting your website traffic in turn. Social networks are starting to look more and more like search engines, and you can't do SEO without taking care of social media accounts on all relevant channels.

When social media is part of your buyer's experience, customers tend to convert at a 129 percent higher rate. Not only that, they are also four times as likely to spend significantly more than those without a social component. See Chapter 8 for more ways to use social media in your digital marketing.

Text Ads

A text advertisement is nothing more than an ad which uses text-based hyperlinks to direct viewers to a given web page. The term is ubiquitous: Google AdWords and Bing PPC ads are text-based, and there's SMS text messaging advertising; but here, we're talking about using text ads in enewsletters to drive traffic to your website.

Text ads also run in online newsletters. Use enewsletter directories mentioned in the section on enewsletters to find the best publications for your audience. Approach the publisher about placing a text ad promoting your content offering.

If you're wondering what you should promote or how it should be promoted, ask the publisher for any past examples of ads that worked well. If they won't give details, ask for more general information, such as types of offers to which their audience responds. Do ads offering free trials get a good response? How about the response to white papers, demos, or samples?

When writing a text ad, be sure to:

- ◆ Have a strong, short call to action.
- ◆ Keep your ad short. Some experts recommend using less than ten words.
- ◆ If you want to repurpose marketing campaigns, look to your top PPC ads. The best PPC ads will give you a better creative start than any graphic banner ad you are using.
- ◆ If possible, tie your ad to the topic of the newsletter issue and ideally to the headline of the issue. Ask the publisher if they will include a mention of your offer in their headline.
- ◆ Despite the assertion that ad images drive conversions, don't think about using an image in your ad. Text-only ads get higher conversion rates than HTML on average in enewsletters (https://blog.hubspot.com/marketing/plain-text-vs-html-emails-data).

◆ Be flexible in ad scheduling. Your offer calendar and the news-letter publisher's open slots may not always match up.

Enewsletter advertising offers unique and significant advantages. First, it's a quick, cost-effective communications channel. Second, enewsletters give you a chance to reach a targeted audience, one which has already given permission to receive the publication and—in effect—given you permission to contact them (within this context).

Enewsletters also give you a chance to educate readers about your products and services. Email provides you with trackable measures with which to assess the success of your text ads. Of course, another measure of success, if your goal is to grow your list, is the number of new subscribers your ad generates.

Webinars

Webinars, or online seminars, are one of the best ways to drive traffic to your website. They can be easily promoted through a number of channels: social media, email marketing, PPC ads, blog-ging, YouTube or Vimeo videos, and your affiliates or strategic partnerships.

Teleseminars, learning events conducted over the phone, are also effective at driving traffic to your website—depending on your niche market.

For example, life coaches looking to expand their clientele often conduct coaching sessions over the phone, so using their phone to learn from experienced coaches is a natural extension of what they do every day. But for those companies and individuals who expect cutting edge technology, teleseminars may not be the best offer.

A webinar hosting service doesn't have to cost a lot, but it does have to be user-friendly. GotoWebinar, a service of GotoMeeting, is a popular choice, as is WebEx. Not sure about a topic? Take a look at your ten most popular blog posts and think about repurposing them as a webinar. If you don't have content to repurpose, see what others in your niche are doing—and then do it better.

YouTube Videos and In-Stream Ads

As mentioned earlier, by 2019, video will account for 80 percent of global internet traffic and 85 percent in the United States. According to a study from video service Fullscreen, young internet users age 13 to 17 are spending less time with text-based online content and more time with video.

That makes video a smart choice for online marketers, and, because of numbers like these, YouTube is the right place to put your attention:

◆ 55 percent of the population watch videos online every day.

◆ 54 percent of senior executives share work-related videos with colleagues every week.

◆ Using the word "video" in your email subject line boosts open rates on average by 19 percent.

◆ Online shoppers who view demo videos are 1.81 times more likely to purchase than those who did not view them.

◆ Eight out of ten 18-to-49-year-olds watch YouTube in a typical month.

◆ Marketers who use video see 49 percent faster revenue growth than companies that do not use video.

In this section, we'll look at two aspects of video marketing on YouTube. First, it's all about the videos themselves; second, we'll focus on driving traffic with YouTube in-stream advertisements.

The first step is to create a YouTube account, and you can't do that without a free Google user account. You can sign up for a free Google account at https://accounts.google.com/SignUp. You'll use that same information to get on YouTube.

YouTube Videos

After you've got a YouTube account, the next step is to shoot the footage. Of course, it can't be a video someone else owns; it needs to be original. YouTube is concerned about copyright violations, so they've got a process in place: when you upload video content, the system will ensure it doesn't violate any known copyrights.

With today's advanced technologies, you can shoot a video with your phone, camera, or webcam. Don't worry about editing right now; once your footage is uploaded, YouTube's video editor makes it easy to edit and add captions or notations. It also offers plenty of free audio, transitions, and titles you can add to your videos. To see some of my videos, go to YouTube and search for the Bob Bly channel.

YouTube accepts a variety of video formats: MOV, MP4 (MPEG4), AVI, WMV, FLV, 3GP, MPEGPS, and WebM. The same is true when it comes to video resolution: you don't have to be too picky about export settings. A larger, higher-quality file will look better on YouTube, but a smaller file will upload quicker.

If your video isn't in one of these formats, you can always use a free video file converter to save it to one that is supported by YouTube. Three come highly recommended: Freemake Video Converter, Any Video Converter, and Free HD Video Converter.

Once your video is ready for viewing, it's time to get to work sharing it. The easiest way to share your video is to copy the URL YouTube assigns to it. Paste the link into an email for list members, share the link in your social media accounts, or write a blog post about the video (you can even embed it directly into your post). Here are other video promotion ideas:

◆ Use a press release to contact bloggers, editors, reporters, and producers to generate free media coverage for your videos in mainstream media, as well as in blogs that cater to your target audience.

◆ Get your videos listed with the major search engines, including Google, Yahoo!, and Bing, and then focus on SEO strategies to get the best possible listing placements.

◆ Start promoting your YouTube channel within your print materials (brochures and other marketing materials), as well as within any print advertisements.

◆ Consider paying for keyword advertising on Google, Yahoo!, Bing, and Facebook. Google AdWords for Video is also a cost effective and powerful tool for promoting YouTube videos.

◆ Hire a YouTube video marketing company to help you plan and implement an online promotional campaign for your videos.

"If you take the time to upload just one YouTube video each week," says Brian Moran of Get 10,000 Fans, "you will see more traffic. It's that simple. Be prolific with the amount of content you put up, and you will get more visitors."

But don't expect to make money right away from your YouTube videos or channel. In April 2017, YouTube significantly reduced how much a publisher can earn: now, video creators won't be able to turn on monetization until their channel hits 10,000 lifetime views.

YouTube In-Stream Ads

In-stream ads run on videos hosted on YouTube or on a collection of sites and apps in the Google Display Network. Ads may also run on YouTube videos embedded on other sites or apps and appear on Android and iOS YouTube apps, m.youtube.com (on iPad and Android), and on connected TVs.

In-stream ads:

◆ Start playing in front of the video your target audience is watching

◆ Are skippable, and the advertiser only pays when a viewer watches at least 30 seconds of the video ad or clicks on a link in the ad

◆ Can be virally shared with one viewer emailing a link to the ad to another, sharing it on social media, or even posting the link on his website

There is a right way and a wrong way to use in-stream advertising on YouTube. First, you need to grab the viewer's attention right away. If you don't get their attention during the first five seconds the commercial appears, they'll skip it. Second, don't make the ad about you and your company but instead about your viewer: focus on their problem, introduce your solution while building your credibility, and send them to your website to complete the CTA you've put in front of them during the in-stream ad.

Online marketing, says my colleague David Meerman Scott, "is about delivering useful content at the precise moment a buyer needs it." That's a tall order, but he's right. To grow your online business and increase revenue, you must match the way you market your products with the way your prospects learn about and shop for them. I've found those marketers whose websites have the highest number of conversion do things differently:

- They clearly state their unique value propositions (UVPs).
- They test their CTAs and headlines regularly.
- They use fewer form fields and also subject all forms to A/B testing.

The value of testing can't be overstated. The late David Ogilvy once said, "Never stop testing, and your advertising will never stop improving."

The study of internet marketing has led me to believe one thing: success requires an experimental mindset. We've got to be willing to try new ways to attract and engage our audience, to rigorously test what we're doing, and to let go of what doesn't work. You'll find out savvy internet marketers are lifelong learners; they are always on the lookout for what's new, what's tried and true, and what's working *now*.

CHAPTER 7

DRIVING TRAFFIC TO YOUR WEBSITE WITH OFFLINE MARKETING

Long before the internet, websites, blogs, and various social media channels, marketing consisted of direct-mail packages, letters, and postcards sent through the postal service. There were also advertisements on radio and TV and print advertisements placed in trade journals, newspapers, and even the Yellow Pages. Offline marketing and advertising worked very well for many decades, and surprisingly, it still works today, albeit with some changes.

You can use the best of both digital and offline marketing strategies and tie it all together to create a well-rounded multichannel marketing program. Any type of offline marketing can have a link back to your website, a blog, an enewsletter sign-up page, or a webinar registration form.

You can also offer a link to an online video that further explains a product or service or gives a phone number for customers to call for an appointment. There are so many options available today, and next year, there will be even more.

Whenever you create offline marketing pieces, you can include your website URL and company name, the URL for a landing page for a specific campaign, and social media text-based hyperlinks. Print your company name and logo on paper marketing pieces as it builds recognition when customers see it on sales letters, brochures, postcards, and ads. In this chapter, we'll discuss the various ways you can do offline marketing and connect it back to your online multichannel marketing program.

Linking Print and the Internet with QR Codes

The Quick Response (QR) code can easily bridge the gap from print to mobile phone screens and to your landing page.

Using QR codes is a quick and easy way to link print marketing materials of any type with just about any online multichannel marketing program you have developed. Customers with mobile phones and a downloaded QR code reader/scanner app can interact with any of your print marketing pieces carrying QR codes. So if you want customers to go to a landing page, put the URL inside the QR code when you create it, and paste the code onto your marketing materials.

When customers open the mobile phone QR reader/scanner, they center the phone app's box edges on the screen to fit over the square code on the paper so that the paper QR code is fully enclosed inside the mobile phone's screen box corners. The app will automatically acquire the code's information, or the customer can tap the phone's Enter button at the bottom to capture the code to the phone.

Once the QR code is scanned in from the print document, a screen pops up on the phone with the information enclosed inside the code. At the bottom of the QR reader app are buttons for browsing that URL address, copying the content (such as to a contact list), sharing the content, or sending a mobile phone message to that website. It is a simple and effective way to convert customers to your landing page, for example, where they can sign up for your emails or buy your product.

It is also easy to track customers when they scan a QR code and then follow their actions. For example, you can customize your code to request location verification. That way you'll know where and when a purchase was made.

In your search for a QR code generator company, you will come across the terms "static" vs. "dynamic" QR codes. In simple language, the static code is there to stay in its original creation, and the website URL it was created with cannot be changed. The dynamic QR code is editable by function and content, such as the URL address. The coding process also shortens the URL address, although you may have to pay for this service with some QR software creators.

Several companies you can check out for your QR code needs are: qr-code-generator.com, goQR.me, QR Stuff, TEC-IT, and Wasp Barcode Technologies, to name just a few.

You can signal boost your digital marketing efforts with several different kinds of print outreach materials. A combination of some or all of these can help drive traffic to your digital footprint. In the next few sections, I walk you through some of the possibilities.

Direct-Mail Packages

Every marketer should be continuously developing a list of potential customers in a marketing database. These are people you have researched and chosen as the most likely contact in a company (if you are a B2B marketer) who will decide to buy your products or services. Included in your database is what you send them, when, and the responses.

A crucial factor in creating and supporting this type of database is making sure your company contacts are up-to-date before sending out a mailing. If not, you must find out who the new contact is and add them to your list.

A positive benefit of growing your list is that you can segment it by variables, such as type of business, or if you're targeting individuals, by age, gender, interests, or locale. Then, you can begin a marketing campaign to bring them in when you have a new service or product geared to them.

You can also rent mailing lists for a one-time direct-mail run based on a specific interest, such as a gardening magazine's subscription list or an arts group subscriber list. List brokers can help you find and rent the right list according to your needs.

It is helpful to have a customer profile already built so you can look at the summary data cards of possible lists to help you decide whether the list is worth testing. List brokers include InfoUSA.com, Mailing Lists Direct, Infogroup Media Solutions, AccuList USA, Reach Marketing, Merit Direct, and many more.

An important part of your marketing and mailing budget is deciding how much you want to spend on mailing out your direct-mail packages. One way to do this is to build a sample package, take it down to the post office, have them weigh it and tell you how much it will cost to mail each packet, and determine whether you need to buy a permit for bulk mail. You can choose from different classes of mail: first class, second class, and third class.

A simple package consists of a marketing letter explaining what your service can do for your customer, a prepaid business reply card the customer can send back to you showing interest in knowing more, and the outer envelope. Self-mailers work well when the primary response mechanism is a URL as it can be printed in large, bold type on the outer panels so the prospects see it even before opening the promotion.

If your URL address is long, you can shorten it first before printing it in your letter or postcard by using www.Bit.ly or www.TinyURL.com. Always test the shortened URL before sending it out in print materials.

The next step of your direct-mail package depends on what your customer wants to see, as checked on the returned postcard: a brochure, white paper, article samples, or samples of your work for other customers. You would then follow up in a week with a phone call or an email message, where you check to see if the customer got the package, has had a chance to review it, and whether they have any questions you can answer.

Postcards

While reply postcards can be included in the direct-mail package, another way to use postcards is as a reminder to a customer who received the introduction package several weeks back. If you do not hear anything back in the first mailing, send a reminder card. After that, it is your choice whether to call them or wait longer before making contact again.

You can also include your postcard in a pack of cards that people find in their mailbox, which includes many other vendors, such as a local dentist, life insurance company, landscaping companies, local restaurants giving a discount on a lunch, and so on.

One side might have copy describing what services or products you offer, including your company name and a website or landing page URL. Be sure you have enough white space so the card is easy to read and not cluttered. Include a place on the reverse side for you to affix a label with the customer's contact information, as in Figure 7–1 on page 114.

Brochures

Brochures are a great marketing tool you can use to present the services or products you're promoting for interested customers. In addition to including these in your direct-mail package, you can carry a few around with you and hand them out to those who are interested, or you can leave them at strategic locations, such as your local chamber of commerce, the doctor's office (if they agree), or any businesses you visit that you think might need your services.

Brochures come in many sizes and may have more than one page. You can take a letter-sized 8.5-by-11-inch sheet of paper, and in landscape orientation, fold the right side over two-thirds towards the left, then fold the left side over the folded right side. The resulting shape is about 3.25 inches wide by 8.5 inches tall, with the edges meeting on all sides. These are called "slim jims."

Alternatively, you can use a legal-size page in landscape orientation, fold each side over to meet almost in the middle, and

Now Own the Latest Edition of Bob Bly's

Business-to-Business Marketing Handbook
– for FREE!

Bob Bly
Copywriter
31 Cheyenne Drive
Montville, NJ 07045

Online: www.bly.com/b2bhandbook/
Or call **973-263-0562**

Now, in your **FREE** copy of Bob Bly's recently updated 181-page e-book *The B2B Marketing Handbook*, you'll discover 35+ years of tested B2B marketing secrets that can double or even triple your clicks, conversions, leads, and sales. Including:

- **10 tips for increasing landing page conversion rates** – page 10.

- Best practices for B2B lead generation – page 54.

- What's working in B2B e-mail marketing today? – page 112.

- 7 tips for more effective content marketing – page 78.

- **The 6 key components of effective B2B offers** – page 19.

- 5 ways to build a large and responsive e-list of prospects – page 29.

- **How to write technically accurate copy for high-tech products** – page 143.

- And more ...

To download your **FREE** Handbook (a $49 value), go to:
www.bly.com/b2bhandbook/

FIGURE 7–1. **Postcard driving recipients to a URL where they can download a free handbook.**

then fold both sides together at the center. You can use a software program such as Microsoft Publisher, Adobe Illustrator, or Adobe InDesign that has templates for brochures, making it easier to create professional brochures on your desktop.

You can add your logo and your company name on the front fold and give a one-sentence description of what you offer to your customers that entices them to open the brochure to see more. On the inside left-hand page, give a brief description of your service or product and add your website URL address at the bottom.

In the center, you might provide a bullet list of your service's features or show benefits of using your product. At the bottom of the center page, add your email address. On the right side, you can show any offers you are making, such as a bonus or discount, including a call to action using a QR code. Include your phone number on this page.

On the back of your right-side page, you can give all your contact information in one place. If you have plans to mail the brochures as self-mailers, then the center back page is where you put the address area consisting of three to four lines of text and a pre-set return address at the upper left side corner. Typically, you can create stick-on mailing labels from your software, such as Microsoft Word and Excel; or if you rented a list, the names and addresses may come pre-labeled.

Print off your brochure at home if you have a good printer and only need a few copies. But if you are including your brochures in bulk direct-mail packages, you could choose to have a professional printing company handle the job. Whichever way you decide, the outcome should look as professional as possible with a clear resolution for images and bleed-free text.

Your professional print specialist can help you choose the right type of paper to use as well as print out a test sample for your approval if you bring along your completed work on a USB flash drive or CD. Using a professional printing company will cost you more money, but if you need to look professional to your target customers, then use their services.

Make sure in the sample your print specialist gives you that all your content is clean and sharp. If you are using QR codes, test each one with your mobile phone QR reader to make sure they go where you intend them to go on the internet. That is another reason why you will want to include the website address underneath (not too close to the QR code), so you can be sure the code is accurately printed. Once you are pleased with the sample quality, then you can approve your printing job.

Many businesses post color PDFs of their brochures on their websites. That way, the prospect can get an instant download, a paper brochure in the mail, or both.

Catalogs

If you have many products or services to offer your clients, then consider creating a catalog, including a picture and an identification code for each product. You may already be selling these items in your online store, so use the same item numbers, or codes, that apply to the online version.

Pre-internet, catalogs were the primary vehicle for selling merchandise by mail, with the response options being an order form or a toll-free number. Nowadays, catalogs are used more to drive prospects to the website for ordering online.

Supporting your website with a print catalog increases revenue an average of 163 percent over sites that are not augmented by a catalog. Men's apparel e-retailer Bonobos says first-time customers who place an order online after getting a print catalog spend 50 percent more than new shoppers who did not get a catalog in the mail first. And nearly one out of three shoppers has a print catalog in hand when making an online purchase.

You can design a sheet, or several sheets, of paper to show each product along with several lines of description and a link to the online store, including a product QR code that goes right to the item online. Depending on whom you send the catalog to and how often, consider using a nice cover so the catalog can be easily stored by the customer.

You can create a cover page with your logo and your contact information and then use a clear plastic front cover. Check with your office supply store to see what they carry in stock, such as a three-prong fold-over cover where you would use a three-hole paper puncher. A slim, hard notebook where you can insert the front cover page into a plastic sleeve on the front face of the notebook also works well.

Another choice is a binding machine that inserts a plastic comb-styled spine onto the pre-cut side of the catalog papers' edge, making it easy for the customer to lay the catalog open on the desk while making an order. Company training manuals are often created using this style of binding.

Also, consider whether you'll send your catalog in a direct-mail package or only to those who show an interest in ordering from the catalog. This can be one of the choices included on a return postcard from a direct-mail package.

Print Newsletters

Newsletters can serve many functions, including offering advice to customers. For example, a group of financial advisors might publish a newsletter that details their predictions of the next greatest stocks to invest in for the long term. Their clients and prospects receive the newsletters once or twice a month, and each issue is three to four pages long. Financial writers give a lot of detail about why they consider the recommended stocks top-rated investments, including a statistical summary of past performance and a forecast, presented in graphs and charts. While the same articles and information may be presented on the company's website, such a newsletter is an informative marketing piece meant to be sat down with and digested slowly.

Newsletters typically encompass several articles. The main stories begin on the front page, where only the first few paragraphs are given, followed by a note to go to another page to read the rest of the article. That way, several top stories of interest can be placed on the front page. Links to websites and landing pages can be given, including the use of QR codes, which are easy to scan from the page.

Your newsletter gives insight in how to use one of your products or services and how this helped one or more of your customers. The newsletter, in general, should not be a total sales piece but rather focus on giving useful information. Including links or QR codes to landing pages for your products is considered proper, however, when it aligns with the content.

Your newsletter layout should provide enough white space between articles, with simple dividers marking the end of each story section. You can create a two-column layout or set it like a regular letter, with dividers between sections. Images are nice, but consider whether you want to use color or black and white images, which may depend on your printing capabilities and budget.

If you are printing and sending your own newsletters by regular mail, you may want to keep them to two letter-sized pages. This way, you can easily fold them to fit into a size 10 business envelope.

To save on envelopes, use the blank back side of your folded sheets to put your customers' address labels, along with the return address at the upper left-hand corner. Just use sticky square or circular labels to keep the sheets closed while in transport, one at the center of the long side, and one at each end of the short sides.

If using the postal permit, it may be easier to use envelopes rather than folding the pages over and sealing them. You can find out from your post office what the most economical practice would be based on your mailing budget. Be sure to bring in a sample newsletter so they can help you make a good decision.

Today, print newsletters are making somewhat of a comeback for two reasons. First, with people's inboxes flooded with online newsletters, print newsletters—which are rarer—stand out and get noticed. Second, print newsletters can be shorter, as key articles can refer readers to company web pages for expanded content on the topic. Here are just some of the topics you can include in your company newsletter:

1. *Product stories.* New products; improvements to existing products; new models; new accessories; new options; and new applications.
2. *News.* Joint ventures; mergers and acquisitions; new divisions formed; new departments; other company news. Also, industry news and analyses of event and trends.
3. *Tips.* Tips on product selection, installation, maintenance, repair, and troubleshooting.
4. *How-to articles.* Similar to tips but with more detailed instructions. Examples: how to use the product; how to design a system; how to select the right type or model.
5. *Previews and reports.* Write-ups of special events such as trade shows, conferences, sales meetings, seminars, presentations, and press conferences.
6. *Case histories.* Either in-depth or brief, reporting product application successes stories, service successes, etc.
7. *People.* Company promotions, new hires, transfers, awards, anniversaries, employee profiles, customer profiles, human interest stories (unusual jobs, hobbies, etc.).
8. *Milestones.* For example, "1,000th unit shipped," "Sales reach $1 million mark," "Division celebrates 10th anniversary," etc.
9. *Sales news.* New customers; bids accepted; contracts renewed; satisfied customer reports.
10. *Research and development.* New products; new technologies; new patents; technology awards; inventions; innovations; breakthroughs.
11. *Publications.* New brochures available; new ad campaigns; technical papers presented; reprints available; new or updated manuals; announcements of other recently published literature.
12. *Explanatory articles.* How a product works; industry overviews; background information on applications and technologies.
13. *Customer stories.* Interviews with customers; photos; customer news and profiles; guest articles by customers about

their industries, applications, and positive experiences with the vendor's product or service.

14. *Financial news.* Quarterly and annual report highlights; presentations to financial analysts; earnings and dividend news; etc.

15. *Photos with captions.* People; facilities; products; events.

16. *Columns.* President's letter; letters to the editor; guest columns; regular features such as "Q&A" of "Tech Talk."

17. *Excerpts, reprints, or condensed versions of.* Press releases; executive speeches; journal articles; technical papers; company seminars; etc.

18. *Quality control stories.* Quality circles; employee suggestion programs; new quality assurance methods; success rates; case histories.

19. *Productivity stories.* New programs; methods and systems to cut waste and boost efficiency.

20. *Manufacturing stories.* New techniques; equipment; raw materials; production line successes; detailed explanations of manufacturing processes; etc.

21. *Community affairs.* Fundraisers; special events; support for the arts; scholarship programs; social responsibility programs; environmental programs; employee and corporate participation in local/regional/national events.

22. *Data processing stories.* New computer hardware and software systems; improved data processing and its benefits to customers; new data processing applications; explanations of how systems serve customers.

23. *Overseas activities.* Reports on the company's international activities; profiles of facilities, people, markets, etc.

24. *Service.* Background on company service facilities; case histories of outstanding service activities; new services for customers; new hotlines; etc.

25. *History.* Articles of company, industry, product, or community history.

26. *Human resources.* Company benefit programs; announcement of new benefits and training and how they improve service to customers; explanations of company policies.

27. *Interviews.* With company key employees, engineers, service personnel, etc.; with customers; with suppliers (to illustrate the quality of materials going into your company's products).

28. *Forums.* Top managers answer customer complaints and concerns; service managers discuss customer needs; customers share their favorable experiences with company products/services.

29. *Gimmicks.* Contests; quizzes; puzzles; games; cartoons.

Article Writing

Writing articles for local and national publications, websites, and blogs is a great way to increase your professional profile as well as your company's digital brand. It also helps build your sample portfolio, showing that you often do guest articles for various well-known publications. In most cases, publications may be both in print and on a company's website.

Either way, make sure you can include a link back to your company website, blog, or social media pages for new readers to follow you. In addition to getting paid for your work, you are also bringing in new leads who may be interested in buying your service or products in the near future.

Whenever your articles are posted online, share links to them on each of your marketing channels and use hard copies as part of your direct-mail package when relevant. If your article is published in a print magazine, have a copy of the article reproduced in color to include in your public relations packages.

Writing and publishing articles for different periodicals, sites, and blogs is like getting free advertising. The more you can guest publish the greater ROI you get, plus you establish yourself as an expert in your field.

Additionally, you'll bring in more customers by linking your articles back to your website, blog, or landing pages. Focus on your industry, and publish as often as you can in related trade publications, offering useful information that encourages readers to want to know more about you and what your business can offer them.

Public Relations

Public relations (PR), whether you conduct it for your business or for a client, is about getting the news out on something new, whether it be a service or a product. For example, you can send a written press release—a one- to two-page overview—to newspapers, bloggers, radio stations, and television stations. Depending on the product or service, you can target your release locally or nationally.

Newspapers may print the release as is, with no editing, or a journalist may call you wanting to do an interview about the product or service and about you. This is a cost-effective method of getting the news out there.

Here's an example. If you, or a client, are seeking support for a new charity for wounded and disabled soldiers, consider upcoming events as possible PR opportunities. If the organization is having a grand opening of a new building where wounded soldiers can get help finding housing, look for jobs, or get financial assistance, write a press release and let your local media know. A story like this would be of great interest to most news organizations and their subscribers, particularly on a local level.

Provide your contact information in the header of the press release, followed underneath by the line, "For immediate release." Create an attention-getting headline, followed by the title of the charity and name and date of the grand opening event. The body of the release offers information about the event, as well as how the charity plans to help soldiers, such as gathering new clothes and household furniture, finding low-cost housing in the local area, and asking for funds to help soldiers and their families with food and other necessities.

Client: The Brownwood Center for Wounded Soldiers www.brownwood.com
Contact: Mr. John Johnson 203-123-4567 jjohnson@brownwood.com

For Immediate Release:
The Brownwood Center for Wounded Soldiers Charity Drive—Grand Opening on July 16th, 2017
123 Brownwood Drive, Anytown, Any State, 10001
Event takes place in the John Pease Auditorium from 9 A.M. to 8 P.M.

***

We are a new charity serving the needs of local wounded and disabled soldiers, who need a helping hand with finding new homes, household furniture donations, new clothes, and jobs available in our local community.

On Monday, July 16th, 2017, we will be signing up soldiers to join our charity so they can be put in line to receive available housing, furniture, or clothing, and be considered for jobs with local businesses that have contacted us concerning current and upcoming openings.

We ask members of our community, along with willing business leaders, to stop by and donate anything that they can, including funds to help with food distribution, for those in our military who have given so much to our great nation. It is time we give back so our soldiers can live in dignity, without worrying about what the next days will bring.

For more information on our grand opening on July 16th, please call the contact number.

Text 454265 to donate whatever you can, to help our soldiers live better lives!

FIGURE 7–2. **Sample press release.**

Of equal importance is the list of soldiers who want jobs, based in the local area, which will be connected with those local businesses looking for soldiers who could fill various positions (see Figure 7-2).

This press release would be typed on a single page and sent to all the local news outlets. It provides enough information to understand the charity's focus but also might interest a journalist in conducting an interview. Most press releases are sent via email. If the recipient does not know you personally, paste the press release text into the body of your email as users do not want to open attached files from people they do not know for fear of getting a virus.

While an editorial journalist would do a story for the paper, probably with a photograph, TV stations could do an onsite interview, possibly including a video tour of the new facility. A fact sheet can go with the press release, giving the news organization more precise points of interest their readers may want to know about, such as how the charity got started and where to send donations.

Send dated press releases, such as Figure 7-2 on page 123, at least two weeks before the event. A week after you send it out, call the editor of those entities you sent the release to and follow up on whether they will be publishing a story.

You can also update them with any news that has occurred since you sent out the release; for example, that donations from the community have reached $100,000. Always let the editors know you will be happy to answer any questions that might come up, and gently encourage them to do a story if they had not already planned for it.

Be sure to use keywords and phrases in your press release. That way, when you post your press releases on the newsroom or media section of your website, people searching those subjects can find it.

Print Ads

Print advertisements remain a very popular part of the mix in many businesses' well-rounded multichannel marketing programs. While we may spend many hours trolling the internet looking for different pieces of information, magazines and other print communications still garner much attention, especially when people want to sit and relax with a favorite magazine.

Be sure to advertise in a magazine that reaches the same target customers you want to reach. There must always be a connection between what you offer readers and the publication you are advertising in.

If you are a specialist in gardening articles and marketing, you can advertise in gardening trade magazines that you help gardening businesses with their marketing and advertising copy. The size of your ad is based on what sizes a publication has available to offer you and what your budget can allow. If you have a print ad in a publication, make sure the online ad version is the same.

Do not forget to put in links to your website or landing pages, if you are selling a product or service, and include a QR code as well for easy access by mobile phone. Also include your email address, phone number, and website URL.

TV and Radio Commercials

Creating, producing, and placing TV and radio commercials is the venue of larger companies with huge marketing and advertising budgets. The hottest spots companies reach for are the Super Bowl advertising slots. Millions can be spent to get that glorifying five minutes or less on the air. Then, there are the costly evening spots on primetime TV. Local businesses pay less because they advertise only in their region vs. major consumer brands who run national commercials.

But all is not lost for the smaller business, who can advertise in a different way—with guest interviews. Interviews with radio and TV hosts do not cost you anything. While this may fall more under the public relations category, it is still free advertising.

If you want to be interviewed on TV or radio, you must offer a compelling reason why a station would ask you for an interview. One such reason is that your new book has just hit first position on *The New York Times* book list. Or maybe you have come up with an invention that is so unusual that news outlets clamor to be the first to interview you about it.

You can also consider creating your own commercial, showing the invention and what it does, and this can be shown during your TV interview. This same video, acting as an online commercial, can also be shown on your landing page where consumers go to buy your invention. During your TV interview, your landing page address can run across the bottom of the screen, including a phone number people can call if they want to know more.

Public Speaking

Public speaking is a great way to share information in your field of expertise—and you will become better known as a consequence. If you have never spoken before in public, try out smaller venues first just to get some experience.

The most effective way to succeed is to plan what you want to talk about first. If you need slides to back up your speech, then check what you need to have, besides a laptop, a connector plug, and the device that will show your slides on a screen or blank wall behind you. Bring along a printed copy of your slides just in case a problem occurs and you cannot use the machine.

Depending on how many people have registered to attend your speech, you can create copies of your slides to pass out to everyone so they can follow along and make notes on each slide.

This is also a perfect time to bring some of your products, such as books, which you can sell during an intermission or at the end of the speech. You can also create marketing material packets, using a paper clip. Do not forget that these materials should also carry all your contact information, including QR codes, which attendees can use while still at the center.

Never forget to market yourself or your company, no matter what venue you are using. Offline marketing aligns well with your online channels as long as you use the right tools to bridge the gap between the two marketing venues.

When I speak, I often hire a videographer to record it. Then, I post the talk on my YouTube channel or my website directly as streaming video or make it available on DVD.

CHAPTER 8

WINNING WITH BLOGGING AND SOCIAL MEDIA MARKETING

Among the many ways of building your website traffic and a community of loyal followers is creating one or more blogs and using multiple social media outlets, which you tie back to your website or landing page.

If you are selling products or services from your website or blog, then it is essential that you know how to bring in traffic from your multichannel marketing infrastructure. For blogs, this means doing some research first to find out the best prices on features in domain registration and hosting sites for your blog.

The first step in building a blog is to decide what you are blogging about. Ideally, the blog disseminates ideas or information relevant to your prospects. Example: a car company blog giving auto repair and driving tips.

Once you know the topic the blog will focus on, then decide what the domain name should be. That name should be easy to remember and closely align with the blog topic. When viewers see the URL address, they know exactly what they will be reading about when they go there to read your blog.

You can wait until you decide which hosting company to use first and have them register your domain name. Or you can go to any accredited ICANN (International Corporation for Assigned Names and Numbers) registrar and do it ahead of time. That way, you have your domain name even if you do not start your blog at once. If you have plans for several blogs, then you can decide on the names, check through your registrar to make sure each is available, and buy them in bulk. You may even get a discount for buying more than one.

Check that you have 24/7 customer support from your hosting service, whether it be through email, phone, live chat, or ticket numbers for ongoing issues. Other things to ask about are whether they offer privacy protection for your contact information (unless they are subpoenaed) and what the fees are for SSL (security sockets layer) certificates to enhance online security for your blog. This is important because you will be protecting the contact information of those who sign up to read your blog.

As you start your research, make a spreadsheet with domain registrar companies listed in the left column. Each column after should list first-year registration fees, annual fees (may be different from first year), privacy fees, SSL fees, level of customer service (phone, chat, email, or 24/7), and whether they host blogs as well.

Here are some domain name sources to look at, for starters: Bluehost, InMotion Hosting, GoDaddy, 1&1, HostGator, Namecheap, Google Domains, Ultracheapdomains, and Register.com. Many of these double as a hosting company as well, so check on hosting fees while you are doing your domain registration research, based on your needs and budget.

You also now have the ability to purchase specific extensions for your blog URL address, such as: .blog, .guru, .buzz, .tech, .club, and many others. Choose an extension that reflects your blog's persona. For example, if you're offering software or hardware advice, then .tech might be reflective of your future messages. GoDaddy is a starting point for customized extensions. Always remember that your website and your blogging site should have as short a name as you can make it.

Hosting Company

Decide what hosting company you want to use after checking around for prices and what blog platforms the hosts will accept. If you have not registered your domain name yet, check to see what the hosting company's annual domain registration fee is as it may be cheaper to register your name through a separate company from your hosting company. One of the most popular is www.hostgator.com.

Find out what kind of software packages are used to build your blog site. WordPress is the most commonly used content management system (CMS) for many bloggers as well as for website design. Many hosting companies that offer CMSs of their own to build websites also offer WordPress as a choice for building websites and blogs.

You can use a different CMS, such as Site Builder, for the website, and the host company can install WordPress for you to use for your accompanying business or hobby blog. If you do use a different CMS for your website, you may not see the blog as part of your page setup because of the two different platforms. Be sure to include the URL link on your website, preferably on each page, so people can get to the blog from your website.

Blogging Platforms

WordPress, an open-source software platform, is the most commonly used platform for creating blogs; some hosts will set that up for you with just one click. WordPress comes with free and paid themes, but also check out others you can use. For WordPress, there is the downloadable version you can get for free at WordPress.org. If you go this route, then make sure your hosting company supports the WordPress platform; most do.

The other version is found at WordPress.com, where WordPress hosts your blogging page but is very minimal in terms of extending it further. Extra purchased options include a custom domain name and added storage. You also cannot use advertising platforms, such as Google AdSense, which is discussed further on in this chapter.

You will also run across the term WordPress Theme Frameworks, which means that the WordPress version you downloaded from WordPress.org has been taken by a company of developers and recoded to be more efficient, using the developer's own toolkits. Some charge fees for their package, while others offer them free, such as CherryFramework.

Whichever way you choose to go, make sure that your framework package has great support, provides regular updates, is easy to install and work with, has many plug-ins and widgets, offers ecommerce capabilities, and supports HTML, CSS, and JavaScript.

Blogger is a Google-owned basic platform where you can tie your blog to your website. This is essential if you want to use Google AdSense to place advertisements on your blog and make some money. One of the conditions for your website, to be approved for AdSense on your blog, is that you must be able to edit HTML on your site. Once approved, you can place the AdSense code on your site or page. Your website must also have been active for at least six months as part of the approval process.

Once you open your account in Blogger, you can decide on the theme you want for your blog and the page layout, create campaigns, create an email for people to contact you, and set the comments parameters. If you already have a Google account, such as Gmail, your Blogger account recognizes you as a Gmail customer and will use the front part of your Gmail email address. You just need to add in the second part in the space provided to you to create the new Blogger email address for your blogging account.

Alternatively, you can also buy a separate domain name to have your blog placed there, unrelated to your website, and you can use Google Domains to get the new domain name and get the Blogger account set up. Your blog continues to be hosted by Blogger, as it does when attached to your website.

YouTube, also owned by Google, is one of the largest global video hosting platforms in social media, and it can also use Google AdSense.

For both Blogger and YouTube, you must go through your created accounts for each to make an application for AdSense approval. Your own website needs a separate AdSense application approval process. (More on YouTube in the social media section.)

Tumblr is another blogging site that is easy to use. You can select the topics you want to see in your feed, and you can re-post to your own blog as well. Your dashboard offers the ability to add posts with text, GIFs (graphic interchange format), audio, photographs, quotes, and links and to conduct chats with other members. While you can blog here, Tumblr also integrates with social media channels, making it easy to cross most platforms with a link.

You can also use Google's AdSense here by getting your code after you make your application through AdSense and then clicking Edit on the title of your Tumblr blog's title. Then, click on Customize Theme on the right side of the page, click on Edit HTML on the left side, add your AdSense code, and click Save. Your Tumblr account must already be approved for publication for AdSense to consider your application. Much like Blogger, you can also buy a custom domain name on Tumblr, which makes it easier to use AdSense.

Ghost is a blogging platform with two options: hosted or as a software package that you can host yourself. Either way, you will spend a bit, as the hosted version is $19 a month, while your self-hosted version will have the annual custom domain fee and monthly hosting fee (as with whomever you have your account). You can also use Google AdSense with this infrastructure.

Typepad is another place to create your blog, independent of a brand like Blogger and Tumblr. You can get a 14-day free trial to see how it works, and pricing starts at $8.95 a month. If you want the choice of multiple blogs, then this may be the place for you. Typepad also supports the use of advertising, but make sure you know which ad networks it allows.

There are plenty more blogging platforms out there, but be sure that you can add on Google AdSense or other advertising networks if you want to monetize your blogs. You can also look at website hosting companies and ask if they offer a blogging platform that attaches to the website account. Companies that offer both website and blogging capabilities include: Weebly, Wix.com, Squarespace, GoDaddy, Aabaco Small Business, Web.com, eHost, HostGator, and others.

To see examples of well-written and successful blogs, check out www.copyblogger.com, www.webinknow.com, www.garyvaynerchuk. com/blog/, and http://sethgodin.typepad.com/.

Integration with CRMs and Shopping Carts

If you want to sell from your blog, WordPress may be your best choice of blogging platform. WooCommerce, a popular WordPress plug-in, can add extensive ecommerce functionality, including online ordering and payment, to your WordPress blog or website (https://woocommerce.com).

Another company to consider for ecommerce is 1ShoppingCart. If you are selling T-shirts, for example, you can have drop-down menus for customers to select the size and color they want, font type, gender type (which affects size), and custom slogans if you are offering that. You can also sell any products, such as books, services, and subscriptions, and it takes all payment types.

Additionally, the platform is screen-responsive to devices, such as mobile phones, making it easy for customers to shop on their phones. Whenever a sale is made, you can set your account to receive a notification by phone or with their desktop notifier.

You can also add on automated discounts, offer coupons, and even offer upsell products. You must always check that there is a mail system connected to the shopping cart, which you can use to send notices to your customers about sales or special events.

Other ecommerce companies to look at are: BigCommerce, Squarespace, 3dcart, Wix.com, Shopify, Big Cartel (good for niche sellers), LemonStand, and many more. Each deserves a look, and you want to make sure that you can get good customer service, that you can expand your shop over time, and that your shopping cart is easily customizable, including the use of AdSense and other ad networks.

If you are building a membership site, consider using MemberGate, which is specifically designed for such sites, as your software platform (www.membergate.com/). It handles all major functions including membership sign-up, payment, monthly billing, email, content management, and more. You can also tie in Google Analytics to monitor traffic, including where customers are coming from, which helps you fine-tune your multichannel strategies to be more efficient.

Writing Blog Posts

If you are just beginning to blog, you may find yourself staring at that blank screen, wondering what you can write about that would interest your soon-to-be followers. You can start with a brief welcome post, which gives a little insight into why you started your blog. You may have a website that offers services or products, so you want to align your copy and content with what is offered on that website.

Pick an issue or problem that your service or product may help with, but give it more of a story about how you had a problem which you solved by creating a new service to address it. Blogging is a storytelling process rather than an attempt to sell something outright. In fact, keep that side of it low-key. Most people coming to your blog want to learn something new rather than just be sold to outright. Blogging is the perfect place to present a more personalized brand—not only of yourself but of your company.

Use a conversational tone when telling your story. If you can add in verifiable research statistics, include those as part of your story. This builds trust and a relationship with your readers because they'll know you are not making it up. Just be sure to use reliable sources and not just a front for someone's own agenda. Government and scientific sites are an excellent (for the most part) place to get statistics.

Depending on the type of company you run, you can be informal and open, or you can decide that the tone of your website dictates that you take a more professional approach. Only you can make that decision as you build your image and brand for both the company and yourself as its owner, or positioned employee, such as the public relations manager of a large enterprise.

When you have finished your draft for your blog, go ahead and set in any social media plug-ins so readers can share your blog for you. However, do not add more than five plug-ins, as it may be confusing for viewers to decide which ones to use. If you need to add disclaimers of any sort, then you should add them at the bottom of the blog.

After you have finished your post, but before you publish it, go through and choose keywords relevant to the post that readers would be most likely to search on Google, and add those in. If you are using WordPress as a blogging platform, you can activate the WordPress SEO Yoast Plug-In.

If you so choose, you can pay to upgrade the plug-in to the premium version where you can get personal help by email from customer service. Another feature in the premium version is the ability to have more than one keyword or term included in your post. This is important if you are monetizing your blog, along with adding in any advertising network on your blog.

The Yoast WP SEO plug-in, used on a WordPress website, also controls the page that shows up in Google search results, such as the home (or index) page of a website, rather than a secondary page. Additionally, it creates XML sitemaps, including images in posts, and sends that information to Google and Bing.

Once you activate the WP SEO for Yoast plug-in, you can also integrate the Linkdex Page Analysis into the WP SEO plug-in and get a content analysis report of your post. This analysis can tell you whether you need to add your focus word in an alt tag for your images or a note that your keyword is not in your page title. But that is only a small part of what you can do with this combination. To find out more about how Linkdex can be used, as described by Joost de Valk, CEO of Yoast, go here: https://yoast.com/content-seo-wordpress-linkdex/.

You can also conduct joint ventures with other businesses by doing guest posts, unless you are paid to do a guest blog. This is another way to promote your website and blog and any offerings you make to your customers. The key is to always link back to your website and blog, or even a landing page, although make sure this is fine with your guest blog publisher. It is just a matter of common courtesy to make sure you can do this, including any links to social media channels, such as Facebook, Twitter, LinkedIn, and other places where you have a presence, particularly if they are monetized.

Useful Blog Additions

This section discusses how to monetize a blog, using several Google tools that add keywords to your blog, as well as how to create internet advertisements using Google AdWords. If you do not have a Google account, then you want to create one now. One way is to create a Gmail account for email, preferably one you could use for business, even as a secondary backup to your business email that is attached to your website.

Once you have your Google email account, then most of your Google accounts can be tied through to this email address. This is helpful when opening Google AdWords and AdSense accounts as your contact information will be sent throughout all accounts automatically, including payment options, unless you want to add a different payment account. That way, you have a Google customer identification number, consistent through all Google accounts, and a Google payment identification number.

A suggestion about Google payment options: when starting out, and if you are managing a small set budget, use a refillable card as your payment choice and fill it with the reasonable amount you are willing to pay, say, for ad campaigns. It is more secure for you in knowing how much money you have set aside for your campaign and that you can just add or transfer more funds when you are ready. You can also follow your ROI by seeing how much you spend to get active customers.

Different Google applications can help you with keywords and advertising to attract customers from the internet universe to your website or blog. You can use AdWords to buy traffic. With AdSense, you are paid when your traffic lands on your pages and clicks on advertisements from AdSense and any other ad networks you are using on your pages.

Social Media Marketing

While people of every age use social media, the heaviest users tend to skew younger (Figure 8–1). Social media can be a way for people to build community, but it can also be a time suck. A University of Pittsburgh School of Medicine study found that people who check social media throughout the week most often are almost three

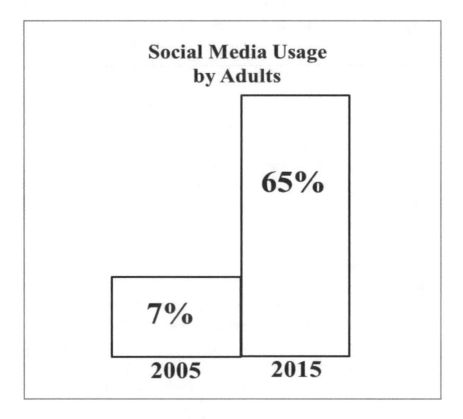

FIGURE 8–1. **From 2005 to 2015, social media usage by adults increased nearly tenfold.**

times more likely to be depressed than those who check it less often.

Facebook, Twitter, and LinkedIn are the three top social media sites, but that does not mean you should concentrate on just those. There are also Pinterest, YouTube, Instagram, Google+, Snapchat, Periscope, Reddit, Tumblr, and a host of others. Each one has a specific platform you should study, including looking at how businesses mold themselves on each platform, such as Amazon, Walmart, Starbucks, and Microsoft, to name some bigger enterprises.

The first step in working with each social media channel is to decide who your target customers are and whether they are likely found in the channel you are looking at. For example, if you are targeting business leaders, you may want to spend more time with LinkedIn and Google+. From there, you can look at other social media platforms, see how they work, and decide if you can create messages or postings that would work well on that platform to bring in your target customers.

Facebook can be a great asset if you are using a business page where all your posts and shares contain business news of interest, with some alternating posts of other news of interest, such as from the scientific community or NASA. Avoid politics, religion, and racial issues as if they were the plague. You can do that on your personal page, but if you have friends who are also business leaders, then leave those topics out over there, too.

This next section looks at the platforms of several social media sites so you have an idea of where to share blogs and also whether channels can be monetized with AdWords and other traffic-boosting tools. You will also want to include analytics so you can see behind the scenes at what your readers are doing and how they react to your messages.

Facebook

Take advantage of creating a business page linked to your website or blog. Fill out all the forms that Facebook asks of you so your business is represented in the best way possible. This is also another good place to employ keywords that reflect what your business does.

You can share links to your blog through a post with the blog link included, which automatically gives a picture of the blog page. Consider adding in a few content details above the link that encourage readers to click through to your blog. This also works for videos you may have done, which are hosted on YouTube as well. If your pages already use AdSense, then you will have more customers linking to those on your websites—and make money at the same time.

If you want to advertise on Facebook, then you can use the Facebook ads feature. Once you set up your business page(s), you will find the choice for creating a Facebook advertisement on your business front page. When creating your ad, you can target your ads to specific customers, such as by certain interests, location, age, and any number of variables relevant to your product or service. You can have your target customers land on your business Facebook page, your blog, or your website, or even your Shopify store on Facebook. You pay for impressions (CPC), which is how many times your ad comes up to be viewed by a targeted customer. You also pay CPC when someone clicks on your advertisement and goes to the link provided.

YouTube

You can find just about any kind of videos on YouTube, and if you are planning a marketing strategy with a video you have created, then you can share this across most social media platforms, especially when you link back to YouTube. You also can use AdSense with YouTube videos, allowing you to make some money in the process, whenever anyone clicks through to view the video.

Add a link underneath the video on YouTube, which leads to your website, blog, or landing page, or as part of your introductory content to the video when you create your post to share across multiple social media channels.

Snapchat

Snapchat, which launched in 2011, has about 100 million users daily. It is used primarily for sending videos and pictures to friends and family that typically are not saved. You take pictures from inside your account and then send them to others. Another tool is the video record chat where you can call someone, and once they join, you can talk through the app, just like a regular phone call. Or they can just see you during the phone call and send you messages. You can also create stories, which last for 24 hours and can be added to over the active period.

While Snapchat is a more informal application, businesses can still use it by creating videos of special events and advertisements. It is also a great way for brands to sell products by mobile phone, as the click rate is about five times higher than on other social media channels, per the Snapchat video on www.Pocket-lint.com. Recently, Snapchat opened its new self-serve ad manager, where you can buy video snap ads; on the Snapchat Mobile Dashboard, you can track campaigns at any time.

LinkedIn

If you are in business selling products and services, then LinkedIn is the place to be seen. One of the ways to put yourself and your business out front and center is by contributing to general posts seen by a person's group of contacts. You can also link to your blog from there as well.

LinkedIn is a more professional business-oriented social media site than any other out there right now based mainly on connecting with potential business partners. You can also create a business page on LinkedIn where customers can reach you rather than just going to your website, although that link is included, too, as well as your blog link. If you are selling products, then consider adding those landing page links in as well.

This is not a place where you would use AdSense or other ad networks, although you can connect with people who work with those companies. Instead, consider sharing links in your posts and on your profile, as well as your company page, if you created one as the owner. These links click back to monetized sites, adding a little money in your pocket over time. You can also join groups you are interested in to become more known in your industry, and if you so choose, you can create your own membership group, charging a fee to subscribe.

Twitter

Tweets are limited to 280 characters, which you can follow below the tweet box where the number begins reducing to zero as you type. You can also add videos and pictures on Twitter, along with links to your website, blog, or landing page.

You can now also create campaigns to grow your followers, gaining a better edge in some of those becoming customers as well. If you want to share news about a new product or service, then you can use the broadcast link or create an advertisement by clicking the link at the bottom of the page.

Do not forget about the hashtag, which Twitter became famous for and which helps put your postings in a searchable category of topics. If you want your post to be found, then check on any current categories first or make your own. More social media channels are also using the hashtag to make posts, videos, and pictures easier to find and comment on and to gain more followers.

Social media channels are always changing and growing, so it is good to stay in touch with new developments and how you can take advantage of those, including how to monetize your marketing channels with AdSense or other services. Share blogs every time you create one, share links to your website where you can, and always keep an active Google AdWords campaign going.

CHAPTER 9

BUILDING YOUR OPT-IN LIST

Experienced internet marketers have a saying: "The money is in the list." An opt-in elist is a list of names and email addresses of people who have registered on your site by filling out a form—and in doing so, have given you permission to email them both content and marketing messages.

The way to build a list is to use the traffic sources shown in Chapters 6 and 7 to drive traffic to a "name squeeze page"—a web page with the sole purpose of getting people to opt into your elist. An example is my page www.bly.com/reports, which has a conversion rate of nearly 50 percent, meaning for every 100 people who click on that link, 50 subscribe to my list. Using this page, I went from a list of zero to 65,000 names in less than a year.

In this chapter, we'll examine the many list-building alternatives available to you, but first, let's look at the ins and outs of choosing an email service provider (ESP).

Picking an Email Service Provider

For our purposes, an ESP isn't Gmail, FastMail, or Outlook. Instead, it's a company that offers email marketing services to businesses. There are dozens to choose from: MailChimp, AWeber, Mad Mimi, Campaign Monitor, Constant Contact, Pinpointe, Bronto,and Emma are some of the most well-known. Any one of these email service providers can:

- ◆ Manage the opt-in and opt-out process: new subscribers will be added automatically to a list and receive a welcome message from you when they opt in, and they can be removed from your list in seconds if they want to unsubscribe.
- ◆ Make sure you are abiding by all CAN-SPAM laws by automatically adding an unsubscribe link and your mailing address to the bottom of every email message you send.
- ◆ Provide you with mobile-friendly templates for your bulk emails so your messages look great on all devices.
- ◆ Handle delivery for you so it's considerably more likely that your emails will actually get delivered to the inboxes of your intended recipients.
- ◆ Give you reports on the results of your email campaigns so you can see how many subscribers have opened (and clicked on the links in) your messages.

Seven Things to Consider When Choosing an ESP

Once you determine whether an ESP makes good business sense for you, you'll want to decide how and with what company you'll choose to work. Keep the following in mind:

1. *First and foremost—even more important than the monthly cost—is the ESP's user interface.* It's a good idea to test several ESPs before you make your final choice.
2. *Second, your budget.* How much money can you spend each month to get the services you need? If you're just starting out, it might be smart to use a free ESP, such as SendinBlue or

MailChimp. You can always upgrade to a higher-level plan if your list grows beyond the limitations placed on their free accounts.

3. *Third, your goals.* If your list-building goals are modest, your ESP choice will be different from someone who plans to send huge email campaigns and autoresponders to thousands of subscribers.

4. *Fourth on the list is tech support.* If you're new to email marketing, you might want an ESP with 24/7 technical support. If you're more tech savvy, you might get by with less.

5. *The fifth thing to consider is the reputation and reliability of the ESP.* You want a service that has been in business for a long time and has a solid reputation.

6. *The sixth consideration is related to ESP reliability: its deliverability.* Most established ESPs have high deliverability rates (that means a high percentage of your emails will make it into your subscribers' inboxes because they aren't blocked by spam filters).

7. *The seventh consideration is important to anyone who already has a list of subscribers: import requirements.* Some ESPs require you to ask all imported subscribers to resubscribe to your list—which could lose you many of your existing subscribers. Stay away from those services as the resubscribe requirement could wipe out most of your list.

Every ESP uses different pricing models, so be sure to choose the one that best suits your list size and expectations for growth.

Email List-Building Best Practices

There are a few cardinal rules of email marketing you should never break. The first has to do with getting a person's permission to send them messages. Permission is given when someone opts into your list, and everyone—without fail—needs to have opted in. Here's the crux of the issue: permission has to be verifiable. This can be taken care of automatically if you use an ESP that tracks the date and time of opt-ins.

Another cardinal rule: always include an unsubscribe link in email messages sent to a list. It's the CAN-SPAM law: you're required to give people a way to unsubscribe from your list in every campaign you send. This further ensures you are emailing in an acceptable manner. A bad email reputation can cause recipients to get messages from their ESPs warning them to be wary of opening messages from you.

Use a double opt-in system to ensure subscribers really do want to be on your list. In a double opt-in, prospects confirm their sign-up via email before they're added to your list.

Elist Maintenance

If a list is full of bad or unresponsive email addresses—if your email messages can't get through—the list is of little value to you. Here are things you can do to ensure your list is "clean":

- ◆ Perform a simple data check to correct typos or misspellings (like kathy@gmailcom, or terry@yaho.com).
- ◆ Track both "soft" and "hard" bounce rates. You can correct a soft bounce, which indicates a temporary delivery problem, by resending the email at a later time. A hard bounce is different: there's nothing you can do for these permanent delivery failures except remove the contact data from the list—immediately. Why? Because internet service providers (ISP) track bounces; if you generate too many, an ISP may block your messages, ultimately damaging your reputation.
- ◆ Closely monitor spam complaints. For lots of folks, it's easier to report your messages as spam than it is for them to unsubscribe from your list. That means you've got to stay on top of such feedback, identify complainers, and remove them from your lists.
- ◆ Remove inactive subscribers to improve ROI. You only want engaged subscribers on your list. Before taking this step, consider a re-engagement campaign. (See "Reinvigorate Stale Lists" later in this chapter for more information on reactivating subscribers.)

MarketingSherpa found email marketing databases naturally shrink by about 22.5 percent every year. Couple that finding with Experian's research showing that every dollar invested in email marketing initiatives yields about $44.25 return, and you've got two good reasons to make sure your list is clean.

Affiliate Marketing and Joint Venture Deals

Affiliate marketing is a business arrangement by which an online retailer pays a commission to an external website publisher for traffic or sales generated from its referrals. But I'm not talking about Amazon Associates, ClickBank, or CJ Affiliate; instead, I'm referring to using this revenue-sharing model with other individual list owners to add contacts to your email list.

Here's a real life example. If you go to the homepage of www.bly.com and scroll down to the footer, you'll see a link to an Affiliates page. Here, those interested in selling my information products can register to become an affiliate.

I added 1,000 names to my email list simply by offering 100 percent commission on the sales of the ebook *Writing Ebooks for Fun and Profit* to an affiliate who owned a list of 450,000 names. All he had to do was send out an email promoting the book. It was a win-win: he earned hundreds of dollars with one mailing, and because every name I gained was a buyer, I got a long list of warm, prequalified subscribers.

Joint ventures are also cooperative enterprises entered into by two or more parties for the purpose of a specific project or other business activity. All that's needed to form a joint venture (JV) is a written agreement that spells out the purpose of the joint venture; how the parties will share in profits, losses, and expenses; and how the parties share in making decisions.

When it comes to affiliate marketing and joint ventures, who should you partner with? No matter the niche market, your goal is to partner with influencers—those individuals known by your audience and who have a degree of leverage within your niche.

Start connecting with individuals at your current level of influence; look for people who are serious about building their brands, and work together to expand your collective influence—and grow your respective lists.

Enewsletter Subscription Offers

An email newsletter can be your most valuable business and marketing tool, but it has to be done well. The content has to be valuable and interesting to your readers.

When promoting your enewsletter, you need to give prospects specifics: why the publication is of value, the publication schedule, and the ease of unsubscribing, should they want to. It can be beneficial to offer a few back issues to prove the publication's value.

Where do you promote your enewsletter?

- ◆ Use your sign-up form as the star of your homepage
- ◆ Place your sign-up form on every page and blog post
- ◆ Make a promotional "squeeze" landing page
- ◆ Use your mailing list landing page URL in your social media profiles and your email signature
- ◆ Link to the landing page from any and all guest posts you write
- ◆ Add the URL to business cards or print marketing

Facebook Ads and Boosted Posts

Facebook offers online marketers an enormous audience: worldwide, there were over 1.94 billion monthly active Facebook users in March 2017 (an 18 percent increase over the previous year). Facebook reaches over two billion people daily who, on average, spend about 35 minutes on the platform.

Facebook advertising is one of the most popular forms of advertising today for many reasons: the variety of available ad formats, the large and diversified audience base, and potential for engagement. You can build your list using Facebook a few different ways: through advertisements seen in the right-hand sidebar of a targeted user's Facebook feed page (or embedded in their feed), through the use of "boosted posts," and via sign-up forms and incentive offers on your Facebook business page.

Facebook advertising isn't as cheap as it used to be; in truth, the average price for a Facebook ad has been increasing 9 percent year over year. (An ad seen by users in the United States and Canada can cost as much as $14.34 per user.)

What Are "Boosted Posts," and How Do they Compare with Facebook Ads in Cost?

A boosted post is a promotional option available to owners of a Facebook business page (you can't boost personal posts). The cost varies depending on how many people you want to reach. If you've got a post you'd like to boost, you can view different budget options by clicking on the Boost Post button. In the dropdown box that follows, you determine your audience and choose one of the budgets that appear or set a custom one.

Boosted posts aren't the only way to use your Facebook business page to promote a list-building offer. It won't cost you a dime to promote offers on your timeline (without paying to boost the post), and it's easy to add a compelling CTA button to the top of your Facebook business page.

Don't be boring! "Sign up for my free newsletter!" isn't very interesting or persuasive, but the energy behind a CTA like "Grab the free ebook: 77 Sure-Fire Ways to Make Money Online!" gets a user's attention. The CTA is linked to a landing page that requires an email address for access to the offered download.

What about Facebook Live Videos?

This addition has generated a lot of interest; in fact, according to Google Trends, "Facebook live stream" search popularity has risen more than 330 percent since its appearance in 2015.

If you're thinking video is the way to go, here are two more facts to prove its worth as a list-building tool: studies show Facebook gets more than eight billion video views every day, and users are spending three times more time watching live videos as compared to the recorded ones.

Again, you'd start with a free resource like an ebook or checklist (relevant to the topic of your live video). You'd direct viewers to a landing page to collect email addresses, and then directly ask users to download it during your Facebook Live session.

You'll also "pin" the landing page link as a comment on your video—and add it to the video description—so that viewers can download it even when you're not live.

Giveaways

There's a fundamental of list building: the more you can engage people, the more likely they are to sign up for your list. And everybody, it seems, loves the chance of getting something for nothing.

Here's a good real-life example: freelance writer Josh Earl grew his list by close to 200,000 quality subscribers in just 11 days by running a giveaway. He already had a list of 5,500 people, all of whom were interested in getting tips on using Sublime Text, a text editing program.

His giveaway: a free license to the text editor, valued at $70. Once the giveaway was set up, using a WordPress plug-in, Josh spread the word about his offer through social media and his current list. After 11 days of promoting his giveaway, he had collected 187,991 email addresses. But there's more: his website received visits from 398,896 unique visitors (significantly driving up his site ranking), and his Twitter following more than doubled.

What does it take to run a successful giveaway? You already know from this example: you've got to offer a prize your audience actually wants—and they should be prizes which are relevant to 1) what your company does and 2) what your audience needs. Here's a caveat: before you step into this list-building arena, consult with your attorney to make sure terms and conditions are properly stated.

In-Mail

What we're talking about here is using social media share buttons in each and every email message you send to your list. In doing so, you make it easy for your current subscribers to share your content across a variety of social platforms: Facebook, Twitter, LinkedIn, and so on. It's a worthy list-building strategy: according to the Social Times, adding social sharing buttons to your email messages may increase clickthrough rates (CTRs) by more than 150 percent.

Email service provider GetResponse affirmed the finding when it studied the trend of adding in-mail social sharing buttons and discovered there's a 158 percent increase in CTRs when you add social sharing—taking it from 2.4 percent to 6.2 percent.

Lead Magnets

Spend ten minutes looking around online and you'll quickly discover the widespread popularity of lead magnets, defined by the folks at DigitalMarketer as "an irresistible bribe offering a specific chunk of value to a prospect in exchange for their contact information."

I mentioned lead magnets in the opening of this chapter (you can see it at www.bly.com/reports). The offer is irresistible: four free reports with a combined value of $100, and half of the people who visit the page agree with me. They jump at the chance to get four wealth-building reports: "Entrepreneurial Retirement: How to Make $100,000 a Year Selling Simple Information Online in Your Spare Time," "Secrets of Successful Business-to-Business Marketing," "How to Double Your Response Rates at Half the Cost," and "Online Marketing that Works."

The titles of these reports teach something: your lead magnets—no matter the type of content—need to have specificity. They must solve a specific problem with a specific solution for a specific segment of people. To get high conversion rates and build your list, your lead magnets must:

◆ Promise to help prospects easily achieve something (and deliver on that pledge).
◆ Have high value, both in the mind of the prospect and in reality.
◆ Be available to the subscriber instantly, either via a thank-you page or through a welcome email message with a download link.
◆ Showcase your unique knowledge and know-how.

Start with one high-value opt-in incentive, which you then promote on your website homepage, at the top of your sidebar, after each blog post, in your website's footer, on your About Us page, or in a pop-up box.

Don't like pop-ups? People love them or hate them, but there's not much doubt they're effective. Michael Stelzner of Social Media Examiner attributes 70 percent of his list of 190,000 subscriptions to the site's pop-up form.

You'll want to test the placement and—in the case of pop-up boxes—timing as you go along. How long after a visitor arrives should a pop-up appear? Not surprisingly, timing does impact conversions: studies have shown if pop-ups are displayed after five seconds, the sign-ups are the highest. In another experiment, opt-ins peaked at ten seconds and were comparatively poor at the five-second mark.

Using a lead magnet as a list-building strategy is efficient. You only have to create one piece of content—although it does have to be something special—and then promote it. For the average small-business owner, the task is manageable.

If the thought of writing scares you, don't worry. You don't have to create the most interesting thing ever written. And if you don't want to write, you can still use this strategy: just hire a freelance writer to create the content. Or choose an alternative to text-based content like a video or audio presentation.

Leverage Social Proof

What's social proof? Also known as social influence, social proof is persuading people a product, service, or thing is good based largely on the fact that it is popular. The classic example is when McDonald's restaurants posted signs with running tally of how many billions of burgers the chain had sold to date worldwide.

Without doubt, social proof is powerful: 63 percent of consumers say they are more likely to purchase from a site that has product ratings or reviews. There are six major sources of social proof:

1. *Customers*: social proof from your existing customers or users (testimonials or case studies)
2. *Experts*: social proof from credible and esteemed experts in your niche
3. *Celebrities*: social proof from celebrities or other influencers
4. *Crowds*: large numbers of people who provide social proof
5. *Friends*: people who are friends of your users or website visitors
6. *Certifications*: a credible, third-party entity which certifies that you are a knowledgeable, high-quality, or trustworthy source

Don't have much social proof to work with right now? Start by leveraging what you have, such as:

- ◆ Social shares
- ◆ Media mentions
- ◆ Ratings and reviews
- ◆ Colleague endorsements
- ◆ Subscriber count

Then, work to get additional social proof from a variety of sources. A few things to remember:

- ◆ *The key to social proof is volume.* The more you have, from a variety of sources, the better.
- ◆ *Negative social proof reduces persuasiveness.* If you've just finished a book about dieting and want to build a subscriber base to promote its release, don't say, "97 percent of overweight people will never lose the excess weight." It only assures the reader there's not much hope for them, so they won't subscribe.
- ◆ *Positive social proof is more influential than money.* This is based on an environmental study examining the effectiveness of four signs on changing consumers' energy-consumption patterns. The most persuasive sign wasn't the one that mentioned saving $54 a month; it was the sign which declared 77

percent of their neighbors were already actively using window fans to save energy.

◆ *It's better to have no proof than poor proof.*

◆ *Social proof,* especially in the form of testimonials, works better with pictures.

Positive social proof should be placed prominently on the pages of your website and your lead-generating landing pages.

List Swaps

Don't think list swapping is about handing over your list in exchange for someone else's. When you think about the sanctity of your subscriber's private information, and the fact your subscribers didn't give you permission to give their sensitive information away, such a trade would be (at the least) highly unethical.

A list-swapping arrangement between two or more parties is a cross-promotional agreement. Basically, each party agrees to promote the other's list-building offer to their own list.

Here's a personal example. I contacted Robert Ringer, bestselling self-help author of *Winning Through Intimidation* (Fawcett, 1984) and *Looking Out for #1* (Funk & Wagnalls, 1977). I had an idea for a list swap: "I'll promote your newsletter, and you promote mine." The first time we did, I added another 900 or so subscribers to my list. And it took very little time or effort.

But you've got to have a list first. Once you've got a small list established—say, 400 or 500—you can start thinking about list swaps.

Who do you swap with? Someone whose mission you agree with and can support; someone you respect and who respects you. Whomever you choose should have a very similar target audience but not be in direct competition with you.

If you each have a lead magnet that would be beneficial to the other person's audience, you list swap by each writing an email to your list about how awesome the other blogger's free lead magnet is.

When engaged in list swapping, think of the service you're doing to your own list by introducing them to valuable information that can help them in a fundamental way.

Offline List Building

So far, we've only looked at online list-building strategies. Now, we're going to review how you can use direct mail (self-mailers and post-cards), conventions, meet-ups and trade shows, and TV and radio spots to grow your list. But first, an unexpected offline list-building strategy: cold-calling.

Cold-Calling

Nobody likes the idea of calling someone out of the blue. Bear with me for a moment: this strategy costs you nothing but time (or a bit of cash if you hire a virtual assistant to do the calling for you). It requires knowing the name of the individual you'd like as a subscriber and a short script:

> "Hi, this is Sarah from ABC Company. I have an important email to send to Mr. Bill Bower. Would you mind connecting me with him to get his permission to send it?"

If that doesn't get you to Mr. Bower, continue:

> "The reason I'm asking is that I work for Kathy Flores, a well-known and respected insurance marketing expert. She puts out a weekly email newsletter that several thousand insurance agents receive, read, and enjoy. The only reason I'm calling is to ask Mr. Bower if he'd be open to us emailing him the weekly newsletter. Our readers tell us it takes about six minutes to read each one and they are finding a lot of value in it. Can you connect me?"

Of course, if you're connected with Mr. Bower right away, you'd use much the same language to convince him of the value of reading the email you're requesting permission to send. (Don't worry about legalities because by getting permission directly from Mr. Bower to send an opt-in email—and not just getting verbal permission and then adding Mr. Bower's name to a handwritten list of email addresses for later list inclusion—you're compliant with CAN-SPAM laws.)

Direct Mail

Self-mailers (folders that can be sent by mail without enclosure in an envelope by using a gummed sticker to hold the leaves together) and postcards are two of the least expensive ways to add names to your subscriber list.

Self-mailers give you more area to work with than a postcard, and since there's no envelope hiding the contents, both self-mailers and postcards make it easy for recipients to see the contents of your mailing immediately.

Postcards are cheap: you'll pay anywhere from a nickel to 15 cents apiece for standard-sized postcards, depending on the volume ordered. Self-mailers will cost you far more, but the advantage of extra selling space may prove worth the cost.

What should you offer? Whatever it is, tie it to a sign-up: make it so the (irresistible) offer can only be redeemed when the recipient signs up for your newsletter.

Networking

If you attend live events like trade shows and association meetings, you'll have many opportunities to add subscribers. Some are passive: your business cards and product or service brochures should feature a sign-up link or, better yet, a QR code. The QR code will allow people to opt into your email list simply by scanning the code.

Is collecting email addresses at such face-to-face events considered "opt-in" by email service providers (ESP)? The answer is yes if you do so using a form that clearly indicates the person is signing up to join your email list. Many marketers have found using a tablet computer with a data collection app to be the most efficient (and ethical) way to gather contact information. Be sure to send these contacts a welcome email as soon as possible confirming their opt-in to your list.

The cost of acquiring subscribers at live events can be difficult to calculate. It's not the cost of printing business cards and brochures; the cost is more in the amount of time spent and the amount of money you spent to attend the event. Still, it's relatively inexpensive—especially when compared to TV or radio promotions.

TV and Radio Advertising

Now, we're in the big leagues when it comes to spending. Radio advertising production costs can run you between $500 and $1,000, to which you'll have to add the cost of airing your radio spot. And what will it cost you to run a local TV advertisement? Rates vary depending on the time of day and year as well as location. You may pay anywhere from $200 to $1,500 for a 30-second spot at noon; but an ad seen between 6 and 7 P.M. will cost you far more. National TV advertising, which can run $100,000 for a 30-second spot, is beyond the budget of most small businesses.

PPC Ads on Bing and Google

Pay-per-click (PPC) advertising is another way to build your list, but it will cost you—and depending on your niche market and the search engine used, it could cost you a lot.

A quick cost comparison between Google and Bing (Figure 9–1) reveals the cost-per-click (CPC) differences.

Keyword	Bing CPC	Google AdWords CPC
Men's boardshorts	$0.48	$1.35
Labor laws	$0.96	$3.30
Medicare supplement insurance plans	$5.99	$11.58

FIGURE 9–1. **PPC ads cost less on Bing than on Google.**

Whether on Bing or Google, every PPC click should end up on a landing page promoting a lead magnet enticing enough to convert a prospect into a subscriber.

Beyond cost, there's another downside to PPC advertising: ad setup and management can be quite time consuming.

Still, by investing some money and time, you can get in front of your audience much more quickly than if you relied on other list-building strategies.

Referral Incentives

Just to be clear, when we're talking about referrals, we're talking about incentivized sharing: you're rewarding existing subscribers for referring your content to their friends and co-workers—and success-fully getting them to sign up for your list. It's about making them an offer they can't refuse: a product discount, ebook, or exclusive special report—as in: "If you get a friend to sign up, I'll give you both something of value in exchange" (a free ebook or video training, for example). Here's how it works:

1. A subscriber receives an email message containing a personalized sign-up referral link.
2. The email is forwarded to a friend (who is not a subscriber).
3. The recipient signs up using the embedded link.
4. Both parties receive the reward.

Many email service providers, such as MailChimp, make it easy to integrate referral incentive links in your outgoing email messages. Also, you'll find a number of referral software-as-a-service (SaaS) providers online: Referral SaaSquatch, RewardStream, and Referral Rock are three that come to mind.

Reinvigorate Stale Lists

Do you have an older list that you think is mostly decayed? Chances are, you're right: experts say you'll lose approximately 23 percent of the contacts in a list each year.

Here's what you can do to re-engage at least some remaining subscribers. Create an enticing opt-in message, and send it to your old list. Offer an exclusive incentive to recapture their attention (like a poll or survey, online competition, discount, or exclusive content available to no one else) and encourage contacts to re-opt-in. If it's appropriate, you can reinvigorate with a product launch email series.

What do you do with the names of nonresponders? Remove them from the list. As these individuals have no interest in what you're offering, their contact details are worthless to you. Remember: the success of an email marketing campaign isn't measured by the number of subscribers; rather, it's measured by the quality of the subscribers and the actions they take as a result of your email.

Surveys and Quizzes

If the widespread popularity of Buzzfeed's personality quizzes (seen on Facebook) is any indicator, people love taking quizzes online. (Who can resist taking a quiz like "Which State Do You Actually Belong In?" or "Are You a Hopeless Romantic, or More Practical and Pragmatic?")

The popularity of interactive media, including online surveys and quizzes, is only growing, and savvy internet marketers are focusing on interactive ways to build their email lists.

Whether you're crafting a personality quiz or a knowledge-based quiz—where an individual's subject matter proficiency is tested, as in "Are You a Content Marketing Expert?"—you need to choose the right title and quiz type for your audience. When it comes to titles, there are three popular options. There's the "Actually" title, as in "How Much Do You Actually Know About SEO?" It's effective because "actually" transforms the title into a challenge—and who doesn't love a challenge?

Then there's the "Which (Blank) Are You?" title; as in "Which Superhero Are You?" And finally The "Celebrity Personality" title: "Which Peter Dinklage Character Are You?"

There are a few best practices for the development of online quizzes and surveys. When creating a quiz, you want to:

◆ Create five to six engaging and entertaining questions.
◆ Be personal toward your audience.
◆ Add images for greater engagement.
◆ Keep the overall experience under five minutes.

Much the same is true for surveys, but as the data collection tool has a more serious tone, there are some logical differences and one major similarity: you want to keep your survey short, taking three to five minutes to complete. Also, you need to:

◆ Make sure every question is necessary.
◆ Ask one direct question at a time.
◆ Avoid leading and biased questions.
◆ Use response scales whenever possible.
◆ Avoid using response grids or matrixes.

Surveys and quizzes alone aren't enough; you want to add an experience into the mix. This can be a feedback form that automatically pops up after someone submits their email in a different pop-up on your site, such as an event sign-up form. You can provide a follow-up survey asking, "What other events would you like to see from our company?" Then use the visitor response to add them to a targeted email list rather than a generic one.

You can promote your surveys and quizzes lots of different ways: through Facebook ads or boosted posts, in PPC advertisements, on your website, in blog posts—even offline.

SurveyMonkey is a popular service for conducting online quizzes to your list. A good incentive is to offer the survey results to people who complete and submit the answers.

Webinars, Teleseminars, and Virtual Summits

Webinars are seminars conducted over the internet, as are virtual summits. Teleseminars, as the name implies, are events conducted over a phone line.

Webinars are one of the most efficient, versatile forms of content you will ever create, and they work like a charm for list building. A solid webinar can be recorded in an hour and serve as a standalone product, a product launch piece, or a cog in your direct-sales funnel.

The average cost of conducting a webinar is between $100 and $3,000 depending on promotion and technology costs. When it comes to cost saving, nothing can beat the teleseminar. If you use a free teleconferencing service like www.FreeConferenceCall.com, the technology side will cost you nothing.

Both teleseminars and webinars are valuable tools—not just for list building but also to:

◆ Share your expertise and position yourself as an expert in your niche
◆ Attract your ideal clients or customers
◆ Sell your programs, courses, and services
◆ Make more money consistently month after month

The virtual summit, of course, doesn't shine a light just on you; it's a showcase for other marketers as well. Every presenter can promote a paid offer or a lead magnet during or after the interview (a link to the offer is also published on the interview page). Of course, all the experts involved promote the event to their own email subscribers.

When creating a webinar, teleseminar, or virtual summit, focus on a specific topic. Select half a dozen or so subject matter experts to interview either live or recorded. These interviews will be made available to registered participants over the course of the summit. The host can then use the recordings to create an information product they can sell.

Coax prospective participants with urgency: use social proof and phrases like "limited spots available" to drive leads to a registration page to harvest their contact details.

There's no debate: an email list is the cheapest way to obtain an audience. Lots of people actually prefer email for commercial communications over any other channel: Merkle, a marketing agency, found 74 percent of adults prefer email for commercial communications.

But to be of value, its integrity has got to be scrupulously maintained. And because you're going to lose close to 25 percent of list contacts each year, your success as an email marketer requires you put attention on growing your list all the time.

If list building doesn't seem important, remember this: newer subscribers are more engaged, adding to healthier open rates and increased revenue per email.

What's the ROI with email? A June 2016 survey of U.S. marketers conducted by the Direct Marketing Association and Demand Metric found that email had a median ROI of 122 percent—more than four times higher than other marketing formats, including social media, direct mail, and paid search.

Email helps you build trust, gives you a way to drive traffic to any page you want, and—unlike direct-mail marketing, for example—email messages can be tested, segmented, optimized, and personalized. With email, you can know exactly what works and what doesn't—and you can replicate what worked over and over again.

CHAPTER 10

HUB SITES, LANDING PAGES, AND SQUEEZE PAGES

The two most important factors in determining internet marketing success are traffic and conversion.

Content and branding are valuable, to be sure. But traffic and conversion are what turn your site from a pretty billboard on the web to a revenue-generating machine.

This chapter shows how to create the websites and web pages these models and funnels require so as to maximize your conversion rates. These are:

- *Hub sites*—also known as portal sites, these are the main websites for your business.
- *Sales-generating landing pages*—also known as microsites, which are simple websites selling a single product or making a single offer.
- *Lead-generating landing pages*—landing pages, also known as landers, generate a lead rather than a direct sale.

◆ *Squeeze pages*—also known as name-squeeze pages, are designed to get people to opt into your elist.

In this chapter, we review each of the four types of sites and pages so you understand the objective, style, look, and functionality of each. You'll then learn how to write and design each of these for maximum conversion rates and sales results.

Hub Sites

A hub site is what you think of as a typical website. Google any business, large or small, by company name, and you are likely to arrive at the homepage of their site.

Think of it as the company's "home" on the web or their main web presence. Broadly speaking, your website should tell the visitor two things: what he needs to know to make an intelligent decision about buying your products and what you want to tell him. The latter refers to things he isn't necessarily asking about but, if he knew, would help make the sale.

Examples of the former include pages with product descriptions, specifications, and order mechanisms, such as a link to your shopping cart. Examples of the latter include customer testimonials and background information on your company.

A website can have a virtually limitless number of pages, but the major pages are usually a homepage, client list, testimonials, case studies, products or services pages, how we work, about us, FAQ, articles and white paper library, blog, press room, contact page, and CTAs.

Homepage

The homepage is theoretically the consumer's first exposure to your site, though tracking in fact shows that a large number of visitors may enter your website elsewhere, most often via product pages or offer pages, also known as CTAs.

At times, it seems there are as many variations of homepage approaches and designs as species of insects—almost an infinite variety.

However, there are three things an effective homepage communicates to the visitor right upfront: who you are, what you do, and why the prospect should be interested.

If you want to increase conversion, put multiple CTAs on your homepage. Mine has four: the yellow "Need Great Copy?" faux sticky note in the upper right corner; the free direct-mail ROI calculator at bottom left; also at bottom, the free offer of a lead magnet, my *Business-to-Business Marketing Handbook*; and a free subscription to my online newsletter (Figure 10–1 on page 164).

The sweet spot on your homepage—the location where a CTA will generate the maximum conversions—is the upper right corner. To make mine stand out, I designed it in yellow, which makes it pop from the rest of the page, which is in blue. I then added a bit more visual interest by putting the push pin in red.

Originally, the homepage did not have the yellow CTA. Once I added it, lead generation from the site tripled. Lesson: put the CTA for which you want the most conversion in the upper right corner of your homepage.

The three other CTAs on my homepage are "gated," which means you have to enter your name and email address before you can access them. Gating offers converts more of your traffic to leads and opt-ins.

Figure 10–2 on page 165 shows my website traffic over a 12-month period for 2016.

Client List, Testimonials, and Case Studies

Click buttons in a menu help visitors navigate to the other pages on your site. Menus can be horizontal at the top and bottom of the homepage as well as vertical in the left or right column.

If you are a B2B marketer, your prospects want to know what companies, especially in their industry, you have served. This information appears on a page where these firms are listed by alphabetical order, industry, or other categories on a page labeled Clients or Customers.

Testimonials are favorable comments of praise from satisfied clients or customers. Case studies are more detailed success stories

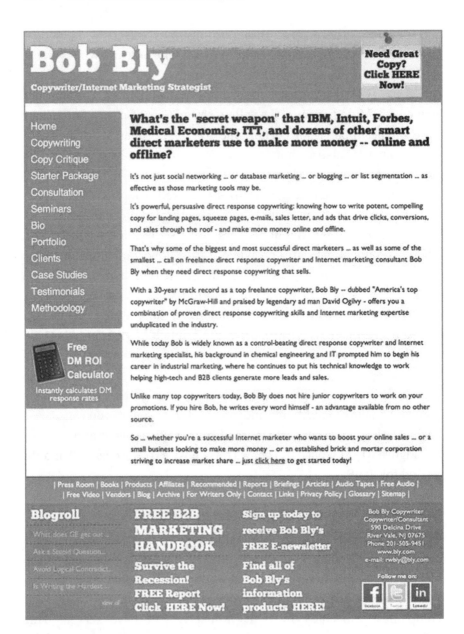

FIGURE 10–1. **The homepage of my website. The site is hosted at the domain www.bly.com.**

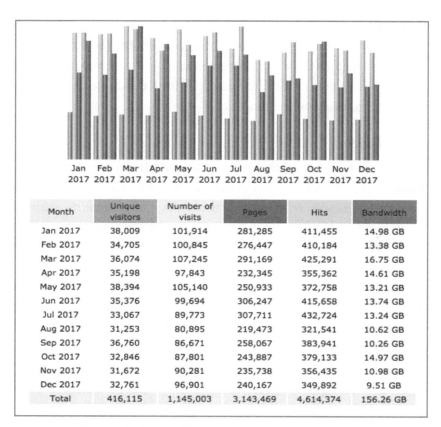

Month	Unique visitors	Number of visits	Pages	Hits	Bandwidth
Jan 2017	38,009	101,914	281,285	411,455	14.98 GB
Feb 2017	34,705	100,845	276,447	410,184	13.38 GB
Mar 2017	36,074	107,245	291,169	425,291	16.75 GB
Apr 2017	35,198	97,843	232,345	355,362	14.61 GB
May 2017	38,394	105,140	250,933	372,758	13.21 GB
Jun 2017	35,376	99,694	306,247	415,658	13.74 GB
Jul 2017	33,067	89,773	307,711	432,724	13.24 GB
Aug 2017	31,253	80,895	219,473	321,541	10.62 GB
Sep 2017	36,760	86,671	258,067	383,941	10.26 GB
Oct 2017	32,846	87,801	243,887	379,133	14.97 GB
Nov 2017	31,672	90,281	235,738	356,435	10.98 GB
Dec 2017	32,761	96,901	240,167	349,892	9.51 GB
Total	416,115	1,145,003	3,143,469	4,614,374	156.26 GB

FIGURE 10–2. **My website traffic.**

of how your product or service helped a buyer solve a problem and gain a benefit such as saving time or money or increasing profits. You should have a case study page, though many sites do not, because some prospects will ask if they can read some case studies about your product or service.

Products and Services

Each product or service you sell should have its own page describing it. Depending on what you sell and to whom, the product or service description should include the name and model number, what it is, what it does, advantages, benefits, color, construction material, options and accessories, sizes, product specifications, and a button the visitor can click to order the item or at least request more detailed content, such as a PDF brochure or fact sheet. For industrial products, high-tech electronics, fashion, travel, and consumer products, include a photo of the item; for example, for a trip to Bermuda, show a couple frolicking on the beach.

How We Work

For service businesses, this page, typically titled How We Work or Methodology, describes your work process to potential customers and clients. Many websites lack this page, but customers want to know and frequently ask how you work with clients. For manufactured products, quality control procedures and certifications (ISO 9002, GMP, FDA) can be part of the methodology page.

This page tells prospects how you do what you do, eliminating the need to verbally repeat to prospect after prospect your methodology, which may be complex. Also, customers like having it written out on a permanent web page they can view at any time and share with others involved in the buying process. I am frequently asked by potential clients, "What is your work process?" I simply point them to the methodology page, and they get the answer they need.

About Us

The About Us or About the Company page is, as the title implies, a profile of your company—or, if you are a solopreneur, of you. It's important because customers not only want to know about the products you are selling, but they also want to know from whom they are buying those products.

Reputation and experience are relevant. Have you been in business for decades or a century? Do you have thousands of satisfied customers worldwide? Or seven service centers nationwide? The idea is to communicate that your company is innovative, service- and quality-oriented, customer-focused, and yet experienced and well established.

If you are a self-employed professional, such as a consultant, the page might be called Bio, and is essentially just that: a biography of you. Your photo is typically placed either on the homepage or, my preference, the bio page.

Frequently Asked Questions (FAQ)

This page consists of questions frequently asked about you and your products by prospects and customers. Answers should provide the information they seek as well as overcome any negatives or objections. You can also use the FAQs to clarify any confusion or misunderstanding buyers have as well as make additional sales points or reemphasize benefits already stated elsewhere on the site. As you encounter new questions you haven't been asked before, add them and your answers to the FAQ page.

Articles and White Paper Library

Articles and blog posts fall under the broad category of content, or useful news, information, and how-to tips related to your products and their applications.

You can start small and then build your repository of articles and white papers all the time. But the goal is to have a lot of both for two reasons. First, the wealth of content helps build your credibility and convince prospects you are expert in your industry, niche, or skill set. Second, articles and white papers, especially when they contain keywords your prospects search to find what you sell, raise your ranking with Google and other search engines.

For instance, when I put up a new site on marketing to engineers, the site itself did not rank on the first screen of the Google search engine results page (SERP) for the keyword phrase "industrial copywriting." However, an article within the site did in fact show as a top result on the SERP. So we added a link from the article to the site homepage.

Blog

The advantage of having a blog is that weekly or daily posts result in more frequent updates to your website content, another activity which Google likes and rewards with higher ranking in its search engine.

Also, the comments feature of blogs enables two-way communication with your visitors, creating more of a sense of community and getting them actively engaged with your ideas and offerings. A more complete discussion of blogging appears in Chapter 8.

Press Room

Almost all large and medium-sized businesses regularly distribute press releases, and many smaller ones send out the occasional release. The press room, also known as media, is an online archive of recent and past press releases. These provide visitors with even more useful content, further optimizing your website for the search engines. They also add content to your site, which is beneficial for raising your search engine ranking.

Contact Page

It's a good idea either on your homepage or on a separate contact page to have your company name, mailing address, phone, fax, email address, social media icons, as well as a form the visitor can complete and submit to ask a question or make a request.

Make it as easy as possible for people to contact you. For instance, if you have your email address on the contact page, make it an active link so if people click on it, they can send an email to you right from the page.

According to an article in *Customer Experience Insight* enewsletter, more than half of customers think that thorough contact information is the most important element missing from company websites. They can't find who, where, or when to contact you.

Solution: Fix it! Put a contact phone number, email address, and social media link on every web page and piece of paper customers see.

Calls to Action

As discussed in the section on homepages, calls to action (CTAs) are pages, boxes, or forms that enable response and encourage it, usually with a free offer. As Figure 10-1 shows, CTAs appear as graphics on the homepage.

But you can also assign to each CTA a unique URL, either an extension of your main domain or a separate domain name you buy, post, and point to the CTA. For example, my *Business-to-Business Marketing Handbook* can be downloaded by clicking on the box at the bottom of my homepage or on this URL: www.bly.com/b2bhandbook/.

The reason to have a URL for the CTA is that, when you are doing a promotion with a specific offer, your ad or email should drive traffic directly to the CTA page and not your website's homepage. So you need to have in your ad or email a hyperlink to the CTA's URL—not the main URL for the whole website.

Why? Because if you promote a specific offer and send the prospect to your homepage, which is general, he will not search for the offer page. He will just give up and click away. You need, when making an offer in your marketing, to drive traffic to a CTA or landing page dedicated to making that offer.

Many web pages use a CTA for enewsletter sign-up that appears as a box or fields right on the homepage. So prospects can fill in their name and email address, then submit the form directly from the homepage, without having to first click to a separate landing page. See the example in Figure 10–3 on page 170; I had this type of newsletter sign-up on my original site.

Pop-Under Page

When people visit your site without opting in or making a purchase, you can use a pop-under (Figure 10–4 on page 171). This is a window that appears on the screen and invites them to get a free gift. They have to enter their email address to get the gift, so you capture their email address and add them to your list. With so many people using pop-up blockers today, these pop-ups are less effective than they once were.

Website Security

If you are selling products and services from your website, you also need to provide secure transaction coverage so your customers' in-

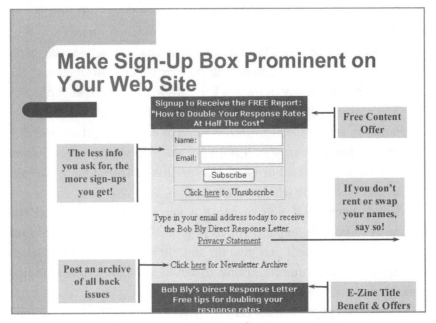

FIGURE 10–3. **Enewsletter subscription form.**

formation remains safe from internet hackers. This is especially true if you are running your own server. In the earlier days of online purchasing, many people feared that credit card and banking information would be seen by less than savory people and bank accounts could potentially be stripped of all their money.

Website owners found that obtaining security certificates from trusted providers helped overcome that fear. VeriSign, for example, was one of the most well-known providers of Secure Sockets Layer (SSL) cryptographic protocols, which secure payments and communications on the internet. VeriSign now operates with the Symantec brand.

In today's world, most websites provide some type of system that protects purchasers from ever losing their money. Certainly, when businesses use a third-party operation, such as PayPal, to handle the financial side of things, then even the business never sees the credit card number or banking information at any point of the transaction.

Don't leave without claiming your FREE Bonus Gift!

To thank you for checking out

www.TheInternetMarketingRetirementPlan.com, we want to send you a FREE Bonus Report, *How to Write Better and Faster*.

In this quick-reading 60-page special report (list price: $29), you will discover:

- **The AIDA formula for writing business letters that get you the results you want. See page 19.**

- 7 steps to writing more powerful and persuasive advertising copy. Page 49.

- **10 ways to improve your technical writing skills. Page 3.**

- How to write more effective sales brochures for any type of product. Page 52.

- **Writing potent cover letters when responding to inquiries. Page 29.**

- Why engineers and other business people can't write ... and what you can do about it. Page 9.

- **And much more....**

Name:	
Email:	

Subscribe

FIGURE 10–4. **This pops up when people leave your site to capture their email address.**

With protection in place for making purchases from millions of businesses online, online shopping is now booming on the internet.

You know when a website is secure because when making a payment, you will note the padlock sign in the website's URL address box.

The SSL certificate provides a recognition protocol between the website (owner) and the provider of the SSL, providing a type of digital handshake as security partners. The data is taken across in packets via TCP and then reassembled at the other end. The SSL certification and protocol process observes any changes along the way and protects the data from outside interference.

There are also different types of SSL certificates, such as WildCard SSL, Unified Communications Certificate, Extended Validation (EV) SSL, and the standard single certificate. Each provides for the different needs for any user. The WildCard SSL covers multiple domains or a domain with multiple subdomains such as the main website, the email domain, intranet, and testing servers more commonly seen in larger businesses.

DigiCert offers a WildCard SSL that also has a Duplicate Certificate interface, which allows for unlimited duplicated certificates. However, this certificate only works with the full domain name such as www.digicert.com but not http://digicert.com. While pricing for one year's worth of coverage for the DigiCert WildCard Plus program is currently $595, you can save money by buying a two-year or three-year subscription, thus saving up to 20 percent. It is also important to note that some server types and mobile devices may not work with the WildCard SSL certificate, so check on this first before making a purchase if this will be important to your business functions.

Unified Communications (UC) Certificate, also known as SAN for Subject Alternative Names, secures up to four domains, websites, and subdomains under one certificate. The DigiCert UC certificate also can be run on as many servers as you want, something which is not offered by all providers. A one-year subscription costs $299, two years is $269, and three years is $239. While all three pricing subscriptions offer four names with each, additional names will cost extra based on whichever plan you go with.

Extended Validation (EV) SSL certificates ensure the identity process through some of the most rigorous verification processes and are most noted by the green website address bar you see on sites where you make actual transactions. The verification ensures the operational and physical entity existence matches the official records and that there is proper certificate authorization. Any fraudulent or phishing activity can usually be detected.

All SSL certificates come in pairs: the public key version and the private key version, which is not seen by either the owner or purchaser. Initially, when first running your own server and setting up shop, you would make a request for a Certificate Signing Request (CSR) from your server to the provider of choice, and when you get the Certificate Authority (CA), you then install the package on your server. This will provide the security you need to conduct credit card and bank purchases on your website, as required by the Payment Card Industry.

The SSL certificate comes with the two keys, as previously mentioned. The public key is the Asymmetric Encryption key which uses algorithms to process data at the point of activity. Most keys will be sized between 1024 or 2048 bits, but anything larger, while it can be done, is a huge strain on computers at this point in time. It is nearly impossible for these keys to be cracked. The decryption key is the private key and remains secret, providing the security needed to protect the data and decipher it at the other end.

Symmetric Encryption uses only one key to both encrypt and decrypt the data. Key sizes run about 128 to 256 bits, and the size is dependent on the server and the client's software. Therefore, it is smaller but still very difficult to crack. While it may seem a complicated subject to understand, this part of conducting business on the internet is one of the most important factors equating success to any online business.

Providing SSL protection to your customers is part of ensuring that they will trust you with their personal information, including their money. In an age where cyber crime is a global problem, providing security is at the top of the list of what businesses must provide to their customers. In fact, you can think of SSL as your own Enigma machine, an encryption and decryption tool the Germans used during

World War II to send messages back and forth across enemy lines. You had to have the key to encrypt and then decrypt the messages on either end. SSL operates along the same principles in scrambling messages so they cannot be read until deciphered at the other end.

When installing your SSL packages, conduct several tests to make sure that all your pages can be seen. If not, you may need to check that your web server, firewall, and network are properly configured to present your pages through SSL. It could be as simple as determining whether port 443 is defined as the SSL port or that it is being blocked by your firewall or router. Additionally, check that your DNS settings are correctly set on the network. Your certificate will work off of your domain name and not your IP address. If you are not a technical type of person, call the company that provided your certificates and get help in walking through a trouble-shooting process.

There are a number of good providers who can offer you the right packages for your purposes, so it is important to do research first by checking out pricing based on offerings. You can go to SSL Shopper first to find more information about SSL and do comparisons between providers using their SSL Certificate Wizard as a starting point. You can also read reviews from previous users of different providers.

Here are a few names of those receiving the highest rankings of stars on the SSL Shopper website: DigiCert, Entrust, GlobalSign, StartCom, and SwissSign. Customer service issues are important to review as, if you are new at implementing SSL certificates, you may need some help ironing out any kinks you discover in the beginning.

Finally, if you need to know more about SSL certificates, there are plenty of books on the subject on Amazon that will help explain more details about the process and even provide information on how to create your own if you are technically inclined to do so.

The Psychology of Websites

With roots based in conversion optimization, online sales psychology goes that little bit further and applies principles of psychology to improve conversions.

Using online sales psychology as a starting point for your website is great if you are designing your first ever website. What do you look for when studying the psychology of existing websites? Start by checking out Amazon and other leading online retailers.

Studying Amazon's website, the core elements you notice are: search bar across the top of the page, login area, and main featured image that rotates through a select few products.

Amazon is conditioning its users to an experience. The company has spent millions and millions of dollars researching the psychology behind its website—what users see first, what they expect to see first, where they click, and why they click where they do. By doing this, Amazon tailors its website around expectations and sets expectations for the rest of the web.

So if you put your search bar down at the bottom of the site, don't include a login, and instead of showcasing featured products you showcase a bit about your company, would this work as well? Does this fit in with what your clients are expecting? Does it get your client from your homepage to a product page to checkout as quickly and smoothly as possible?

If a user searches for a product and the drop-down menu offers suggestions such as "search for Formula 1 in books" or "search for Manchester United in DVDs," this helps remove a little friction for the user. Instead of typing in Formula 1 and then selecting books from a secondary menu, the user's journey is simpler and they get the same end result with minimal confusion.

On product search result pages, the search filter options are typically down the left hand side, as is the case with Amazon. Why? The Western world reads left to right, and the web has conditioned people to expect this feature down the left hand side. Try adding yours to the right side of your website and see not only how odd it looks but how confusing it is and how it affects your conversions. Moving it to the left should give the user a better visual appearance and improve sales.

Always remember to keep your key elements "above the fold." This means keeping information that is important, such as images, headlines, sub headlines, and CTA buttons such as "Buy Now" clearly above the fold. You don't want to make your users search or have to think; just place a nice big "Buy Now" button right in front of them and get that sale!

To aid your online sales psychology studying, consider software such as www.inspectlet.com. It records visitors to your website and the actions they take from start to finish. Analytics may tell you there's an issue, but screen recording software such as Inspectlet will show you exactly what the problem is.

Sales-Generating Landing Pages

Also known as sales pages, online sales letters, or microsites, these are usually single-page websites dedicated to selling one product—typically a product suited for ecommerce, meaning you can directly order it from the page using your credit card or PayPal.

Figure 10–5 on page 178 shows the sales page for a $19 ebook I sell on how to make money by writing, publishing, and selling PDF ebooks. It is worth studying because we know it works: the page gets a 32 percent conversion when I drive traffic to it from my subscriber list. This means for every three people who click onto the page, one purchases the product.

In the upper right of the page, you see a sketch of a little man. This is a frame from a short sketch video. A sketch video, or white board video, is narration accompanied by a visual presentation that is a sketch rather than videography. Video on web pages can often improve engagement and sales; when I add these short sketch videos to my product sales pages, conversion goes up around 10 percent to 15 percent.

The email I use to drive traffic to this sales page is reprinted in Chapter 12 on email marketing. Both the email and the sales page follow one of marketer Mark Ford's copywriting techniques, which he calls "the power of one."

In the power of one, your copy focuses on a single idea, clearly expressed, with lots of proof. In the case of this promotion, the idea is simple: the easiest product to sell online is an ebook, as stated in the headline and lead. This is immediately followed by a list of points supporting the claim that ebooks are the best and easiest product to sell on the web.

In landing pages, it pays to build credibility early, right on the first screen. Reason: people have always been skeptical of advertising, and with the proliferation of spam and shady operators, they are even more suspicious of what they read online. Therefore, your landing page copy must immediately overcome that doubt.

One way to do that is to make sure one or more credibility builders is clearly displayed on the first screen the visitor sees. In the banner at the top of the page, use your logo and company name if you are well-known; universities, associations, and other institutions can place their official seal in the upper left of the screen.

Within or immediately under the banner, put a strong testimonial or three above the headline on the first screen. Consider adding a credibility pre-head. This is a line of copy that comes before the headline. It sums up in one pithy sentence or phrase some key credibility of the seller.

Testimonials build credibility and overcome skepticism, as do case studies and white papers posted on the website. If you invite customers to a live event, ask if they would be willing to give you a brief testimonial recorded on video. Have a professional videographer tape it, get a signed release from the customer, and post the testimonial on your website as streaming video. Require the customer to click a button to hear the testimonial, rather than have the video play automatically when the visitor clicks on the page.

For written testimonials, customers may suggest that you write what you want them to say and just run it by them for approval. Politely ask that they give you their opinion of your product in their own words instead of having you do it. Reason: what they come up with will likely be more specific, believable, and detailed than your version, which might smack of puffery and promotion.

For this sales page, I reserved the domain name www. myveryfirstebook.com. I recommend picking domain names that are both relatively short and easy to remember. Each of my sales pages has a unique domain name, making it easy for me to promote the offer online, in print, and even when giving webinars and seminars, as I am able to recall the domains from memory because of their simplicity (see Figure 10–5).

© 2017 CTC Publishing

Bob Bly, author of 80+ books and the man McGraw-Hill calls "America's top copywriter," reveals how you can make money with...

The World's Easiest - and Most Profitable - Product to Create and Sell Online!

Order Now

Affiliate Program

Free Newsletter

An e-book is the ideal product to sell on the Internet. And now, you can create your first e-book ... and start making money by selling it online ... in 90 days or less.

About Bob Bly

Bob Bly is a full-time freelance copywriter specializing in online, direct response, and b-to-b marketing. He earned more than $700,000 last year from his freelance writing, and became a self-made multi-millionaire while still in his 30s.

A copywriter for more than a quarter of a century, Bob has written promotions for over 100 clients including Phillips, Agora, KCI, 21st Century, Weiss Research, EBI Medical Systems, Sony, IBM, AT&T, Grumman, Crain Communications, McGraw-Hill, Intuit, and AlliedSignal.

Bob is the author of more than 70 books including *The Copywriter's Handbook* (Henry Holt) and *Internet Direct Mail* (NTC Business Books).

Dear Internet Marketer (or Aspiring Internet Marketer):

May I share a secret with you?

This secret, known by nearly all successful Internet marketers, is that there's no product easier to create or sell online than an e-book.

Why are e-books the perfect information product to sell on the Internet?

Well, just consider the advantages of e-books over every other type of product being sold online today:

Virtually 100% profit margin -- your e-book is delivered as an electronic PDF file over the Internet, so the payment you collect for its purchase is nearly pure profit.

No printing costs, no big cash outlay - compare that with self-published books where you can easily spend $9,000 or more on a first print run of 3,000 copies.

No inventory to store ... it's just a PDF file you keep on your server. By comparison, the inventory of just one or two self-published print books can take up your whole garage or spare bedroom!

Quick and easy to update - you can correct errors or add new information at any time - without spending a dime.

No shipping costs or delays - the buyer gets it within minutes of placing his order online.

FIGURE 10–5. **Sales-generating landing page hosted at the domain www.myveryfirstebook.com.**

Lead-Generating Landing Pages

In B2B and consumer lead generation marketing, the landing page does not ask for an order but rather captures a lead. The offer is often a special report, ebook, or other digital content.

In Figure 10–6, you see the landing page you are taken to when you click the box Free B2B Marketing Handbook at the bottom of my homepage. Notice in the right-hand column, you are given three check boxes, each making a different offer.

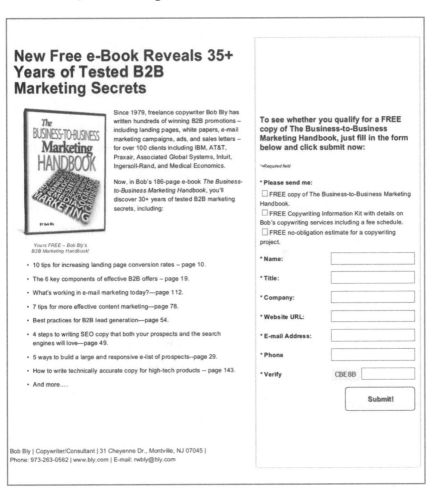

FIGURE 10–6. **Lead-generating landing page hosted at www.bly. com/b2bhandbook/.**

Visitors who check the first box get the free handbook. These are semi-qualified leads for me. On the one hand, they have an interest in B2B marketing, which is something I help clients with. On the other hand, they are just asking for a free lead magnet without explicitly saying they want me to write copy for them.

The second box allows them to ask for an information kit on my freelance copywriting services. Prospects who check this box are somewhat more qualified as they have expressed interest in learning more about my services.

The third box enables the prospect to request a cost estimate on a copywriting project. Prospects who check this box are the most qualified because they have indicated a need for my copywriting services and are interested enough that they are willing to talk with me via phone or email to get a quote.

Notice the two-column layout with the headline, image, and copy promoting the handbook at left and the response form in the narrow column to the right. The reason for this is you want the response form to be visible on the first screen of the landing page. A common mistake is to put the response form under the description of the lead magnet. Doing so forces prospects to scroll down to find the response form, and we know from long experience that this reduces conversion rate and leads.

Squeeze Pages

Figure 10–7 on page 181 shows the squeeze page I use to get people to opt into my list by subscribing to my enewsletter.

We call this a "free on free" squeeze page because we are using a free gift (the library of reports) to bribe the prospect into accepting another free offer: a subscription to the newsletter.

In the early days of the internet, there were not many free enewsletters being offered, so the fact that a valuable and informative publication was yours free for the asking was enough to get people to subscribe and opt into your elist.

But today, the market is flooded with free enewsletter offers. Many people get too much email, so they are hesitant to subscribe.

Get 4 FREE Special Reports from Bob Bly Worth Over $100!

*Email Address

[   ]

Sign Up

Sign up for a free, no-commitment subscription to my e-newsletter on direct marketing -- *The Direct Response Letter* - and get 4 FREE Bonus Reports ... over 200 pages of valuable marketing advice that can double or triple your response rates:

FREE Special Report #1: Entrepreneurial Retirement: How To Make $100,000 A Year Selling Simple Information Online In Your Spare Time
(list price: $29)

- 10 tips for increasing landing page conversion rates.
- Best time of day -- and day of week -- to send e-mail marketing messages.
- 7 steps to selling more newsletter subscriptions online.
- Give your information products the "loose-leaf test."
- 5 steps to building a large and profitable opt-in subscriber list.
- Should you avoid hype in online marketing?

FREE Special Report #2: Secrets of Successful Business-to-Business Marketing
(list price: $29)

- 50 lead-generating tips.
- 5 things I know for sure about marketing to engineers.
- How to write more effective product brochures.
- 23 tips for creating B2B mailings that work.
- 10 ways to stretch your advertising budget.
- What makes B2B different than consumer?
- 29 article ideas for your next newsletter.

FREE Special Report #3: How to Double Your Response Rates at Half the Cost
(list price: $29)

- 9 strategies for improving your outer envelope.
- The magic of false logic.
- Uncovering your customer's core complex with the "BFD" formula.
- The 3 elements of a successful USP.
- My 10 favorite marketing books of all time.

FREE Special Report #4: Online Marketing That Works
(list price: $29)

- 10 steps to online marketing success.
- Copywriting secrets of the search engine optimization (SEO) pros.
- 8 affordable ways to drive more traffic to your Web sites.
- A proven way to increase landing page conversion rates.

FIGURE 10–7. **Squeeze page hosted at www.bly.com/reports.**

To overcome this reluctance, you have to bribe prospects into subscribing by offering them a free bonus report or other premium.

First, people go to your squeeze page. They think, "I really want the free bonus gift, but I don't know about the newsletter. So I will sign up, grab the free report, and then I can unsubscribe." But, when they get the first newsletter, if they find it interesting and informative, they in fact will not unsubscribe. So you have a new prospect added to your elist, which is a valuable asset to you as an online marketer.

I have a collection of special reports I sell for $29 each on my website. But I also give away these reports as bonuses for various offers. For signing up for my enewsletter, you get four of these reports. I settled on four because four reports cost $116, which allows me to say that the bonus gift has a value of over $100, creating high perceived value. The proof that this gambit works: the page has a 49 percent conversion rate, which means nearly half of the people who click on it enter their email address and sign up, joining my list.

As with my other landing pages, the squeeze page can be reached by clicking on a box at the bottom of my homepage; this one says, "Sign up today to receive Bob Bly's free enewsletter." But it also can be reached through the URL www.bly.com/reports. I feature that URL, rather than my homepage URL of www.bly.com, in most of my marketing. That way, I build my opt-in elist, which currently has 65,000 subscribers.

Search Engine Optimization (SEO)

SEO is a method of increasing the ranking of your website on Google and other search engines.

The objective of SEO is to help prospects find your site. A recent email from the Specialized Information Publishers Association notes, "For most of your customers and prospects, your website is your company. So if they can't find it (or can't use it) on your website, you don't have it."

You get more traffic when your site shows up on the first screen of Google's search engine results page for the most important keywords potential customers search when looking for what you sell.

To get that high ranking, you must deliberately practice SEO, which involves taking these four important steps that can help search engines find you on the web more readily:

1. *Keyword research.* The first step is to come up with a list of keywords and phrases for which you want to optimize the page you are writing. These should be the keywords and phrases people use when searching for your product or service on the internet.

   You can brainstorm what these words might be, then use any number of online tools to find out which ones are the most popular. Two tools I use are www.wordstream.com and https://adwords.google.com/home/tools/keyword-planner/.

2. *Write the best copy you can—for the human reader.* Just sit down, and write the best damn copy you can about the topic. Don't even think about keywords as you write. Concentrate 100 percent on sounding like one human being talking to another about a subject you are enthusiastic about and want to share. If you are writing strong, specific copy and content, your text will contain the right keywords naturally.

3. *Insert keywords from your keyword list.* Now, go back and insert keywords from your list into the copy, wherever and as frequently as you can, without disturbing the style, tone, meaning, and persuasiveness of the copy. If forcing a keyword disrupts the flow of the copy, don't do it.

   For instance, on www.bly.com, one line of the original homepage copy read: "Call on freelance copywriter and internet marketing strategist Bob Bly." I like the sound of strategist. But our keywords research showed that people search for internet marketing consultants, not strategists. So we changed the copy to read "internet marketing consultant."

In another paragraph, we talked about my experience as a copywriter, saying that I know "how to craft landing pages that drive conversions through the roof." Once again, I like the variety of using "craft" as a verb. But to optimize the sentence with the keyword "copy," I changed it to "how to write potent, compelling copy for landing pages that drive conversions through the roof." Another keyword phrase that came up in our research was "make money online," and so we added that to the sentence: "landing pages that drive conversions through the roof—and make more money online."

One of the keyword phrases that ranked highly in our research was "online copywriting." Any time you can replace a non-keyword phrase with a keyword phrase, with no harm to the copy, you should. So we changed, "they call on Bob Bly to write their most important online marketing campaigns" (people were not searching for "campaigns") to, "they call on Bob Bly when they need online copywriting that sells."

4. *Write keyword-rich meta tags for each web page.* Meta tags are HTML code specific to the pages on your site. This code is not visible to the viewer and is in effect hidden behind what you see on the screen. Yet the search engines use this code in ranking your site.

The most important meta tags are the title and description tags. The title tag is what your visitors see at the top of their browser windows when they visit your site, as well as what they see in their bookmark lists. Failure to put strategic keywords in the title tag can result in pages being poorly ranked. The title tag should be a maximum 95 characters including spaces but ideally no longer than 6 or 7 words. The description tag should be a maximum of 220 characters with spaces. You can read more details about tags in Chapter 6.

When your website comes up in a Google search, the description tag is what the user sees on the search engine results page (SERP). It should incorporate strategic keywords and clearly communicate what you offer, who it is for, and the key benefit. Your major keywords should also be placed in the keywords meta tag, though Google pays less attention to the keyword meta tag than to the title and description tags.

Mobile-Only Index

Many mobile websites contain less content than their desktop counterparts. Because most people search with a mobile device, Google has rethought its approach. Moving forward, its algorithms will primarily use the mobile version of a site's content to rank it in search results.

Those with responsive sites, where the content and the way the pages display on the screen is the same across mobile and desktop, will have the advantage. But even then, you may need to adjust to accommodate mobile searchers. Today, voice search makes up almost 20 percent of all searches. And the words they use are typically different than what they might type into a browser. That may make you want to rethink your SEO approach.

What should you do? If your mobile website content is lightweight compared to your desktop site, consider moving to a responsive site. Use long-tail keywords (keywords containing at least three words), and optimize titles and meta descriptions for natural language queries. But how do you know what keywords to use? By doing keyword research.

Keyword Research

The use of keywords is a marketing strategy that brings potential customers to your website. If you specialize in website design, then adding words such as web design, website design, WordPress designer, HTML, and PHP will bring more interested consumers your way. When you first sit down to design the content and structure of your new website, adding keywords should be part of that process, too.

Make a list of words that could relate well to what you do, and then begin doing some research on those words. One place to begin your research is by going to http://freekeywords.wordtracker.com

where you can enter words and see how they rank in popularity of web searches. For example, "website design" pulls up 2,209 searches, whereas "website design company" pulls up 328 searches. You can do a trial version to see how it works; if you plan on researching keywords often, then a full subscription might be worth your time.

The idea is to make a comprehensive list that really reflects what you and your business, products, and services are all about and what areas of web design you might specialize in to differentiate yourself from the pack. The reason why you need keywords on your website is so it can be pulled up on the first or second page of a search engine result by a customer looking for what you offer.

Once you get your website up, then using keywords in extended marketing and advertising will become just as important for the same reasons as what you put on your website. You want to be found on the internet so you can sell your product or service. Pay-per-click (PPC) ads can be put anywhere you see as relevant for catching the attention of potential customers.

Customers see your ads because they did a search using the same keywords you are using in the ad, or the Facebook ad you created using those keywords popped up on their Facebook page as part of their indicated interests. If you see ads on the right-hand side of your Facebook page, those are Facebook ads created by businesses which are keyed to your indicated interests on your profile page. The business owner does not know their ad is going to your page, but Facebook does.

PPC means that you can create these ads and you only pay a fee when someone clicks through on your ad link, which goes to the product landing page. The linked-through landing page is where you sell your product or service, and its contents should also utilize many of those same keywords.

If you have leveraged your keyword strategy efficiently, then you will get lots of attention and sales. If not, and you are getting clickthrough actions but not sales, then a review of your marketing campaign, including the keyword strategy and the landing page, should be conducted.

Additionally, you can monitor the ratio of clickthrough actions to actual sales or inquiries made. You can also determine other factors such as time of day that more clickthrough actions were done, especially for successful sales or inquiries. Know what limit you want to make on your credit card for PPC services so that you do not find yourself with a huge bill.

Most people will be surfing the web or engaging their friends on Facebook early in the morning or in the evening hours. Consequently, in more developed strategic marketing, you might like to put out ads and notices using one type of message for the morning crowd. Then, send out another round of messages and ads for the evening crowd using a different approach, maybe utilizing a video ad in the evening when people have more time to sit, relax, and watch. Each of these advertisements must continue to use those keywords.

Keyword strategy means place them in highly visible areas on your website. Your homepage is where customers land first when arriving at your site, so load that page with as many keywords as possible.

Keywords must all fit the content of what you put on your page, however, so crafting the content correctly is important to search engines picking up those keywords. Your other pages should have them, too, but they will be more particular to actual products and services that you provide, maybe a blog that you update often, and other content which is refreshed every now and then, plus the call-to-action page.

Your website will be a work in progress because you are adding in new content all the time. Consider linking with other reputable websites, which bring added information to your website.

These links should reflect keywords in some manner as well. In other words, if you market your services as a website builder, then do not put links to horse racing blogs on your site. However, if you built that main horse racing website—even if it's not related to your main business—then add a link to it in your online portfolio to show off your variety of website design skills. It is worth your time to become an expert in keyword research and development because you can create your own website advertising for free by understanding and utilizing SEO.

There are a number of places to look at for information on PPC advertising and marketing. Try SpeedPPC to find out who are the current leading search engines that offer PPC advertising. You can also visit Google AdWords, Yahoo! Search Marketing, and Goclick to get a quick overview of some of the top leaders in PPC advertising.

For more help on keywords, try out keyword software tools like Wordtracker and Keyword Discovery. You can also type "keyword software tools" in the Google search box to get the latest list of companies providing keyword research help. Start your research and build that keyword list.

Another great way to quickly get ideas is to type a keyword into Google and then scroll down to the bottom of the SERP to see the "Searches related to [keyword]."

For example, if you discover via keyword research that "supplements for weight loss" is generating more than 5,000 monthly searches, then you can think about writing some blog posts that offer information on the subject of weight loss supplements.

You can also edit some existing pages on your site to make use of variations of that phrase to help search engines understand that these pages really are all about weight loss supplements. That's how you'll get your pages ranked higher in the SERPs.

Your goal as an SEO writer is to improve your online presence (or that of your clients) so customers can find products and services when they search for specific keywords.

For example, let's say you're a health and fitness supplement ecommerce store—we'll call your business Norman's Nutrimart. You (Norman) sell all kinds of weight loss supplements, protein powders, energy drinks, vitamins, and minerals.

Sally (your soon-to-be customer) is gearing up for the Boston Marathon and wants to make sure she's getting all the nutrients she needs to be at peak performance. She's just popped onto Google to start searching for an energy drink that is safe and effective. As Norman's SEO copywriter, you'll crawl inside Sally's psyche to understand her thought process and determine which keywords and phrases she's most likely to type into that search box.

Why? Because incorporating a variety of phrases into the web copy—word and phrase variations that fit under the umbrella of the keyword theme—is how you're going to ensure that Norman's Nutrimart shows up at the top of the SERPs for Sally to see . . . and click!

CHAPTER 11

PUBLISHING AN ONLINE NEWSLETTER

Promotions work best when sent to a warm list of prospects—that is, a list of people who have some relationship with you or have at least expressed some interest in the product or service offered. This fact is why savvy marketers spend a small fortune on specially targeted lists of buyers who match the marketer's ideal customer profile.

Why are warm lists so much more responsive to your marketing messages than cold lists of people with whom there is no previous relationship? First, because the biggest factor in getting someone to buy your product or service is that they know, like, and trust you. Generally speaking, the closer you are to your market, the better off you'll be. Well, when people subscribe to and then regularly read your online newsletter, they feel they get to know you better, and they start trusting you, your expertise, and your advice.

The second reason marketing to warm lists is more successful is that warm prospects are demonstrably interested in what you have to offer. Why should you prefer a cold list of prospects with no prior relationship with you to a list that has explicitly given you permission to market to them?

The best way to build both your own warm elist of prospects and a strong relationship with them is by publishing your own enewsletter.

Opt-in Elists Are Permission Marketing

Marketer Seth Godin calls this kind of marketing "permission marketing." Think about when you're watching your favorite TV show and the commercial break comes on. Your favorite show has been interrupted. And now marketers are trying to convince you to buy their products, which you may or may not be interested in. At best, this process is an annoyance. But when prospects have explicitly given you permission to market to them, they look at your marketing not as annoying or a burden but as valuable and exciting information.

For these reasons, I recommend building an opt-in elist of interested, prospective buyers and keeping in touch with them by email. The fastest way to build a large elist is to offer a free online enewsletter or ezine (online magazine) in exchange for their email address. Offering a free online enewsletter is also the best way to turn those email subscribers into money. The enewsletter allows you to keep in touch with your best customers—indeed, with all your customers—at virtually no cost. Because it's electronic, there's no printing or postage expense. Also, by offering potential customers a free subscription to your enewsletter, you can capture their email address and add them to your online database. You can then market to these prospects, also at minimal cost.

Let me show you specifically how having an ezine helps bring in business for me as a freelance copywriter.

I once gave a speech on software direct marketing. It was recorded, so I had audio cassette copies made (this was when we still used cassettes instead of CDs or digital mp3). In my ezine, I offered the cassette free to any subscribers involved in software marketing— potential clients for my copywriting services.

Within 24 hours after I distributed the ezine, we received over 200 inquiries from marketing managers at software companies requesting the tape, many of whom needed copy written for direct mail and email to promote their software.

By comparison, most copywriters tell me that when they send postal direct mail to a list of prospects, they average a 2-percent response. At that rate, they would have to send out 10,000 pieces of mail to generate the 200 leads I got in an hour for free.

That's what an ezine can do for you. Once you build your subscriber list, you have an incredibly powerful marketing tool and the most valuable asset your business can own: a database of buyers with email addresses and permission to email them at any time.

Here's the basic strategy in a nutshell: you build an elist of subscribers by offering a free enewsletter—and a free bonus, as I'll explain—in exchange for their email address. You then routinely email these subscribers with free, valuable information. You then do one of two things: a) you place small online ads in the regular issues of your enewsletter linking to a page on your site where the subscriber can read about and order a product; or b) you send stand-alone email messages to your subscribers, again promoting a specific product and with a link to your site. Then, you count your money.

With 65,000 subscribers, my monthly ezine, *The Direct Response Letter* (go to www.bly.com/reports to subscribe), is not the most successful or widely read enewsletter on the planet. Far from it. But marketing results and comments from subscribers tell me my simple formula for creating the ezine—which, including copy and layout, takes me just a half hour or so per issue—works. In this chapter, I want to share the formula with you so you can produce an effective enewsletter of your own, sitting at your computer, without hiring a writer or designer, in just a single morning or afternoon.

How Much Is Your Opt-In Elist Worth?

On average, each subscriber on your elist will bring you between a dime and a dollar or more of gross revenue per month. So, let's say you have 1,000 people on your list. That should generate you between $100 and $1,000 a month—between a dime and a dollar each. It won't always work out this way since much depends on how qualified your elist is as well as the quality of your copy. If you sell expensive products it can be quite a bit higher than a dollar a month.

Should you ever charge for your enewsletter? If your objective is to build a large elist to sell your products, then make the newsletter free. Charging for the enewsletter will drastically reduce the rate at which people subscribe. However, if your enewsletter contains particularly time-sensitive and valuable information such as daily stock tips, for example, then you can consider charging for it. You might charge a monthly fee of $10 to $20—but it really depends on the nature of the information. In most cases, offer a free enewsletter for the purpose of building up an elist of prospects to whom you can market your products and services.

Use a Free-on-Free Subscription Offer

I highly recommend offering a free bonus as an ethical "bribe" for subscribing to your enewsletter. This bonus can be a free special report or ebook in PDF form, an MP3 audio file, or something else altogether. The bonus can be repurposed content that you've published before (as long as you own the copyright). I call this a "free on free" offer because you're offering both a free enewsletter *and* a free bonus in exchange for their email address.

I encourage you to make a free-on-free offer because years ago, a free enewsletter was an exciting offer; but now that there are so many free enewsletters, people can be somewhat negative about them. They think, "Another enewsletter?" But when they see the free bonus, they say, "You know what, I'd like to have that bonus. I'll sign up for the enewsletter, see if it's any good, and get the bonus—and if it's not, I'll just cancel or unsubscribe." But if the enewsletter is decent, they won't unsubscribe.

Choosing a Name for Your Enewsletter

I call my enewsletter *The Direct Response Letter*. That's because I'm a direct-response copywriter and want to attract people interested in direct-response marketing. Most of my emails are about direct-response marketing, though some are about time management, goal setting, and related business issues.

The important thing is to name it in such a way that your readers will understand the main theme of the enewsletter. Make the name related to the topics you'll be writing about in your emails. You can include your name if you'd like, as I do. Name it something simple, explanatory, and unique. Don't get too creative, but you do want to stand out since there are many enewsletters out there.

Your Enewsletter Publishing Schedule

The frequency with which you email your subscriber list is really up to you. Some marketers email once every other week. Some, weekly. And some send daily. I email on a schedule that works out to three or four times a week.

But the key is that you're offering valuable content. You do not want to be hitting up your list with sales pitches too frequently, or they'll unsubscribe in a hurry. As a rule of thumb, more than half of your emails to your list should be useful content, and half or less sales messages.

Designing Your Enewsletter

What works best in enewsletters—text, HTML, or text in an HTML shell? Here are a few guidelines that can help.

Send a text enewsletter if:

- ◆ Your audience is used to text
- ◆ They are information seekers
- ◆ Image is not important
- ◆ Your product is not "visual"

Send an HTML enewsletter if:

◆ Your audience is used to HTML
◆ Image is important
◆ Your product is "visual," and you want to show photos of it
◆ Branding is key
◆ You want to track open rates

Years ago, I sent text enewsletters. But these days, I send text enewsletters in an HTML shell—meaning, the email itself is HTML, but the enewsletter looks like it is text. With this format, I can track open rates. Pure text enewsletters cannot be tracked.

I don't make a production out of it; it's just straight type. Many readers have told me they like it this way and that they don't like HTML ezines, which look a) more promotional and less informational and b) seem to have more to read.

Use a good email marketing program that will help you with most of the formatting. I use Constant Contact, but some other popular ones are MailChimp, Infusionsoft, and AWeber. You can format your enewsletter in the program.

You can use one of two enewsletter formats. The first is a continuous narrative format (see Figure 11–1): Just one continuous narrative—no

---

Which subject line is best?
A—Subject: Why I am an "Essentialist"
B—Subject: The Essentialist Way
C—Subject: The key to success is to stick to essentials
D—Subject: Why selectivity is the key to success
E—Subject: Why I am a born-again Essentialist

Dear Direct Response Letter Subscriber:

In his best-selling book "Essentialism: The Disciplines Pursuit of Less" (Crown Business), Greg McKeown preaches his philosophy of Essentialism as the path to having a better and more rewarding life.

FIGURE 11–1. **Single-article enewsletter format with continuous narrative.**

After reading it, I am a born-again Essentialist!

The core idea of Essentialism is, in McKeown's words:

"There are far more activities and opportunities in the world than we have the time and resources to invest in.

"And although many of them may be good, or even very good, the fact is that most are trivial and few are vital.

"Only when you give yourself permission to stop trying to do it all, to stop saying yes to everyone, can you make your highest contribution towards the things that really matter."

If you know people who pursue a primary goal, activity, or mission with laser-like focus—whether it's building a business, mastering the violin, or accumulating wealth—they are almost surely, with rare exceptions, Essentialists.

If you know people who volunteer for everything, have a calendar filled with diverse activities, pursue a dozen hobbies and interests, and volunteer for every committee in every worthwhile organization under the sun—I can virtually assure you that they are not Essentialists.

I only came across McKeown's book a couple of months ago. But I have been an Essentialist my entire adult life.

I focus, to the exclusion of almost everything else, on just the few things that matter most to me—my business and my clients, writing, and my family.

Yes, I would like to do more. But as McKeown correctly points out, our time, attention, energy, and bandwidth are shockingly finite.

So if you try to do everything, you accomplish—and get good at—almost nothing.

"The overwhelming reality is: we live in a world where almost everything is worthless and a very few things are exceptionally valuable," McKeown writes.

"We can choose how to spend our energy and time. We can't have or do it all."

He quotes John Maxwell: "You cannot overestimate the unimportance of practically everything."

Marcus Aurelius says it this way: "If thou wouldst know contentment, let thy deeds be few."

The way I put it is this: If you are someone who is "all over the place," you will never really get to the one place you want to go.

FIGURE 11–1. **continued**

The key to Essentialism is laser-like focus on one or two things. Steve Martin said:

"I did stand-up comedy for 18 years. Ten of those years were spent learning, four were spent refining, and four were spent in wild success. The course was more plodding than heroic."

I have always described myself as a plodder, too. If you write, as I have, 12 hours a day, 5 days a week for more than 3 decades, you can't help but get better at it!

Sincerely,

Bob Bly

P.S. My Essentialism does not mean I make zero contribution to worthy causes outside my small number of core activities.

But I do so in the most time-efficient manner—by donating money rather than my time to these worthy causes.

By focusing just on my business, I make more money . . . which in turn enables me to make bigger contributions to curing cancer, feeding the hungry, and other things that are important but that I do not have the bandwidth to participate in directly.

FIGURE 11–1. **continued**

sections. I tend to use this format in most of my issues. Continuous narrative is for when you want to focus on one topic per issue. It gives you the space you need to tell your story and get your point across.

The second format you can use is a segmented narrative format with independent sections addressing distinct topics. These sections are separated by either dashes or asterisks. I used this format more often in the past but still use it on occasion. The segmented format allows you to write about a variety of topics and gives your reader more variety (Figure 11–2 on page 199).

There's no reason why you can't alternate between the two formats. I use the continuous format most of the time and the segmented format once a month at the beginning of each month.

Finally, there's the format for your sales email that will link to your landing page (see Figure 11–3 on page 200). The sales email is

Show your Facebook posts to more people....

You don't need to buy boosted posts or ads on Facebook to get your message across on social media. Just pay attention to the latest algorithm changes announced on the Facebook Newsroom link below:

https://newsroom.fb.com

Then adjust your Facebook content to widen distribution by delivering content the updated algorithm favors. For example, in autumn 2014, Facebook announced that it was going to start favoring link posts with images attached over photo posts with URLs in their captions. By February 2015, link posts were getting as much as 3X the organic reach of photo posts.

Source: PR Daily News Feed, 5/22/17.

...because Facebook gets people to buy!

A recent Animo survey shows that 64% of Facebook video ad viewers say it influences buying decisions. These consumers report that watching a branded video on Facebook has affected a purchasing decision made in the last month. Also, 84% of consumers use their mobile devices to view social video, and 81% of marketers are meeting that need by optimizing for mobile

Source: IAB SmartBrief, 6/7/17.

Boost your mobile website's ranking on Google

FIGURE 11–2. **Multiarticle enewsletter format.**

basically in the continuous narrative style with the addition of the links to the landing page. Consider it a miniature version of your much longer landing page that will do most of the selling job.

Ideal Word Length for Your Enewsletter

Don't make the issues too long. I am convinced that most subscribers do not print out the enewsletter, take it home, and curl up with it on

Dear Direct Response Letter Subscriber:

In the early 1980s, thousands of small business owners bought, read, and used a little book that was, for them, their "small business marketing bible."

It focused on low-cost/no-cost ways they could promote their businesses on their own:

www.offlinemarketingmagic.com

No Madison Avenue advertising agency. No million-dollar ad budget. No Superbowl TV commercials. No celebrity endorsements. No blogs. No Facebook or Twitter. No web sites. No e-mail.

Just proven, rock-solid strategies for producing great marketing results on a shoestring that worked like gangbusters!

Now you can profit from dozens of these "lost" 20th century power marketing techniques!

For more information ... or to order this out-of-print marketing classic on a risk-free 90-day trial basis ... just click here now:

www.offlinemarketingmagic.com

Sincerely,

Bob Bly
Copywriter / Consultant
31 Cheyenne Dr.
Montville, NJ 07045
Phone 973-263-0562
Fax 973-263-0613
www.bly.com

Follow Bob:

FIGURE 11–3. **Promotional email sent to enewsletter subscriber list.**

the couch later to read. Therefore, I use a quick-reading format designed to allow subscribers to read my enewsletter online right when they open it. You can see the most recent issue at www.Bly.com to get more of a feel for the length and content of these articles.

I tend to make my issues between 300 and 700 words. I wouldn't make them much longer than that. Most of my subscribers either read them or not on the spot. Some tell me they save the issues, but I wonder if they ever read what they have saved.

I generally make my sales emails even shorter than that. A recent email of mine was only 127 words not including the header and footer. The reason for the brevity of the sales email is that the email links to the product landing page, which is considerably longer and does the full selling job. Your objective for these emails is simply to get them to click the link to your sales page. Let the fuller sales letter do most of the selling.

Answering Questions and Queries from Your Subscribers

I always include a section below the signature of my email where I ask my subscribers if they have any questions, suggestions, or comments about my ezine as shown in Figure 11–4.

I frequently receive such feedback, which I often include in the ezine, using just the person's initials to preserve their anonymity. I solicit feedback for a number of reasons. First of all, I enjoy connecting

I welcome your feedback! Did you like today's message?

What other topics would you like to see covered in my e-mails?

Please let me know at: rwbly@bly.com

As always, please feel free to forward this e-mail to a friend!

FIGURE 11–4. **Feedback request.**

with my readers and learning about their perspectives. Second, they are more likely to buy my information products after connecting with me. Third, this feedback from readers provides ideas for future editions of my ezine. And finally, the feedback gives me ideas for new products.

For these same reasons, I recommend that you answer questions and queries from your subscribers. The more you connect with your list, the better your sales. Remember, your list is a list of people and not mere email addresses. They're real people with real concerns and preferences—and that includes buying preferences. The more you address their concerns and interact with them, the more qualified your list will be and the warmer the reception for your sales offerings.

14 Things You Can Put in Your Enewsletter

The question arises: what do you put in your enewsletter? Here are 14 things I typically put in my enewsletter, and you can too:

1. *How-to tips.* How-to information should be the foundation of your enewsletter. Teach people how to do what they really want to do, quickly and easily (if possible). How-to tips are especially important if you're a consultant or freelancer—or if you want your enewsletter to provide leads for your service business. How-to information helps to establish you as an expert, which is how you want to position yourself to sell your information products and other services. Here's an example: let's say you offer an enewsletter on Facebook marketing. You might offer "5 Ways to Make Your Headlines Stand Out." Most of my ezine editions focus on how-to tips.

2. *Dialogue with the reader and soliciting feedback and participation.* You can ask their feedback about something specific. For example, let's say you're engaging in market research for a new book. You might ask what they'd like to see in the book, which will provide you information you can use.

3. *Tips from friends and colleagues.* You can highlight how-to information from those you know and admire. Of course, always make sure to attribute their information to them and perhaps provide a link to their site.

4. *Plugs for friends' and clients' books, ebooks, reports, products, and services.* Link to their site and encourage a purchase, explaining why you think they're qualified and describing their credentials.

5. *Reader feedback and contributions.* Here, you can address reader concerns that you've received for the benefit of the list at large (answer people privately first). Sometimes, readers' ideas can be used as a launching point for how-to information or as a counterpoint to something you've already written. You may even disagree with your reader, and you can explain why. But try to keep your reader anonymous in most cases. I use their initials only.

6. *Upcoming speaking engagements, seminars, and webinars.* You can promote upcoming events in which you or others are involved.

7. *Updates.* You can write about what you've been up to lately—whether projects or some relevant personal issue. I wouldn't make updates the focus of the email too often, but if the update is something interesting, relevant, or a good story, include it. For instance, I recently had a health scare and was relieved to find that I was all right. I included the story as the focus of one of my emails to offer a lesson about having perspective in life and being grateful to be alive. I received a number of kind replies.

8. *Recommended vendors.* You can include this as part of your message—or, on occasion, you might even make this the focus of your email.

9. *Useful and relevant websites.* You can point out some good websites that may help your readers—something that will make their life easier, make them money, or help them in some other way.

10. *Capsule book reviews.* I sometimes include recommendations or reviews for books I've read. One of the secrets of success is reading every day to enhance your skills. Offering your readers summaries or reviews of important books can be a fantastic way to engage them.

11. *News nuggets of interest.* Topical issues related to the news can be a great choice for your enewsletter *if* they're not divisive as they can prompt discussion. Then again, some marketers specifically target a particular political market. For instance, small-business marketer Dan Kennedy's ideal market is conservative, and he announces this unabashedly. He finds that many of the small-business owners he markets to are strongly anti-tax and so on and that this works well for him. In general, however, divisive political and religious issues can alienate segments of your list.

12. *News about your new books or publications.* If you publish books or magazine and trade journal articles, you can announce this to your list at least in part of your email. You can link to the Amazon page or to the article.

13. *Plugs for your own products or business.* Of course, building an elist is ultimately about selling your products and services, and about 20 percent of the time, your enewsletter can link to your sales page. However, once in a while, you can plug your product within the body of your informational email. To generate tons of leads for your business, put free offers in your enewsletter editions.

14. *Quotations.* You can always include quotations from others in your enewsletter or even comment at length about an idea contained in a quotation—something that your readers will find engaging, thought-provoking, or motivational.

31 More Topics for Your Enewsletter

The options for enewsletter topics are almost unlimited. You have the opportunity to get really creative with your enewsletter editions—all the while remembering to provide what your readers are interested in. Here's a convenient list of additional topics you can include in your enewsletter:

1. *Product stories.* New products; improvements to existing products; new models; new accessories; new options; new applications.
2. *Company news.* Joint ventures; mergers and acquisitions; new divisions formed; new departments. Also, industry news and analyses of event and trends.
3. *Product tips.* Tips on product selection, installation, maintenance, repair, and troubleshooting.
4. *How-to articles.* Similar to tips but with more detailed instructions. Examples: how to use the product; how to design a system; how to select the right type or model.
5. *Previews and reports.* Write-ups of special events such as trade shows, conferences, sales meetings, seminars, presentations, and press conferences.
6. *Case histories.* Either in-depth or brief, reporting product application successes stories, service successes, and the like.
7. *People.* Company promotions; new hires; transfers; awards; anniversaries; employee profiles; customer profiles; human interest stories (such as unusual jobs or hobbies).
8. *Milestones.* For example, "1,000th unit shipped"; "Sales reach $1 million mark"; "Division celebrates 10th anniversary."
9. *Sales news.* New customers; bids accepted; contracts renewed; satisfied customer reports.
10. *Research and development.* New products; new technologies; new patents; technology awards; inventions; innovations; breakthroughs.
11. *Publications.* New brochures available; new ad campaigns; technical papers presented; reprints available; new or updated manuals; announcements of other recently published literature.

12. *Explanatory articles.* How a product works; industry overviews; background information on applications and technologies.

13. *Customer stories.* Interviews with customers; photos; customer news and profiles; guest articles by customers about their industries, applications, and positive experiences with your product or service.

14. *Financial news.* Quarterly and annual report highlights; presentations to financial analysts; earnings and dividend news.

15. *Photos with captions.* People; facilities; products; events.

16. *Columns.* President's letter; letters to the editor; guest columns; regular features such as "Q&A" or "Tech Talk."

17. *Excerpts, reprints, or condensed versions of company materials.* Press releases; executive speeches; journal articles; technical papers; company seminars.

18. *Quality control stories.* Quality circles; employee suggestion programs; new quality assurance methods; success rates; case histories.

19. *Productivity stories.* New programs; methods and systems to cut waste and boost efficiency.

20. *Manufacturing stories.* New techniques; equipment; raw materials; production line successes; detailed explanations of manufacturing processes.

21. *Community affairs.* Fundraisers; special events; support for the arts; scholarship programs; social responsibility programs; environmental programs; employee and corporate participation in local/regional/national events.

22. *Information technology stories.* New computer hardware and software systems; improved data processing and its benefits to customers; new data processing applications; explanations of how systems serve customers.

23. *Overseas activities.* Reports on the company's international activities; profiles of facilities, people, markets.

24. *Service.* Background on company service facilities; case histories of outstanding service activities; new services for customers; new hotlines.

25. *History*. Articles about the company, industry, product, or community history.

26. *Human resources*. Company benefit programs; announcement of new benefits and training and how they improve service to customers; explanations of company policies.

27. *Interviews*. With company key employees, engineers, service personnel; with customers; with suppliers (to illustrate the quality of materials going into your company's products).

28. *Forums*. Top managers answer customer complaints and concerns; service managers discuss customer needs; customers share their favorable experiences with company products/ services.

29. *Gimmicks*. Contests; quizzes; puzzles; games; cartoons.

30. *Links to relevant URLs*.

31. *Free downloads*.

Six Tips for Writing Enewsletters

Here are six tips for writing an enewsletter that will help increase your readership and sales:

1. *Write for surfers and scanners*. Your readers will not open your email and gobble up every last word. At least, most of them won't. Most of your readers will be skimming your enewsletter first before reading it more thoroughly. Some will do nothing but skim. Thus, you want your enewsletter to appeal both to those who read thoroughly and to those who "surf and scan." You might consider using subheads in your enewsletter to help captivate and focus the scanners' attention.

2. *Provide information quickly and easily*. Make your enewsletter extremely easy to read: make it short (no more than 400 to 500 words), write conversationally, and think both verbally and visually. How will your enewsletter first appear to your reader? Is it intimidating to read? Make it a single-column in Arial or another easy-to-read sans serif font (studies have shown that sans serif fonts such as Arial and Verdana are

easier to read on computer screens, while serif fonts such as Times New Roman are easier to read in print). The column width should be 60 characters, so you can set your margins at 20 and 80. However, to make sure the lines come out evenly, you must put a hard carriage return by hitting return or enter at the end of each line. Your email marketing program will help with this.

3. *Use lots of lists and bullets.* Lists and bullets work well in enewsletters. Bullets are short bursts of information that appeal to your reader. Lists easily organize your information. In fact, some of your enewsletter editions can be simply a list: "10 Reasons You Should Invest in Gold Immediately." Using a list is an easy way to organize an enewsletter edition. Even more, lists and bullets break up the monotony of text and make it easier to read.

4. *Write in chunks.* Use frequent line breaks. Line breaks make the enewsletter easier and less formidable to read. The shorter the paragraphs, the better.

5. *Use hyperlinks.* Naturally, in your sales emails, you'll link to your sales page. In these sales emails, include a link above the fold—in the top area before the reader scrolls. Link to your product landing page high up in the email. Then, include periodic links to the sales page throughout the email—three or four times total. Link several times because the more links you include, the more likely your reader will end up clicking. Don't get too link-happy, though. When you include too many links, you risk spam filters intercepting your emails. In your information enewsletters (not your sales ones), still include a link to your basic website at the bottom.

6. *Give readers a chance to talk back.* As I mentioned before, always give your readers a chance to offer feedback since this lets you connect with your readers and can even prompt new ideas for future enewsletters and products. You can include a regular area at the bottom of your email in which you explicitly encourage feedback in an inviting way, as I show in Figure 11–4.

When to Email Your Subscribers

When you're working with an email marketing program, you can automate the emails so they are sent out on a predetermined schedule. The program will include instructions on how to do this. It's relatively easy. But you'll have to write the content and put it into the program. Occasionally, you can send live emails (emails that you've just written). You could make all your emails live; however, this option can become unmanageable. Try to automate the majority of the emails but include a live email here or there to keep your enewsletter current and fresh.

I tend to send out my ezine between 10:30 A.M. and 12:30 P.M. EST on weekdays. Some marketers send emails on Sundays. You'll have to test to see which days of the week and which times work best for your subscribers.

How to Get Subscribers

When you launch an enewsletter, you'll obviously need subscribers to send it to. There are many ways to gain subscribers, and I'll go over several in this chapter. First, I want to point out a promotion that got me 982 new enewsletter subscribers at no cost in 24 hours.

First, there's the "Internet Loss Leader" strategy, in which you essentially give away one of your products to the customers of another marketer in exchange for adding those customer names and email addresses to your subscriber list. An example is the promotion I discussed in Chapter 9 (see page 145)—the one in which I went to someone who had a large list with several hundred thousand names. I explained to him that everyone who buys is added to my list. He would get all the revenue from the sale, but I would gain subscribers.

We sold almost 1,000 copies. Within 48 hours, I had 982 new people added to my list—at zero out-of-pocket cost. And not only that, but these new subscribers had paid for my book, so they weren't freebie seekers; they were proven buyers.

The merchant was happy. He made nearly $19,000 for a single email blast. And because I sold to his list, the names were added to *my* list. I was able to grow my list without having to pay anything out of my own pocket.

This story shows that you can be really creative in the ways you go about adding subscribers.

Here are some standard ways to grow your elist:

- ◆ *Search Engine Optimization (SEO)*—make your website key-word-friendly so people will find it through search engines. Make your enewsletter sign-up box prominent on your website so when people visit, they'll be prompted to enter their email address to receive your free enewsletter and bonus.

- ◆ *Banner ads*—you can pay to advertise your free enewsletter on other companies' websites.

- ◆ *Pay per click (PPC) advertising*—here, you pay only when someone clicks on your ad. A couple of the most popular PPC advertising venues are Google AdWords and Microsoft Bing. Facebook ads can also work well.

- ◆ *Direct mail*—send postcards to prospective subscribers promoting your enewsletter.

- ◆ *Affiliate marketing*—promote your products to other people's lists.

- ◆ *Co-registration*—here, when people subscribe to or buy something, they sometimes have an option to receive related promotions. You can pay to be in the registration slots to get leads from the traffic that came from the primary offer. For more information on co-registration, visit www.MyCoRegSecrets.com.

- ◆ *Books and articles*—you can link to your website in the byline or in the body of the content. Again, make your enewsletter sign-up box prominent on your website so that when they visit the site, they'll be more likely to sign up.

- ◆ *Pop-ups and floaters*—you can make your enewsletter sign-up box even more prominent on your website by making it pop up on the screen to get the sign-up. Many email marketing programs let you do this in a way that is resistant to modern pop-up blockers.

Build Your List with "URL Substitution"

You have created a sign-up page for your online newsletter with its own URL; for instance, my main website URL is www.bly.com, and my enewsletter sign-up page URL is www.bly.com/reports. One way to get many more subscribers at virtually no cost is with the URL Substitution technique.

Here's how it works: As a digital marketer and businessperson, you will have countless requests and opportunities to share your URL. When you're at networking functions, you pass out your business card imprinted with your company URL. When you are a speaker at an industry event, your bio in the program includes your company name and URL. When you write an article for a business or trade magazine, it carries your byline and a brief bio, including your URL, and the publication typically has many thousands of subscribers,

In all such situations, the choice of which URL to list is up to you. So instead of using your main URL, which connects to your website's homepage, instead use your enewsletter sign-up page URL. You can just list the URL without saying what it links to. You can say "To subscribe to Bob's free online newsletter on direct marketing, visit www.bly.com/reports." Or even better, highlight the bonus gift instead of the newsletter itself; e.g., "For a free special library of marketing reports worth over $100, visit www.bly.com/reports now."

Stop People from Unsubscribing

Sometimes subscribers forget they subscribed to your enewsletter and end up flagging it as spam or unsubscribing. So I like to remind them at the top of the email that they opted into my enewsletter and are free to unsubscribe at any time. Any good email marketing program will require you to comply with CAN-SPAM laws, but I include a message reminding them that they voluntarily opted in. This reminder notably reduces spam complaints and keeps my emails being delivered.

So here's the strategy:

1. Write an enewsletter.
2. Use PPC ads, banner ads, co-registration, or other means of generating traffic to build an elist of subscribers with your free-on-free offer.
3. Email these subscribers regularly with free, valuable information.
4. Advertise your products and services and link to your sales pages.

Every marketer who wants to make more money online should create an enewsletter and start building an opt-in elist of prospects as soon as possible. Your elist is truly the most valuable asset your business can own.

CHAPTER 12

GENERATING LEADS AND SALES WITH EMAIL MARKETING

Of all the online and offline marketing channels, email is proven to have the highest return on investment (Figure 12–1 on page 214)—seven times greater than ads or websites. The best results are obtained by sending emails with product offers to your own elist; second best is emails to the lists of your affiliates and joint venture partners (see Chapter 14). The lowest response comes from sending emails to rented elists. An article on *MediaPost* observes that you are six times more likely to get a response from an email than from a social media post.

No wonder *ClickZ* reports, "Email marketing continues to be the best digital channel for ROI." The Data & Marketing Association (DMA) found that email marketing is the top profit generator with the lowest cost per acquisition among widely used digital marketing channels—just $10.32. Half of the 592 marketers polled by the DMA expressed a plan to increase their use of email.

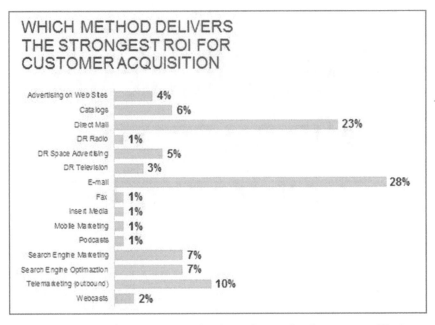

FIGURE 12–1. **ROI of various marketing channels shows email's is the highest—four times more profitable than search engine marketing.**

The email itself does not sell the product. Rather, its primary objective is to get the recipients to click on a hyperlink. When they click the link, prospects are immediately taken to a landing page—which, as discussed in Chapter 11, does the actual selling, elaborating on the product features and benefits, showing a photo or video of the item, and giving prospects a mechanism for ordering online.

Despite all the buzz about Snapchat, Twitter, and other social media, email is still the most widely used way people communicate at a distance in writing, whether personally, as consumers, or in business. Ascend2 marketing reports that more than half of companies surveyed said email marketing worked well for them, outranking social media, advertising, and search engine marketing.

According to market research firm The Radicati Group, in 2015, there were over 205 billion emails sent and received daily worldwide—

about 7 million emails zipping around the digital superhighway in the time it took you to read this sentence.

The average office worker gets 121 emails a day. FierceCMO says that 98 percent of consumers age 18 to 64 check their email address at least one to three times per day. And an article in *Chief Marketer* notes that millennials expect email to remain their preferred method of communication at work for the next five years.

You get your best results emailing to your own opt-in email list—people who have registered on your site and agreed to get emails from you. Your opt-in list is also known as the house file or house list. Chapter 9 showed you how to build a large and profitable opt-in elist and why, for many internet marketers, the house list is their most profitable asset.

Why does emailing to your house list generate better results than any rented opt-in elist you could use? As shown in Chapter 1, in our discussion of the Agora Model, email to your house file—and the house files of your affiliates—works best because the recipients have already agreed to receive emails from you (or from your affiliate if you are emailing to their list). They also know who the sender is (again, either you or your affiliate) and are therefore much more receptive to emails from these familiar correspondents than they are to emails from total strangers.

For many internet marketers, email is the killer sales app for their online business, and sending email marketing messages to their list is how they generate the bulk of their orders. In this chapter, we focus on how to write emails that drive more traffic to your landing pages, which in turn, results in more opt-ins, leads, conversions, orders, and sales.

Six Important Email Metrics

There are half a dozen key metrics that you should keep track of to determine how well your email marketing messages are working and how much money you are making from them. They are bounce rate, opt-out rate, open rate, clickthrough rate, conversion rate, and gross revenues. They can be measured and reported using either analytics or integrated shopping cart software, listed in Appendix B; I recommend 1ShoppingCart.

Bounce Rate

A bounce is an email that does not get delivered to the recipient because the email address you sent it to is not valid or active. The cause can be a typo in the email address, a change in the recipient's choice of internet service provider (ISP), or closing down a domain, server, or email account.

On a well-maintained elist, the bounce rate should be small—ideally, about 1 percent or less. MailChimp, a large email services provider, tracked millions of emails and found the typical bounce rate was around a little under 1 percent. A bounce rate of 8 percent or above means either the list is old and outdated, or you have a quality problem with the list or possibly your method of email distribution.

Opt-Out Rate

Every time you send an email to your opt-in list, some of the people on the list will decide they no longer want to get email from you and will opt out or unsubscribe, which simply means they will ask you to remove their name and email address from your list and send no more emails to them. For this reason, unless you are constantly and proactively building your elist, these opt-outs can cause the size of your elist to shrink by as much as 25 to 30 percent a year.

So in addition to continually building your opt-in elist, you must work to reduce your opt-out or unsubscribe rate, defined as the percentage of your subscribers who opt out of the list each time you send an email to it. Throughout the rest of this chapter, we will look at email marketing practices that keep prospects engaged with your email messages and in doing so keep the opt-out rate low.

Ideally, your opt-out rate should be 0.1 percent or below. That means if you send an email blast to your list of 5,000 subscribers, a maximum of five and preferably fewer will opt out from that single email.

Open Rate

The open rate is the percentage of people receiving your email that click on and open it. According to Constant Contact, open rates can range from 5 percent to 20 percent, with the average being around 10 percent to 15 percent. Mine varies from 8 percent to 25 percent depending on which of my lists I am sending to.

Some marketers feel the open rate is very important. I am much more concerned for each email I send out about the next three metrics: clickthrough rate, conversion rate, and gross revenues.

Clickthrough Rate

The clickthrough rate (CTR) is the percent of people receiving your email marketing message who respond to your offer by clicking the hyperlink to reach your sales page for more details and possibly to order. Typical CTRs range from 1 percent to 5 percent and sometimes more for each email blast. And a study from Marketo found that *text emails on average produce 17 percent higher clickthrough rates than HTML emails.*

Conversion Rate

The conversion rate is the number of prospects who reach or land on your sales page and accept the offer, whether it's to download a free special report, register for a webinar, or buy a product.

Depending on whether you are trying to generate a lead with a free offer or sell a product, the conversion rate on a landing page can be anywhere from 1 percent to as high as 80 percent or more. If you are selling a $29 ebook and get a 5 percent conversion rate, then for every 100 people who clicked on your email hyperlink and went to the landing page, 5 bought the product and 95 did not.

Gross Revenues

The gross revenues are determined by four factors: the size of your elist, the price of your product, the clickthrough rate, and the conversion rate. Let's say your elist is currently 10,000 names and you are

Clickthrough Rate	Conversion Rate	Numbers of Orders	Gross Revenues
1%	1%	10	$390
10%	1%	100	$3,900
1%	10%	100	$3,900
10%	10%	1,000	$39,000

FIGURE 12–2. **Boosting both clickthrough and conversion rate has a multiplier effect that yields maximum sales when selling a $39 product to a list of 10,000.**

selling them a $39 product; and for today, the list size and product price are both fixed.

You could increase your gross sales by improving either the CTR or the conversion rate, but if you boost both, it has a multiplying effect that can take your revenues from modest to spectacular.

In Figure 12–2, we see results of sending an email to a list of 10,000 subscribers with an offer of a $39 product. When the CTR and conversion rate are each 1 percent, we get only ten orders for $390 revenues on the email.

If we can boost either CTR *or* conversion tenfold from 1 percent to 10 percent, our sales from the email go from $390 to a respectable $3,900. But if we boost both clickthrough *and* conversion from 1 percent to 10 percent each, we multiply our results a hundredfold and make a whopping $39,000 in sales from a single email.

Content vs. Sales

One thing that holds us back from making $3,900 or $39,000 from every email we send is that if you send your subscribers nothing but sales pitches, they will resent it. Many will ask to be removed from your list. Many others will stay on the list but stop opening and reading your emails. Your list will shrink, and your sales will plummet.

To maintain good relations with your list and keep them reading your emails, you must offer a mix: some of the emails can be sales messages, but others must be pure content—tips, advice, news, or other useful and interesting information. I have found that you can maintain good sales and readership when at least 50 percent or more of your emails are content while half or fewer are sales pitches.

If you send even more content, your subscribers may like it better, but you will have fewer opportunities to send them sales messages, and your online revenues will go down.

Email Frequency

Your safest bet is to start with once a month and gradually increase the frequency to twice a month, then once a week, twice a week, and so on.

If the opt-out rate remains low, your subscribers are telling you they are happy to get your messages more frequently.

On the other hand, if you increase emails from once a week to twice a week, and the opt-out rate spikes higher, your subscribers are indicating you are sending too many emails, and you should drop back to the previous frequency, which in this example would be weekly.

A big mistake online marketers make, though, is sending too few rather than too many emails. When I raised my frequency gradually from monthly to four times a week, my opt-out rate remained steady. And by sending more emails, I made more sales.

Ideal Word Length for Email Marketing Messages

There is no ideal length, though as a rule of thumb, emails tend to be on the shorter side.

The reason short copy works here is that when you are using email marketing to make sales, the email does not make the whole sales pitch. The selling is done, whether with short or long copy, primarily on the landing page. Therefore, the email's only job is to generate enough interest or curiosity to get the recipients to click on the CTA link to the landing page. This can often be achieved with very short copy.

Which Email Format Is Best?

Many entrepreneurial internet marketers use text emails because they are quicker and easier to create. This is especially true for internet marketers selling information products because text looks more like information than a sales pitch. It also looks more like personal email. The width of the text should be no more than 60 characters per line; if it is longer, it becomes difficult to read and unappealing visually.

HTML emails are primarily used by companies to whom branding is important (e.g., Chevrolet showing their logo) or whose products are more persuasively sold when the prospects can see what they look like (e.g., a resort in the Bahamas, fashion, cars, jewelry).

If you do choose HTML because of its ability to include pictures in your email, be warned that images are also used by spammers and hackers to transmit viruses. For this reason, many ISPs automatically block or request permission to load pictures in email correspondence.

Because ISPs view pictures in emails as opportunities for malicious events, emails with too many photos can cause it to be tagged as spam and not be delivered. The best advice is to either do text emails—which eliminate the concerns of images altogether—or, if you do use HTML for the visual, keep the number of pictures to a minimum. Text is always safer to send than images.

In my information marketing business, we use a hybrid format of text in an HTML shell—the email looks like text but is coded in HTML. The reason is that it allows us to measure the open rates on HTML, which we cannot do with text-only emails.

Designing Emails for Mobile Devices

According to software company Cvent, the average mobile user looks at their smartphone 220 times a day. And more than 80 percent of subscribers report that they will delete an email if it doesn't look good on their mobile device. As a result, it is vital for you to optimize your emails for mobile subscribers—especially if they are a big chunk of your audience. Using mobile email best practices ensures that designs are legible and easy to interact with not only on mobile devices but also on tablets and desktop environments.

Here are some tips for making your emails look great on mobile devices:

- *Enlarge fonts.* It might not seem obvious to you, but readers in their mid-50s and older often have trouble reading tiny text on mobile devices. Fortunately, the Apple-recommended font size of 17 to 22 pixels in mobile emails satisfies most readers. Tiny text is even hard to read on a desktop computer. To avoid illegible fonts, a size of 14 pixels as a minimum for body copy and 22 pixels for headlines is recommended. Apple's IOS automatically resizes fonts under 13 pixels, making them larger on your behalf.
- *Use thumb-friendly buttons.* As the descriptive model of human/computer interaction known as Fitts's Law suggests, increasing the size of an interaction target decreases the time and effort required to click it. That means you'll want to use thumb-friendly buttons for your "Read more," "Buy now," and social media links. Big buttons are not only more visible on a mobile screen; they're also easier to interact with.
- *When it comes to reading emails on mobile, CTA must be touch-friendly.* It's recommended you put the CTA front and center and, if you're using a button, make it a minimum size of 44 pixels by 44 pixels.
- *Streamline content.* Evaluate the content in your email, and get rid of the less useful or relevant links, copy, and images. Also be concise, but still cover the key points. The shorter the copy, the easier it is for people to scroll on mobile.
- *Use single-column layout.* While many online newsletters are multicolumn, mobile-friendly emails should consider

switching to a single-column layout. This approach accommodates smaller screens and can help increase legibility.

◆ *Ditch detailed navigation bars.* When viewed on a mobile device, navigation bars can break, are too small to tap, or simply aren't relevant to the content of the email.

◆ *Use alt text.* Like webmail and desktop clients, there are numerous mobile email apps that block images by default. As a result, it's important to optimize your emails to be viewed without images. Luckily, there are a number of strategies to help combat image blocking. Alt text, short for alternative text, is one of the best ways to get around clients that block images by default.

What Offers Work Best in Email Marketing?

For generating sales leads or to get someone to opt into your elist or subscribe to your enewsletter, a free offer works best. The most common free offer is content, usually a downloadable PDF such as a special report or, especially in B2B lead generation, a white paper.

For generating orders, the ideal offer combines a product discount, free bonus gift (also called a "premium"), and a money-back guarantee of satisfaction. That applies whether you are selling merchandise or information products.

From Lines and Subject Lines that Boost Results

If you are emailing to your own opt-in elist, the from line should have your name or your company name, whichever the recipients are more familiar with. You can also use both; for example, "From: Carol Jones, IBM."

When you are emailing to rented lists or affiliate lists, the email will be from the list owner. They will often introduce you with a sentence or header that says, "Here's a special discount offer from our friend John Smith at XYZ Valves" or something similar.

Subject lines are written to arouse curiosity and generate enough interest to get prospects to open the email. If you have a large enough email list—thousands of names—you can profitably split test, or A/B test, two different subject lines. In these tests, I have seen subject line A generate as much as 25 percent higher CTR than subject line B with the remainder of the email identical for both test cells.

Run your email copy through SpamAssassin at http://spamassassin.apache.org. This free tool will show you whether your email as written will trigger spam filters. It also makes recommendations for fixing the email so the recipients receive it directly rather than in their spam folders.

Writing the Email Body Copy

The key to writing a good email marketing message is to focus not on selling the product but on the benefit to the prospect of clicking on your CTA hyperlink. Some of the ways to do this include:

- ◆ Identify your prospect's main problem, fear, or concern in the copy; e.g., "Worried about a notice you got from the IRS recently?"
- ◆ Offer free and useful content; e.g., "Click here to get our White Paper: How to Reduce IT Costs 25 percent this Year."
- ◆ Offer a product discount with a time limit on it; e.g., "50 percent off on all DVDs—this week only."
- ◆ Tell prospects the benefits they will get when using the product you are selling and back it with a guarantee; e.g., "Lose 10 pounds in three weeks with the 21st Century Rapid Weight Loss Program or your money back."

Renowned direct-marketing expert Drayton Bird says, "There's one thing an email or letter must have: well-written, persuasive copy. Don't have it and you're sunk before you start."

Hyperlinks and Calls to Action (CTAs)

The CTA is copy that tells your email readers to click the hyperlink in your email and gives them a reason for doing so. Example: "To download a free copy of Bob Bly's 186-page *Business-to-Business Marketing Handbook*, click here now: http://www.bly.com/b2bhandbook/."

The CTA and hyperlink should appear at least twice in the email: once within the first couple of paragraphs and again at the end.

The reason to include the hyperlink in the lead is to get clickthroughs from prospects who are immediately interested based on the lead and subject line but do not want to bother to scroll down to read the rest of the message or find the response link.

Include the link again toward the close, which is where the reader logically expects to find it. If you use a P.S., add a third CTA and hyperlink below that as well as the P.S. gets a lot of readership.

Should You Personalize Your Email Messages?

I do think it is better to personalize your emails, and I advise you to do so. You should personalize the salutation ("Dear Bob" or "Dear Bob Bly"). It can also be effective to personalize the subject line ("Bob, did you see this?").

Unfortunately, when I built my elist, I did not capture names, so it's not an option for me. All I asked for on my opt-in form was email address—not name. I did this not because I thought asking for just the email address would increase sign-ups but because I was new to internet marketing back then and just did not know any better.

So now my list has no names, which makes it impossible to personalize my salutations. Yes, I could start collecting names now, but that would only give me names for new subscribers. It would be much more difficult to get existing subscribers to submit their names.

One thing that might work, but would be a bit expensive, is to offer a free audio CD for registering their names. This would also enable me to capture street address, city, state, and zip code since I'd need a snail mail address for mailing the free CD. Less costly would be to offer free PDF content such as a special report and to require subscribers to give me their name to get it.

But for the CD, it makes logical sense to the subscriber to give me their postal address because without it, I couldn't very well mail them their free gift. There is no real logic in asking for just their name for downloadable PDF content.

How to Handle Subscriber Questions and Complaints

The only response you want is for the customer to click the hyperlink that brings her to the sales page where you advertise your product and enable her to order it if so desired.

If your email gets a 2 percent clickthrough rate, it means that for every 100 people who get the email, two of them did as you had hoped, which is to click the hyperlink that takes them to the sales page.

That means 98 out of the 100 recipients did not click the hyperlink. They either deleted the email without opening it, or they did open it but were not interested enough to click the link and read your sales page.

A few of them, however, may take one of several other actions. Some of them may ask you a question about the product. Should you take the time to answer?

My policy is to answer short, simple questions that I can reply to with a brief answer.

If the answer is long and it is given in one of my blog posts, articles, books, or other information products, I provide a hyperlink the person can click to either read the post or article or buy the book or course.

If the question is not easily answered in a short email or in one of your information products, you can offer to advise the customer on a paid consulting or coaching basis.

How to Handle Refund Requests

All refund requests should be handled promptly and politely, without argument, and with a full refund as promised in your guarantee.

Be generous with your guarantee and have an unwritten grace period. If you offer a 30-day money-back guarantee, and customer Joe asks for a refund on day 35, give it to him. Don't quibble over the five days past deadline for refund. On the other hand, if Joe asks for a refund a year later, he doesn't get one.

Many internet marketers do not want to keep customers who keep buying products and then return them for refund. Top information marketer Terry Dean says that if it is the first refund request from a given customer, then he gives them the benefit of the doubt; maybe the product truly wasn't right for them.

But to Terry, and me, too, if there is a second refund request on the next purchase, we assume our products are not a good fit for that person, and we do not want them as a customer. I remove the person from my newsletter subscription list. And the shopping cart software I use allows me to block their IP address so they cannot place any further orders. You can get the shopping cart software from www. BobsBestCart.com.

Sample Sales Email

Figure 12–3 is a sales email I sent to my list for my ebook *Write and Grow Rich*, which was my first foray into online information marketing.

When I decided to test the waters of internet marketing, I looked for a way to put together my first information product quickly and easily.

As it happens, I had written about a dozen columns for *Writer's Digest* magazine on how to earn six figures as a freelance writer.

The articles had all been published in the magazine, and I owned the rights to them.

I emailed all the articles to Dennis Rome, a graphic designer who was just starting out in his own freelance business.

"Turn them into an ebook, please," I asked Dennis. He did so, and the first edition was born. He charged me $175.

I priced the ebook deliberately low—$29—because I had never sold anything to my enewsletter subscriber list before, and I was worried they wouldn't buy anything expensive.

Subject: The 22 habits of financially successful writers

Dear Direct Response Letter Subscriber:

A recent survey revealed that writers who earn more than $60,000 a year consistently do 22 things that writers who earn less money don't.

To get your hands on this list of 22 habits of highly profitable writers . . . and master dozens of additional strategies for earning six figures as a freelance writer . . . click below now:

http://www.freelancewritingprofits.com/

Sincerely,

Bob Bly

FIGURE 12–3. **Email marketing message selling an ebook.**

The book sold well. I gave Dennis additional content to make the book more substantial, including some of my cartoons, and released a second edition at $39.

The email shown in Figure 12–3 offered the first edition at $29, and did very well. It generated a clickthrough rate of 5.2 percent and 120 orders for gross sales of $3,480, from a 75-word email that took me less than five minutes to write.

Why did it work so well? Two reasons. First, it's a short teaser email that understands its purpose is to generate a click—not make a sale.

The goal is not to get prospects to buy anything. It is to tell just enough to whet their appetite, and to make them click on the link to learn more.

Second, the number 22 in the headline arouses curiosity. Readers start to make a list of qualities of successful writers. They cannot come up with 22 and want to know what they are missing. Or they do come up with 22 habits and want to compare their list with mine—again, to see what they might be missing.

CHAPTER 13

AUTORESPONDERS AND UPSELLS

Email, as part of your multichannel marketing program, is one of your best tools for gaining new clients, followers, and purchasers of your products. You spend a lot of time building content for your emails, which you hope will engage most of your readers, including adding in the links to landing pages where they can buy your services or products.

Designing your email content is an ongoing process because each time you do an email send-out to your list, you offer prospects new material to read. If you are sending out notices about a new product or service, you may send that information again in another two to three months, but the content is repurposed so that it is fresh and interesting just as it was the first time the message was sent. Out of any of your marketing channels, email will be the one channel you spend the most time creating original material for on a regular basis.

Once you have set up your email schedule, such as sending an email twice a week or five days a week, then you should have an autoresponder email system that takes over to handle the job of responding to your customers whenever they take an action.

Whenever one of your readers clicks on a link and makes a purchase, signs up for a newsletter or membership in your program, or even when first subscribing to receive your email, there should always be a response sent via autoresponder from you to show your appreciation for their efforts. The autoresponder system you set up comes into play whenever one of your customers takes some type of action, sending a trigger back to your email system to activate and send a response.

Simply put, an autoresponder is software or SaaS (software as a service) that sends a sequence of emails to a person who has taken some action. You write the emails, enter them into the autoresponder system, set the action that triggers the sending of the autoresponder email series, and also schedule when each effort goes out.

How many emails should you have in an autoresponder series? The number varies. Three is usually the minimum, and seven is typical. Some marketers do much more.

How effective are autoresponder email series? On average, if you send an autoresponder series of seven emails to people who visited a sales page and entered their email address but did not buy, you can convert 10 percent to 30 percent of them to a purchase.

A single thank-you email is often sent as the first effort. It is your customer service in action and part of building trust and loyalty with your audience, who like to be recognized and appreciated for believing in you. A personalized thank-you email note goes a long way in building those first steps. The autoresponder email system helps you to do this while avoiding hours of having to manually respond to each customer. It also means you can leave your office, take a vacation, or do whatever you need to do without worrying if you need to tend to your customers.

Autoresponder Fundamentals

Once you sign up with a commercial email provider, such as Constant Contact, MailChimp, or AWeber, then you upload your current list of subscribers. An example of an autoresponder email you might have received if you directly sent an email to someone in a company is the out-of-office email, which that person set up to automatically cover incoming emails while gone on vacation. The response email tells how long the person will be out of the office and whom to contact—with contact information—if the issue is urgent. This makes it easy for the recipient to continue forward in taking care of an issue. This type of autoresponder is the oldest one around, along with email address bounce backs when an email does not reach its destination because the address is faulty.

We also get automated notifications by email based on calendar applications. There are medical notification autoresponders set to remind patients that they need to come in for their annual visit to the doctor. Autoresponder emails also remind customers that a monthly or annual payment is coming up and requests that customers update their payment preferences, just in case they have changed since the last payment.

As bulk email providers come up with more tools and processes for customers to use in their administrative control center, the more evolved email marketing will become in the coming years. Marketers are already designing multiple systems to segment customers so that they receive targeted emails based on past purchases even while still receiving the regular emails that everyone else on the master list gets.

Or maybe readers show interest in the product or service but have not yet made a purchase. Then, those readers go into a group that gets an occasional email about the product or service, keeping them involved, at least for a while, until they do make the purchase or are moved into another list.

This becomes part of upselling to the customer: showing them new products and services related to a purchase they made a while back. For example, if a customer buys a photo-editing software program today and you have developed a training program around this same software, you can first upsell this training to the software purchasers at the time they buy the software. The first upsell moment occurs at the point when checking out at the shopping cart but before they click to complete the software purchase.

The upsell notice can be prominently located at the top of the shopping cart checkout page, with a check box to select it, so it can be included in the final purchase amount. Putting such offers at the top means the customers see this offer first as they arrive on the checkout page. Add in a few lines of content about the training program and its features, and that adds to the value of the training program as something the customer needs. Why not get it now and save hours trying to figure out the software program on your own, right?

If they do not buy the training program at the time of purchase, you can send them the occasional email that offers tips on how to use the software, highlighting some of its special features. This is the continuation of the first upsell, but expanded to be teaser emails— giving just enough information, but not so much that the goal to upsell the training program is defeated.

When you start making sales on your website or get people to sign up for your newsletter, the crucial component you need to keep it all together is your autoresponder, which will send messages to your customers after any transaction is completed. If you have made a purchase online and received an email saying, "Thank you for your purchase and here is your download product," then you've just been contacted by an autoresponder system.

The system can be tied to your newsletter sign-up landing page or hooked to your online shopping cart, whether by you personally or through a third-party vendor that is providing a full merchant account with integrated shopping cart, payment gateway, and the autoresponder that adds a little bit of personal attention to the customer.

Your autoresponder can accomplish the following services for you and your customers: the order confirmation message when the transaction is successfully processed, shipping confirmation, conversion messages to the customer providing other connected products they might be interested in, welcome and thank-you letters, reminders to take certain actions, monthly reports of all send-outs, and even contests and surveys. Automating this part of your business leaves you free to devote more time to your business, creating products and devising marketing campaigns.

An example of how an autoresponder works is when a customer signs up for your newsletter, an email is sent to them as soon as they hit the Submit button on the sign-up page (Figure 13–1).

Any messages you send must always have the opt-out option at the end or at the beginning where subscribers can unsubscribe if they

---

Dear (auto-inserted name),

We are delighted you have signed up to receive our newsletter which will be sent to you once a week! Additionally, we would like to have you visit our website for more information on the product information you have shown interest in on our sign-up page. Here are some links to information you might really enjoy! Feel free to also browse around our website and see what else we offer our clients! Here are your links for today's visit to get you started.

- MarketingPlace.com/writing-booksfastandeasy
- MarketingPlace.com/KeepYourFinancesOrderly
- MarketPlace.com/WhenYourClientWon'tPay

We are looking forward to having you as one of our valued subscribers and we hope you will also sign up for our forum as well to give us further insights into things you like about our website and what you think we should improve.

Very Sincerely,

Tom and Janice

The Marketing Team

MarketPlace.com

*This publication is never sent unsolicited so if you feel you are receiving this message in error, and would not like to hear from us any further, please click here to unsubscribe. ***

FIGURE 13–1. **Autoresponder email sent immediately to prospects who sign up for a free online newsletter.**

don't want to receive any more messages. This keeps you protected from CAN-SPAM issues that could possibly crop up. This also is a good way to measure your marketing campaign's effectiveness by tracking if there are groups of people who unsubscribe whenever you send out certain types of messages.

Other types of autoresponder messages can be an upsell or cross-sell type, which provide additional sales for you. For example, your customer signs up for your free newsletter on best practices for raising a healthy puppy. In the subsequent cross-sell autoresponder thank-you note, provide a few links to free articles such as "What to Look for When Choosing a Vet," or "Natural Ways to Keep Fleas off Your Puppy." After that, you might promote the new book you just wrote and published called *Healthy Foods for Healthy Dogs: Providing a Healthy Diet for Long Life.* Your message can look like the one in Figure 13–2 on page 235.

In the upsell, we will use software as an example. If a customer has bought a software program from a company, that company may come out with a new version of that program after two years that the customer might be interested in it. That new software takes advantage of new technical capabilities on the market such as integrating with iPhones, iPads, and other sales components now available on the internet marketplace. As the old software is not capable of upgrades to the new version, then this would be considered an upsell situation.

Autoresponders can also convert customers to paying customers from one type of free service to a paying service that provides much more to the customer than if they were still in the free zone of a membership.

As an example using software again, Adobe.com has carried a wide range of software programs considered essential for people working in publishing and graphic design. For some people, buying the programs outright is far too expensive, so Adobe created the subscription arrangement for each software package. Autoresponder messages put this information out to the public, and for those who couldn't buy the program before but could make a monthly payment

Dear NAME,

We now have the latest and greatest "cookbook" guide that will provide a long and happy life for your new puppy or even the middle-aged dog that has been a treasured member of the family for so long! It's a lifestyle manual for a healthy pet you'll want to keep handy—always within reach!! Not only will you have a healthy dog, but you will save money on veterinarian bills too!

As veterinarians for over 20 years, we have seen many dogs with health problems that could have been avoided with a different diet. We have spent the last five years researching the latest findings in scholarly papers and adding in our own findings from our years of treating many different conditions to come up with the complete dietary manual for bringing up and keeping your favorite member of the family happy and healthy.

For a modest fee of $19.95, we hope you will find this information manual valuable and one you will keep handy over the lifespan of your loyal member of the family. Just click here to make your purchase and your guide will be sent immediately. "The Cookbook Guide for Providing a Long Healthy Life for Your Dog."

If after 30 days, you don't feel our guide to a healthy dog offers you what you need, please feel free to send the book back for a prompt refund. No questions asked!

FIGURE 13–2. **Autoresponder email for a cross-sell.**

now, it has been a real boon, especially to small businesses with limited funding.

When Adobe brought out its Creative Cloud subscription package, current customers could get in on a year's subscription for a nominal monthly fee; while new Adobe customers paid a little more, the fee was very affordable. This was a great example of conversion and upsell, and again, the message was sent by autoresponder to current and past customers as part of the marketing strategy.

Newsletters are sent by autoresponders and set for delivery at specific times designated by the writer after the content is added. It is important to balance content with providing free and interesting information as opposed to just sending out notices concerning products you are selling.

No subscriber wants to feel that every message is just a ploy to get money. The intention should be more subtle; therefore, adding free content with a high value should be a major factor of your newsletter. When subscribers get valuable information and reports for free, it is like getting a gift. When the messages finally come regarding products for purchase, customers are more likely to sit up and take notice.

These messages should also give a brief overview of the product but then provide a link that goes right to the actual specially designed marketing piece that explains all the benefits and features of owning the product. The autoresponder is essential in getting that message out and getting the customers to the marketing page.

Some companies offering autoresponder systems you can review for pricing and features for your business include AWeber, SendFree, 1ShoppingCart, and Constant Contact. Once your autoresponder is up and running, you can devote your time to building your business as the leads and sales begin to roll in.

Autoresponder Benefits

Autoresponders, ultimately, exist to respond to an action that a reader or customer makes by clicking on a link or call-to-action (CTA) button found in an email or on a website, blog, social media channel, or landing page. When a reader fills out a form, or a customer makes a purchase, then clicks to send the information forward, a series of email autoresponders are triggered relevant to those actions. A new subscriber receives a thank-you note for signing up to a newsletter or membership, or the customer receives the invoice after payment and an email thank-you note. Finally, both might receive an email bonus link to a special report, related to what was signed up for or bought.

The obvious benefits of having a finely tuned autoresponder email system is that, first, you save a tremendous amount of time (and money) in not having to individually send out emails to each customer that makes a purchase or signs up for something. Second, when you integrate the autoresponder system with your shopping cart, the customer receives the invoice, a thank-you email, and a bonus link email, if you offered one as part of making the purchase. Any of these actions can take place at any hour of the day, leaving you free to earn money while you are busy elsewhere or sleeping in your bed at night.

You can create multiple campaigns from your email admin center, easily keeping track of each one, including statistics on how well they are doing—aside from sales numbers. Autoresponder tracking systems with analytics also help you figure out if you have a weak link anywhere in your multichannel program such as one of your social media accounts. It can be as simple as adding hashtags to your content so it can be found more easily when people do searches for that topic.

As you build your email list of subscribers, you can conduct analyses on who your readers are, where they are located (region or country), their product or service preferences, what they do while on your various marketing channels, and a host of other interaction variables. This can be done right inside your bulk email admin center. Add that data in with your Google Analytics from your website, blog, or landing pages, and you can get some robust insight into who your customers are and what they want.

This will help you build your business and design products and services that your readers want to see. Your business can build exponentially if you really think this through, and your autoresponder email system can help you do that. It can automate just about every step in that process, and you can personalize each autoresponder email, which is an important part of making your subscribers feel they are a special part of the world you are offering to them. Another important benefit of using your autoresponder email system is that you can conduct A/B testing on any part of your emails and landing pages, giving you valuable analytical information on what works well and what does not.

Types of Autoresponder Emails

Types of autoresponder messages include:

- ◆ Calendar-based automated reminders (medical visits, billing renewals)
- ◆ Out-of-office responses by email
- ◆ Thank-you emails, welcome emails for signing up to your emails or a membership, bonus link emails after a purchase
- ◆ Sequence emails (creatively leading your customers)
- ◆ Lead-nurturing (drip) autoresponder emails (people who have not bought yet)
- ◆ Webinar email autoresponder series (first notification, sign-up, verified attendance notice, reminders, and after it is over)
- ◆ Customer service autoresponders (auto-generated claim numbers, product return verification)

Sequence Emails

Do not presume that just because readers bought your book on canning fruit that this is all they want to know about. Expand on that field of interest further. You can do a sequence of emails, with one on best types of cookware to do canning with, the next email on types of natural pesticides to use on your fruit in the garden before picking them for canning, a third email on how to optimize soil mixtures for best fruit production, and so on.

You can set up a whole automated sequence email campaign on just that leading to a landing page for your new book that incorporates all that information—and more. You can call it, "The Complete Guide to Growing and Canning Your Fruit."

Now that readers know how to can their fruits, including how to grow fruits, they may want to also know how to market their homemade products. When customers bought the expanded guide on how to grow perfect fruit and then can the fruit, you could have included the first upsell notice for the marketing book at the time they were checking out of the shopping cart.

Remember, you can put that first upsell notice right at the top of the shopping cart page. While that may not guarantee they would have bought it at once, the seed is sown in that they now know there is a marketing book they can buy to help them sell their canned fruits.

There is a whole other line of products you can create for just that purpose of marketing canned fruits. You can lead your readers on with sequenced emails giving that information, a tidbit at a time, such as how to build a Facebook page for their product, even while giving a link each time to a landing page for your book on how to market canned fruit. This way, you give value in each of your emails, even while offering a link, or CTA button, to buy your *Marketing for Selling Your Canned Fruits* book.

Follow the statistics on these emails to see how readers act when they read your emails, starting with the email open action and following through to clicking on the link for the book's landing page. Do more sales conversions occur after the first, second, or third email you send? Do most readers always click on the CTA to go to the book's landing page and buy it? Or not buy it? If not, does your landing page need more work? All these answers can be found in your analyses of what your customers are doing at each part of your multichannel marketing system.

Lead-Nurturing (Drip) Autoresponder Emails

People who sign up for your emails can fit into several groups: those who are ready to buy something from you, those who are thinking about it but want more information, and those who are interested in being on your list but do not know if they want to buy anything right now.

For this group of readers, sending out automated emails on interesting subjects related to your products and services is the most important part of keeping readers engaged with your brand and learning more about what you offer. It is not so much about direct selling to this group, although you can slide in a link or CTA just in case they want to find out more about a product or service.

A starting point about the content you offer these readers is first learning what marketing channel they came from to get to you (e.g., a social media campaign or your blog) and then finding out if they bought something or not. Let us say that, no matter what channel it was, you had a recent campaign to capture more leads by offering a free small white paper which discussed one of the components of the new service you are offering.

This new group receives the same emails, which show engaging content about how this service was created to solve a common problem that many readers had found while running their business. You may give a case study in one email, then another in the second email, rather like story-telling sessions.

At the bottom of these first two emails, you give a short piece of content about the book and a link, or CTA button, to a landing page for the book you wrote about how to solve this problem for your readers. Yet they still need to hire you to get the solution implemented properly, because this issue is technically complex for most readers.

At this point, you might split the readers into two groups (or email channels): those who bought the book (Group A), and those who did not (Group B).

Group A now receives automated emails referencing components of the book shown in emails as to how hiring you can help them be more successful. Your service, as presented in the book, is a one-stop business that can get it all done for your customers so they do not have to do it themselves. From here, once they have received a few of the supporting email sequences that may also have links to videos, you can offer your readers a product demo and a free consultation.

Meanwhile, Group B is on another track, and they receive the occasional email like Group A got, but they also get other emails with different content about other services you provide, including links to content with more information such as a video. For those more interested in these other services you offer, rather than the problem that the book discussed, you could then separate those interested readers into Group C.

Now, they are in an email channel that supports their interest, which they showed you when they clicked on those links but not the book link. Those in Group B who click on the book link show that they are still interested in the book and, potentially, your personalized service but just may not be ready yet. They stay in Group B.

The Group B example in sequenced emails can also be called a "drip campaign," aside from nurturing your new leads. The process can be complicated, but the autoresponder emails help you do all of this very easily. Your biggest efforts in building this come at the beginning as you design it.

Even if your system is not complete when you start the campaign, as you watch your statistics from the autoresponder link clicks, you can continue to build on to your system to accommodate your readers so they stay active and interested. If you are new to building email autoresponder campaigns, feel free to consult with your bulk email provider because this is what they do best, and they can help with tips in segmenting your readers.

Webinar Autoresponder Email Series

Webinars are very popular for marketers who like to show their followers how they can carry out something in their business that will help them make more money. In the earlier lead-nurturing email example, a webinar can be offered at some point for Group A because they showed the most interest in the product. So, let us see how one fits this into the channel.

Group A has already seen a video or two as part of the sequence emails they received. You can then send an email inviting readers to attend a webinar where they can see the service in action and how it can help them decide on hiring you. Once the webinar invitation goes out, readers fill out the form and send it back. This generates the reservation acceptance email that carries a link that is automatically code-created with that person's identification and takes the person to the webinar link when the time comes to join up.

The acceptance email also offers a capability to have the webinar event inserted into whatever calendar system the reader uses, such as Google Calendar or Microsoft Outlook. Readers just click on whichever one they want it to go in, and their calendar pops open with the link and event inserted.

A reminder email is sent a day before the event, again on the morning of the event, and again right before the webinar event begins. All your readers need to do is click on the link several minutes before it starts, which goes right to the webinar page where each reader is recognized as a pre-registered attendee (because of the ID link code).

Once inside, each attendee's name pops up to the right side of the screen where the attendee list is. This also tells you who showed up and who did not based on your registered list of intended attendees. As you will see, it is important that you reach out to those who did not show up. They are not lost to you yet.

Once the webinar is over, get the list of attendees—including those who did not attend—and create two separate channels: one for each group. For now, we put aside those who attended but did not sign up for the service.

For the registered nonattendees of Group A in the lead-nurturing campaign, now moved into a Group A short-term email subset, you send an autoresponder saying that they were missed at the webinar but there is a link for a replay if they would still like to see it. Of course, they cannot ask questions or make replies because it is recorded, but they may still want to take advantage of whatever offer you made at the end of the webinar such as a price discount to hire you within 48 hours of viewing the webinar.

If your short-term subset group members clicked on the replay link but did not click on the provided link to get your service, you can have an automated email go out several hours later, asking if they would like to have a consultation to know more. They can click on a link in the email to generate a callback from you or set up an appointment to meet with you.

After 24 hours, you can send out another autoresponder that reminds them that the discount will be over in 24 hours, so they need to act now. From there, if no actions were taken, you can move nonresponding people into another email channel to receive regular emails of interest in products and services you have to offer, including emails that just offer valuable content without any sales approach.

Just keep them engaged even though they are not candidates for hiring you for your service right now. The key phrase in that sentence is "right now." Potentially down the road, you may re-engage them again if they click on one of those links within the campaign that leads to hiring you for your service.

Customer Service Autoresponder Emails

Most of us have received autoresponder emails when making a complaint to a company about a product or service that did not work right. A company's reputation, aside from great products and services, is also judged by how it handles customer service issues. If your company does not have excellent response systems in place to handle customer issues, you will lose out on customer loyalty and, ultimately, more sales—a bigger loss than trying to get in new customers.

While every company wants to engage more new leads in hopes of bringing in more money, taking care of the customers you have is essential to keeping your brand's persona at a high rating. With the internet and social media in place, you will not get away with bad service for very long. What used to be gossip between family and friends is now out there on the internet for everyone to see.

Once a complaint is made to a company, whether by chat, email, or phone call, an auto-generated claim number is created so the company can record every step of the process in taking care of the issue. The customer receives the claim number by autoresponder email, or if the customer does not have email, a letter can be sent out with the claim number included. This claim number is used every time contact is made between the company and the customer.

While the claim number is auto-generated, along with the corresponding autoresponder email or letter, each point of contact from then on should be made between the customer and a specific customer service person, who has a name and contact information, along with hours of operation given in the email or letter.

A level of urgency should also be applied to each issue, such as a software function that is not working properly, leaving the customer who needs it to work perfectly for business in a position of losing money and time while the software is down.

Once the problem has been solved to the customer's satisfaction, an autoresponder email is sent out asking if everything has been taken care of properly and if the company can now close out the claim. Once the customer clicks on the approved link provided, the case is automatically closed on the company's side.

When you are handling the issue, do whatever you told the customer you were going to do for them. There is nothing worse than a company that lies, saying they will do something like send a replacement product, and then nothing happens. In truth, this is more likely to happen with companies that have a monopoly in the marketplace, leaving customers with few other options to find the service they need.

With that in mind, make sure you have a system in place to address customer issues at every level of interaction. If you always offer a link in your emails that customers can click on to get customer service for a problem that leads to a page where there are links for chat, calling a phone number, or sending an email, then you are already a powerhouse in offering customer service. Provide a customer service link on your website and even on your social media channels.

You can also offer a level of urgency list on the landing page, such as one through five, with five being the most urgent. The customer selects the level and the issue is pushed up the chain of service for immediate response. Wherever the claim notice lands in the system, the autoresponder email sent back reaffirms the claim, gives a claim number, shows the issue the urgency level applied for, and when the customer can expect to be contacted back.

The message is also personalized, using the customer's name, which gives more of an impression that the company cares about the customer. Whenever you write up these autoresponders, be sure to use content that is friendly and caring but also matches the company tone you use for communicating with customers. You must remember your brand is at stake.

Other customer-based autoresponder emails you may need are for failed renewal payments, such as monthly fees for a subscription. Be kind in the automated response. There is probably a good reason why it did not go through, and the customer can get it fixed quickly.

Finally, here are some other tips on what types of autoresponder emails you can set up, which work very nicely with your customers and readers:

- Birthday greetings, including a one-time discount for one item in a certain range of products
- Holiday greetings, including half-price sales, discounts, and the like
- Running a survey and offering a bonus or incentive to readers who complete the survey
- Abandoned shopping carts, for reminding customers they did not finish their order (do it nicely)
- Abandoned emails. Subscribers (hopefully only a few) who do not open your emails for months may need to be resubscribed. Send out an autoresponder asking the reader if they would like to still be on your list, especially as you have new content coming up. Give them that link. Also give the link for them to unsubscribe, and they can choose which way to go.

Next, I'll talk more about upsells, an important part of your autoresponder communication system that, if done correctly, will bring you more revenue than just banking on what you bring in with direct sales.

Upsells

Upsells on a smaller level have already been discussed, such as having a short upsell notice on the shopping cart page before the customer gives the credit card information and closes the purchase. In this case, the upsell is positioned at the top of the page, visible to the customer as he or she lands on that page. The customer can take a moment to look at what it is, decide to click the check box, and add it to the shopping cart or else say no. The purchase continues from there with filling out shipping and credit card information to complete the purchase.

In addition to free bonuses that I usually offer to my customers when selling them one of my PDF ebooks, I connect an upsell to some of my products that might help them based on the ebook or program that they are buying.

One of the great ways to bring in more customers is giving speeches to customers who need your expertise in a certain area of business. Your talents can range from developing software programs or creating educational online courses to offering personal development coaching or building wonderful websites.

People who have never given speeches before balk at the idea of doing so. Yet it is really not that hard to do, and it will help your brand, and yourself, to do it. The next several pages give the upsell I provide to potential customers.

When you are offering your products and services online, one fairly simple way of generating even more income is to provide different upgrades or versions of the same product. This is commonly seen in software products, as an example.

Buying a software program means also buying the license to run it on your computer. There may be add-ons that you can purchase, such as in IBM's SPSS program, which comes as the basic version and then charges additional prices for several types of add-on components for your analysis needs.

If you are selling copywriting books on your website, you can also sell connected four-week programs along with that book at the checkout point. This is considered an upsell when the products are connected to each other. The book purchased might be called *How to Write Great Leads for Any Type of Client You Get*. The upsell is the four-week program that walks you through the process and fully engages you in practicing what the book offers, which also happens to be the textbook for the course.

Upsells also occur, as in software, when you can upgrade your current version to the latest version on the market, for a small fee, at the same time that you are renewing your annual license.

This is not to be confused with cross sales, which typically offer other products and services that the customer might be interested in based on the type of product or service being purchased at the point of sale. Maybe you decide to purchase a new tablet, and for an additional fee, you can purchase three movies at a smaller cost than if you were to buy them independently of the tablet. You may also get one free video game if you purchase two new ones, making a total of three video games you can now play on your new tablet.

Amazon.com provides numerous benefits when someone purchases the Kindle Fire HD and then also gets the Prime membership package, which allows for Prime purchasers to view any number of movies and TV shows for free.

In a specific example of upselling, Amazon sells the original black and white Kindle reader but also points out all the wonderful benefits that the Kindle Fire HD, particularly the 8.9-inch version, will provide to those who love books, movies, and video games. That is a case of upselling from the black and white reader-only version to a more comprehensive high-definition color version with greater capabilities.

The idea is to set up your point of sale page to determine from the shopping cart just what products and services the customer is purchasing and then automatically trigger pop-ups that show better versions of the same product or service, such as newer versions of a book being purchased or extended services that can be added on to the main service being purchased.

In the case of buying a book online, other books can be shown at the point of purchase that also are variations of the same subject or may reflect a behind-the-scenes monitoring of what the prospect was looking at while on the site before making the final choice. This would be more a case of cross sales rather than upsells, unless the newer edition of a book is promoted as the alternative purchase. That would be an upsell.

It is also important at what point these alternative options for upselling are made because people can become irritated if too much stuff is pushed at them when they are ready to leave. The best strategy is to have pop-ups show when the customer puts the product or service in the shopping cart.

At this point, they are still browsing and may be more willing to look at upgrades. If they are being shown these right at the time that the credit card is being entered, this might be confusing and maybe even irritating, as they are now ready to complete the purchase. If they get irritated with pop-up upsells, then they may just dump the whole purchase. Then, you have lost the sale. Too many choices at the wrong time can cost you, rather than adding to your revenue.

Another good tactic that Amazon utilizes is showing what other people are saying about their products. Generally, these are people who have made purchases of a product and are so happy with it, they come back and review the product. This can be in the form of book reviews, movie reviews, or product reviews. Some customers would rather see what others say before finalizing a purchase.

Potential buyers want to know what the best points about the product are, according to the reviewer, and whether they will match up with what the customer is looking for. Knowing that the newer version or edition aligns more with what the customer wants to have, based on a customer review, is a big selling point. In fact, that is an upsell. The nice part for Amazon is that they do not have to pay for this type of marketing. It is created for them for free by their own customers.

In this case, the layout of Amazon's product pages provides the reviews with the product when you scroll down the page. If you look a little further past that, there is a scrolling bar that shows comparative products along those same lines, some of which may be cross sales and others upsells.

There is another part to efficient upselling, and that is maintaining a customer relationship management (CRM) system, which keeps information about your customers handy so you can do analysis on what they bought and when they bought it.

This is particularly important if, as a software provider, you are coming out with a new version of a software product that has many more perks attached to it than the previous version. You will want to approach these customers with information about the new product and how it will add to their software operations if they upgrade to the new product. For those who have a license, they can go to a particular link, present the license, and get an upgrade, which will be far cheaper than if they were buying the product for the first time.

What is important about this group of consumers is that once they have the product, you can get feedback and reviews about how well it is working for them. This information is then passed along on the website (with their permission) as testimonials on how wonderfully the new version is working for their needs. For those who are new to the product, upsells can include purchasing online classes so the new customers can learn the product and get up to speed quickly without having to suffer through self-training, which is haphazard at best for most people.

The CRM system is one of the most important tools to utilize for just about any business that consistently upgrades products or creates new editions of books. CRM systems provide all the information you need to determine how to upsell to current and past customers so that revenue continues to come in on a regular basis.

The greatest results from upsells come at the exact moment when the initial purchase is made, and this is done by sending the buyer to an upsell page as shown in Figure 13–3 on page 250.

This is also an important part of the behind-the-scenes working processes that should be built by you, or your webmaster, into any website as an actual customer database. This, in turn, can be downloaded into your computer's CRM system for future reference and analysis in market research and strategy projects that generate future revenue.

As an added benefit, you can also create an upsell at the point of purchase for a new or upgraded product by offering extended two-year or three-year licenses, which make it cheaper in the case of upgrading a software program and license for that span of time.

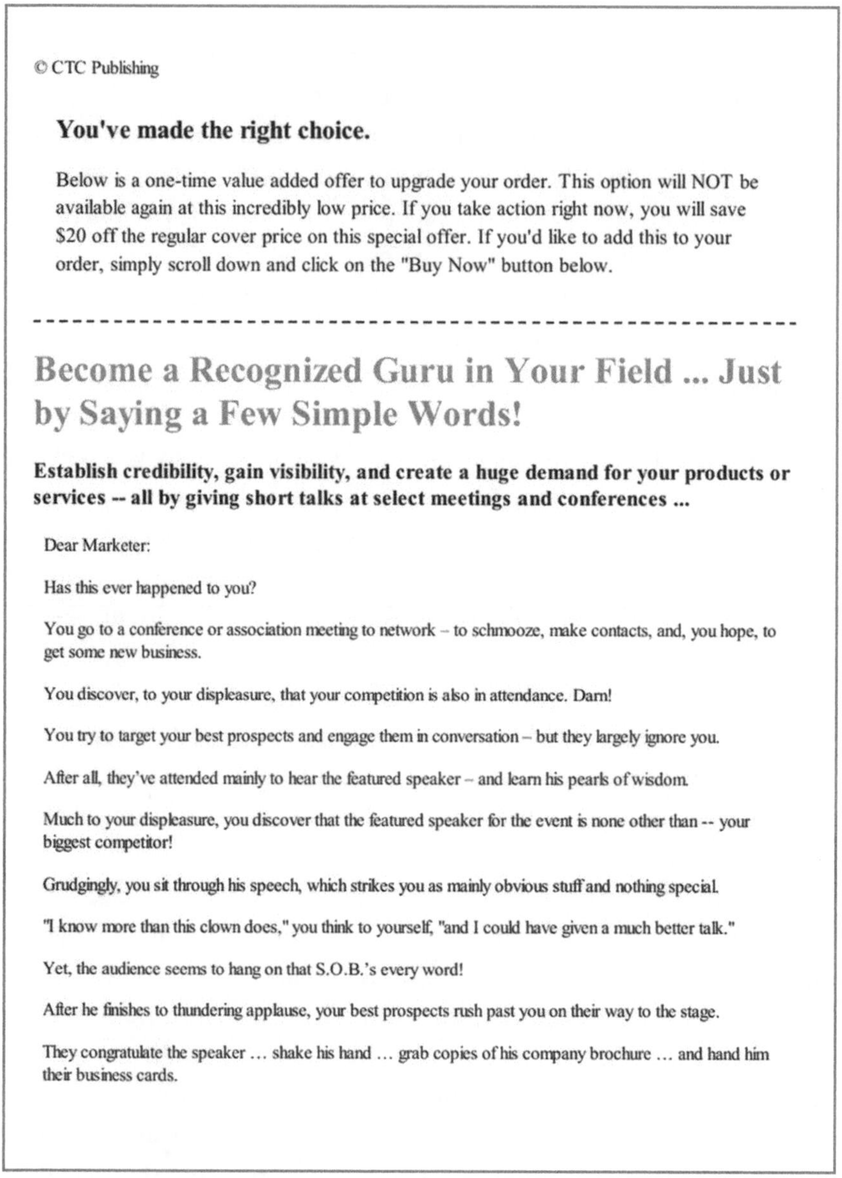

You've made the right choice.

Below is a one-time value added offer to upgrade your order. This option will NOT be available again at this incredibly low price. If you take action right now, you will save $20 off the regular cover price on this special offer. If you'd like to add this to your order, simply scroll down and click on the "Buy Now" button below.

Become a Recognized Guru in Your Field ... Just by Saying a Few Simple Words!

Establish credibility, gain visibility, and create a huge demand for your products or services -- all by giving short talks at select meetings and conferences ...

Dear Marketer:

Has this ever happened to you?

You go to a conference or association meeting to network – to schmooze, make contacts, and, you hope, to get some new business.

You discover, to your displeasure, that your competition is also in attendance. Darn!

You try to target your best prospects and engage them in conversation – but they largely ignore you.

After all, they've attended mainly to hear the featured speaker – and learn his pearls of wisdom.

Much to your displeasure, you discover that the featured speaker for the event is none other than -- your biggest competitor!

Grudgingly, you sit through his speech, which strikes you as mainly obvious stuff and nothing special.

"I know more than this clown does," you think to yourself, "and I could have given a much better talk."

Yet, the audience seems to hang on that S.O.B.'s every word!

After he finishes to thundering applause, your best prospects rush past you on their way to the stage.

They congratulate the speaker ... shake his hand ... grab copies of his company brochure ... and hand him their business cards.

FIGURE 13–3. **After the customer selects a product from the shopping cart, she is taken to an upsell page that offers a related product.**

And you can't help but overhear them all telling your competitor, "We need to work with you ... please call me tomorrow morning so we can book you!"

Maybe your competitor even looks up from his adoring "fans" ... sees you glaring at him from your seat ... and winks at you with an infuriating smile – as he continues to steal project after project from you.

You go home frustrated, having wasted a day, and no richer to show for it.

Your competitor goes home elated – and with more work booked than he can handle.

What made the difference?

You and I know that clients want to deal with vendors who are considered the top experts in their field.

And what do top experts do that their less respected competitors don't?

They give talks: speeches ... seminars ... lectures ... workshops ... college classes ... training sessions ... podcasts ... tele-seminars ... you name it.

Well, let me tell you a little secret, which perhaps you've already figured out: the speakers you hear at industry meetings don't know any more about your specialty than you do!

But they've done two things you haven't ...

First, they've taken the time to organize their knowledge into a clear, informative talk – one that conveys valuable ideas to the audience – and makes them sound like knowledgeable pros.

Second, they've actively marketed their free talk to organizations their prospects join – and to meeting planners in charge of sessions their prospects attend.

As a result, they – not you – get asked to deliver the important workshops, keynotes, break-out sessions, and after-dinner speeches in your industry.

And they, not you, get all the attention ... applause ... recognition ... visibility ... and exposure from these events.

But it doesn't have to be that way, because now you too can ...

...speak and grow rich!

If you sell a product ... solve a problem ... or offer a service, you have valuable expertise that others want to know about.

By sharing your knowledge in short talks -- given at the right venues to the right audiences -- you can take

FIGURE 13–3. **continued**

your business to the next level.

Your prospects attend the meeting. They see you are the guest expert. They hear your content-rich talk. And suddenly, they decide *you* – and not your competitors – are the one they want to buy from!

Plus, you can do it without awkward "networking" ... without complicated Internet marketing ... and without a labor-intensive PR campaign or costly advertising ... just by giving short talks, for free, at select industry meetings and events.

Now, in my how-to guide, *Getting Famous Through Public Speaking: How to Market Your Product or Service Through Free Seminars, Workshops, Speeches, and Lectures,* you get step-by-step instructions on how to promote yourself by giving talks.

Including:

- How to absolutely guarantee your talk gives listeners what they want and need to know from you. Page 43.
- The "green sheet" method for ensuring that every potential customer in your audience leaves with your name and contact information in their hands – without pushing business cards on them. Page 28.
- Why your talk should be shorter, not longer, than you think. Plus: a fun gimmick for making sure you don't run over – it will have your audience rolling in the aisles. Page 20.
- 10 reasons why giving speeches is a more powerful self-promotion than direct mail, space advertising, e-mail, or any other marketing method. Page 31.
- The 8 secrets all great speakers know – and practice – that boring, mediocre, and unsuccessful speakers don't. Page 16.
- "No-brainer" for getting audience members to give you rave reviews and testimonials you can use to promote your talks, your services, and yourself. Page 51.
- 7 ways to bond with the audience – and get them on your side – before you step up to the podium. Page 34.
- Must you offer a handout at all your speaking engagements? The answer may surprise you. Page 26.
- 41 techniques that can transform you from a nervous amateur into a smooth, confident, engaging public speaker. Page 21.
- Want to really become an "instant guru" in your field? Become a college professor – without getting your PhD. Page 38.

- How to promote yourself by giving talks – even if no one asks you to do so. Page 30.
- Thousands of meetings take place in the U.S. every business day. Here's how to find the ones where you can gain visibility in your marketplace as a speaker. Page 4.
- The most important part of your talk – and an easy technique for making it instantly engaging. Page 14.
- PowerPoint mistakes that can quickly send even the most interested audience into a coma ... and how to avoid them. Page 40.
- The organization says they can't pay even an honorarium for your talk. But don't worry. There are 8 things you can ask for even better than cash. Page 8.

FIGURE 13–3. **continued**

- 10 situations in which public speaking is the most engaging, and effective, way to get your message across to your customers and prospects. Page 3.
- What Spiderman can teach you about promoting your business with special events. Page 37.
- Most speakers get business cards from fewer than 10% of prospects in the audience. This little trick gets 80% to 90% or more of prospects in the audience to give you their card. Page 29.
- 5 incredibly powerful ways to get more leads, and close more business with members of your audience, whenever you give a talk. Page 35.
- Want to give a hard-sell pitch for your product to a captive audience of interested prospects who actually want to hear it? Page 33 shows you where – and how – to get away with it.
- 6 questions to ask before you accept an invitation to speak. Ensures you don't waste your time talking to people who aren't potential customers. Page 7.
- Tips for preparing visuals that "knock 'em dead" -- instead of putting them to sleep. Page 24.
- 8 simple steps for organizing a powerful – and persuasive – speech or presentation. Page 12.
- Best ways to close your talk. Hint: It's NOT by making a sales pitch. Page 15.
- And so much more ...

Praise for Bob Bly and *Getting Famous Through Public Speaking*

Getting Famous Through Public Speaking is a quick-reading, 50+-page e-book available for immediate downloading as a PDF file.

That means no shipping or handling charges ... and no waiting. Order today, and start promoting your business by giving talks tomorrow!

Here's what people have said about earlier editions of *Getting Famous Through Public Speaking*....

"This guy really knows his stuff. An excellent and practical primer."
--R. John Slade, President, Knowledge Garden

"An invaluable marketing tool that all business owners or entrepreneurs should have ... even just one of the many innovative techniques in this book will pay back its cost many times over."
--Fred Weiss, Chairman (retired), Studebaker-Worthington Leasing

"I found so many valuable ideas in the book, which I am putting to immediate practical and exciting use. This book is the key to Fort Knox."
--Dottie Walters, President, Walters International Speakers Bureau

"I have been speaking in public since 1958. That's why I bought Bob Bly's book. A professional in any field needs only one tip to convert a $39.95 specialized how-to book or report into ten times that much money -- maybe in just one speech. He will always spot at least one tip that he forgot or ignored or never considered. That's why a professional keeps buying how-to books in his field."
--Gary North

FIGURE 13–3. **continued**

Use it risk-free for 90 days

Very few speakers' bureaus, lecture agents, or publicists can guarantee that they can get you speaking engagements.

And virtually none promise you increased leads, orders, or sales from the speaking gigs they book for you.

But with *Getting Famous Through Public Speaking,* you get both. I guarantee it -- or you don't pay me!

That's right ...

If *Getting Famous Through Public Speaking* doesn't help you get more speaking gigs, resulting in more business for your or your firm ...

Or you are dissatisfied for any other reason ... or for no reason at all ... just let me know within 90 days.

I'll refund your $19 payment in full. No questions asked. And, you can still keep the e-book free.

That way, you risk nothing.

In 90 days or sooner, you could be in the spotlight at an industry event or association meeting as a featured speaker – as I frequently am -- while your competitors turn green with envy, wondering why they were overlooked.

Or, you could be attending yet another networking function ... where you're just another vendor looking for business ... while the speaker – also a vendor – grabs all the glory – and the new business.

It's entirely up to you.

So what are you waiting for?

Don't miss out on this one-time offer of a $20 savings off the regular cover price of $39, and order *Getting Famous Through Public Speaking* on a 90-day risk-free trial basis, by clicking below now:

Sincerely,
Bob Bly

P.S. **Quick-Response Bonus!** Order *Getting Famous Through Public Speaking* today and you get a FREE 60-page Bonus Report, *How to Do Your Own Public Relations.* (list price: $29).

FIGURE 13–3. **continued**

In it, you will discover:

- 29 great story ideas for the next issue of your company newsletter or e-zine. See page 17.
- Promoting yourself, your company, or your product through public speaking? Here's how to make your talk more memorable, engaging, and persuasive. Page 26.
- How to use "DR PR" – direct response press releases – to generate new leads, prospects, and business opportunities. Page 14.
- 4-part formula for writing business letters that get you the results you want. Page 50.
- Want to position yourself as an expert by writing a book? 5 ways to write a book proposal editors say "yes" to. Page 29.
- Fool-proof formula for writing articles and getting them published, under your byline, in the trade publications your customers and prospects read. Page 14.
- Plus: a special library of sample press releases and query letters. Easy-to-follow templates guide you in writing your own PR materials. Starts on page 58.

Web Design by: Filipino Webmasters Inc.

FIGURE 13–3. **continued**

Always take advantage of the opportunity to upsell by providing benefits to the customer but without a lot of pressure. Being subtle about upsells is the best approach to success.

This upsell to several of my reports, ebooks, DVD, and CD programs that I offer customers has sold very well, and many customers have come back over the years to thank me for this product that gave them the kick they needed to become better known in their field of business by becoming speakers.

Upsell vs. Cross-Sell

Both approaches add value to what the customer has bought, but the upsell offers a better version of the same product, such as a premium software package over the starter version of the software package. A cross-sell would be to add on more value to the software package by showing a software book that trains readers on how to use the software.

The two terms are sometimes interchangeable, depending on the circumstances. In my example, because I do not have two versions of any product, the term "upsell" is more proper, especially as I have offered a onetime discount to buy at the moment of the original sale.

Either way, upsells can be added at any time during or after the buying process of one product. Once the customer has completed the purchase, an autoresponder email will arrive, giving a similar upsell like the one presented above.

When that purchase is completed, another autoresponder email arrives, thanking the customer and giving the link to download the new purchase. In the case of a physical product, the thank-you autoresponder email also states that the product is being readied to be sent out, and as soon as it is shipped, the tracking number will be forwarded to the customer.

Any upsell products or services you link to should be a complement item to whatever your customers bought before receiving the upsell offer. Offering the above upsell adds extra value to the item originally bought by showing another way to expand and grow the customer's business. It also shows that you care about the customer by thinking of items they might need to develop their business better, based on what the customer just bought.

Finally, always stay in touch with your autoresponder email system to check that each part of your system is working well; when it is not, get it fixed quickly. Always keep your eyes on your analytics, which can give you the first warning of a problem in the system, such as a large number of unsubscribes in one area. Make sure you take advantage of offering products and services at different stages of your autoresponder marketing system, but do not oversell.

CHAPTER 14

JOINT VENTURES, AFFILIATE MARKETING, AND LICENSING

Joint ventures, affiliate marketing, and licensing are powerful tools all internet marketers can use to their advantage. I think of these tools as applications of Napoleon Hill's Mastermind principle, which he referred to in his seminal work *Think and Grow Rich* (The Ralston Society 1937). Here's what Hill wrote about the Mastermind:

> Economic advantages may be created by any person who surrounds himself with the advice, counsel, and personal cooperation of a group of men who are willing to lend him wholehearted aid, in a spirit of perfect harmony. This form of cooperative alliance has been the basis of nearly every great fortune. Your understanding of this great truth may definitely determine your financial status.

In this chapter, you'll find an introduction to joint ventures, affiliate marketing, and licensing so you can know how to use them efficiently and profitably.

Keep the following in mind before you begin: *do your research first*. I've mentioned this before, but it's worth repeating: research is the first step for any marketing venture. Know your product or service thoroughly. And know your market thoroughly. What you find important as a business owner or marketer is almost never what your prospective customer or client finds important. Conduct the proper research to find what they're really looking for and what they really want. That means research the keywords related to your business. Keyword tools can tell you how many searches for that particular keyword are made per month (the search volume) as well as the competition for that keyword and the cost per click (CPC)—an estimate of what each click on your website would cost you if you advertised through Google AdWords.

The Google AdWords Keyword Planner has become more complicated to use recently, so I recommend Keywords Everywhere, which is a free browser add-on that automatically shows you the search volume, CPC, and competition whenever you search for a term on Google. Simply go to www.KeywordsEverywhere.com, and download the add-on for either Chrome or Firefox. From then on, all you need to do is search for a term on Google and the search data will appear right below the search bar.

When you type in a keyword phrase and see your data, you want a monthly search volume between 4,000 and 40,000. Anything beyond that means that the competition is too high.

Most of this chapter will focus on joint ventures because affiliate marketing and licensing are forms of a joint venture. If you don't already have a product, you may want to try affiliate marketing first. With affiliate marketing, someone else provides the products and services to promote, as well as the marketing tools. But you can use any of these tools to expand your existing business or create a new one.

Joint Ventures

A joint venture is a mutually beneficial relationship between parties engaged in some economic activity. Here, you have an equity share in a project but not in someone else's company.

Here are a few of the benefits of a joint venture:

◆ Low cost for everyone involved
◆ Minimal increase of staff, facilities, and equipment
◆ Shared work and risk among partners
◆ Sharing of ideas, expertise, and inspiration

A common example of a joint venture is a freelance copywriter and freelance website designer working together on a project for a client. They provide a turnkey service that provides clients with both the copy and the website. The copywriter and website designer may even team up with a freelance graphic designer or photographer.

Here's a specific example of a joint venture in the internet marketing space: Glazer Kennedy Insider's Circle (GKIC) and Infusionsoft. Infusionsoft provides software for business owners and marketers to automate much of their marketing and sales process, while GKIC educates its customers on marketing and sales. Each company introduces its audience to the others and even receives affiliate commissions, which I'll talk about later.

Rich Schefren, founder and CEO of Strategic Profits, says joint ventures are limited by only six things:

◆ Your creativity
◆ Your sense of what's possible
◆ Your pre-programmed limiting beliefs
◆ Profitability for everyone involved
◆ Legal guidelines
◆ Operating in an ethical manner

As you gain experience with joint ventures, you'll strengthen your goal-setting muscles and improve your ability to make and implement practical plans. The power of joint ventures is virtually unlimited.

Here's the golden rule of joint venture partnerships: do as much as possible for your joint venture partners so it is as easy as possible for them to participate, contribute, and benefit.

But there's a flip side to this rule: each party in a joint venture must contribute equally. Make sure to invest your time, energy, money, and other resources in a joint venture only if the other parties are equally willing to invest their resources.

Their contribution won't necessarily be in the same domain or comprise the same tasks, but the contribution should be of equal weight. This equality of investment arises naturally when the joint venture is a good fit, based on your shared values and the mutual benefits of the joint venture. But it's important that you enter into a written agreement with your partners, in which all responsibilities, expectations, and potential penalties are laid out and clear to all partners.

The Five Main Types of Joint Ventures

Within the broad category of marketing gambits encompassing joint ventures, there are five specific variations most commonly used by successful online marketers:

1. *Marketing Joint Venture*. Someone with a list promotes you and your product (or vice versa). The revenue split can be anywhere from 50/50 to 100/0 depending on the purposes of the joint venture. For instance, you may be willing to give up all the revenue upfront to gain customers or sell on the back end.

2. *Co-Marketing Joint Venture*. Here, each partner promotes the joint venture to their customers. This is what GKIC and Infusionsoft do.

3. *Co-Branding Joint Venture*. You partner with someone to create a new product altogether. Both your names are on the product, and you essentially create a new brand for the joint venture.

4. *Sales Joint Venture*. Here, you're partnering with people who do not ordinarily promote that kind of product. You could say that Salvation Army soliciting donations at Walmart is an example of this.

5. *Affiliate Programs.* This is what the next section is all about. Running an affiliate program means you have the product or service and recruit people—affiliates—to promote it for you.

Any of these five options can work for you depending on your goals and where you hope to take the structure of your venture.

Four Big Goals for Your Joint Ventures

There are four main benefits you can get in your business by participating in joint venture deals:

1. *Customer acquisition.* You're obviously looking to acquire as many customers as you can reasonably expect to service or fulfill orders for. Depending on your business model, you may not need to gain a profit from a first sale. If you've figured out the lifetime value of a customer, you may find it's better to gain a customer than to make a profit from the first sale.

2. *Successful event or product launch.* Cultivate strong relationships with major players in your industry online. Make it beneficial for everyone who promotes your event or product launch. You might offer a basic level of compensation and then increase the forms of compensation based on performance. For example, every participant can receive:

   ◆ A promotion for one of their products to the list of buyers
   ◆ Their name or logo on all promotional materials
   ◆ An affiliate commission for each person who buys or registers

3. *Ask your joint venture partners what they would like.* Their feedback can give you some ideas for compensation.

4. *Positioning or branding.* The two are related. Positioning is, generally speaking, how people see your product or service, especially relative to competitors. Branding is creating awareness of your offering. Make sure you choose your joint venture partner carefully. Keep in mind that their reputation will likely affect the positioning and branding of the product or service.

Write your joint venture goals clearly, and provide a deadline for attaining them.

Three Types of Joint Venture Partners

There are three different types of joint venture partners:

1. *Similar companies*—they are in a complementary or related industry. For example, let's say you sell information products in the golf market, and they sell golf clubs. The natural compatibility is obvious. Each company's products can complement the other's.
2. *Competitive companies*—they do the same thing you do. For instance, you sell information marketing products in the golf market, and your joint venture partner does, too. Don't overlook the possibilities for a joint venture just because a company is the competition. You may be surprised to find how willing they are to enter into a partnership with you.
3. *Unrelated companies*—you do different things but have similar customers. For instance, sticking with the golf example, you sell golf information products, and your joint venture partner sells outdoor clothing. Most businesses look at demographics (age, sex, income, and so on) and stop there. Smart business owners look at psychographics as well. What interests and needs do your customers have beyond what you supply? The businesses that supply those interests and needs are good joint venture partners.

Think about what makes the most sense for you. If you choose to go down the joint venture route, how can adding a partner to the mix best enhance what you already do and help build on what you want to do?

Three Criteria for a Joint Venture Partner

Here are three criteria for a joint venture partner:

1. *List quality.* Are these qualified, proven buyers? How large is the list?
2. *Product quality.* Are there testimonials? How about online reviews? What is the refund rate?
3. *Reputation quality.* A simple Google search can help you discern the person's reputation. Go deep into the Google search and do some detective work.

Rate your prospective joint venture on a scale of one to ten on each of these three criteria.

They don't have to be a perfect ten on everything. Having a mix of seven, eight, and nine is sufficient.

Four Questions to Ask About a Potential Joint Venture Partner

Ask yourself the following questions:

1. What resources do I need for my joint venture, and who can provide them?
2. What are the benefits for my joint venture partners and their customers?
3. Can I add even more value?
4. Can this joint venture generate ongoing monthly income for everyone?

Keep your answers in mind when finding prospective partners.

How to Find Joint Venture Partners

Plan to start with 25 prospective joint venture partners. Trying to start with more is overwhelming. Break this list up further by looking for ten similar companies, ten competitive companies, and five unrelated companies.

You can use Excel or Word to keep track of your prospective partners and your contacts with them. Keep track of their contact information, website address, Alexa.com ranking (to see how their website ranks with search engines and how many visitors they get), and social media profiles, as well as anything important they mention during your conversations.

Throughout your search, keep in mind your three criteria for good joint venture (JV) partners as well as your answers to the four questions above. Let your values and goals guide you in your search.

Finding Prospects in Your Network

Your personal network of contacts is the first place to look for potential JV partners. You already have a relationship with people in your network and probably know their businesses. Go through your address books, social media profiles, business cards, and so on, and identify those who might be a good fit for a joint venture.

Finding Prospects Through Research

You can use websites to research people and companies who might be a fit. Here are a few examples:

- *Google*—search for keywords related to your joint venture topic
- *LinkedIn*—browse those in your first-degree connections, ask for introductions to second- and third-degree connections, and use keywords to find people to contact. (Experiment with the advanced search option, but keep in mind that with a free version of LinkedIn, you have a limited number of searches before LinkedIn requires you to purchase the premium version)
- *Facebook*—use keywords, and look for groups related to your joint venture topic
- *Forums*—search Google for forums related to your topic, especially for forums used by those similar to who you're looking for—marketing directors or information marketers, for instance. You may also get some good ideas or inspiration from these forums.

Finding Prospects Through Events

You can often find prospective joint venture partners at internet marketing conferences. Internet marketing conferences are best for meeting "super affiliates," as I'll explain later. There are two different methods you can use to find joint venture prospects through events. You can either work the room—or you can become a speaker for an event.

Working the room is what people usually think about when they think about networking. Drink in hand, you go around introducing yourself to different people. Now, you don't want to bring up your joint venture right away, but while talking to a person and asking them questions, you can get a sense of whether the person might be a good partner for you.

Simply introduce yourself, show interest in them, and ask about their projects. People love to talk about themselves and their passions. Dale Carnegie's famous book *How to Win Friends and Influence People* (Simon and Schuster 1936) is based on just this notion. Show people you're interested in them, and they'll love you.

On the other hand, you could become a speaker for an event. When you're a speaker, people come up to you when you're done speaking and engage you in conversation. I prefer speaking at events rather than working the room because I'm introverted and find it easier to have people come up to me rather than having to go around engaging in small talk.

It may be easier than you think to get booked as a speaker. With some conferences, especially the big ones such as GKIC's, getting booked as a speaker is difficult. But many others need speakers willing to speak for free. Think about it this way: if you were in charge of finding speakers but couldn't pay them for it, would you pursue the most famous? Of course not. Famous and powerful people typically charge speaking fees. So there is a chance you may be able to get booked as a speaker at some conferences.

Keep networking and researching until you've found 25 prospective joint venture partners who you think you might want to partner with.

Ranking Joint Venture Candidates

Ask yourself a couple of questions about each:

1. *Do they have a large customer or subscriber list?* A large list is anything over 10,000. A high page rank with lots of back-links and a high daily visitor rate is a good indication of a large subscriber list (check out Alexa.com).
2. *Do they have presence or a platform in the marketplace?* Are they active on social media sites? Do they have a lot of followers, likes, and shares? Do they have podcasts, videos, or articles online?

Now, look over your list and rank them from the person you most want to work with down to the one you least want to work with. Here are four criteria you can use to rank your list:

1. List size—the money is in the list.
2. How well do your target markets complement each other?
3. Reputation—are you comfortable with their ethics and business practices?
4. Are you enthusiastic about working with them?

Now that you've figured out who you want to contact and have ranked them, it's time to contact your prospective partners.

First Contact

At this point, sales and copywriting skills will come in handy. First, determine how you will contact them. Will it be by phone, email, or letter? Much of this depends on how well you know the person. For someone you already know, you probably have an idea of the most comfortable way to contact them. So I'll speak about cold contacts—those whom you've never contacted before.

A phone call is great for immediacy. Plus, they hear your voice, which helps with familiarity. (The biggest factor in whether someone will do what you want is simply that they like you). The downside of calling is you're likely to hit the voicemail or assistant. You can always leave a voicemail or message if you're unable to get through to the assistant, then follow up through another means.

I wouldn't just drop by someone's place of business without first scheduling an appointment. Professional people are busy, and it's likely you'll irritate them if you just drop by. Not a great first impression. Then again, some salespeople (Tom Hopkins comes to mind) insist that by dropping by you stand a better chance of meeting them in person than by asking for an appointment over the phone. How you want to approach them is really up to you.

Write an email or send a letter if you have some copywriting skills. In writing you can carefully state your case. Ask them to set up a phone call with you so you can discuss their priorities and determine how to craft your proposal.

I won't go into everything that goes into a perfect pitch, but you'll want to get their attention with some benefit. Don't expect that just because you're excited about a project, they will be, too. The reality is that even for close friends, you have to sell them on why you should be joint venture partners. Always answer in your mind, "What's in it for me?" That is, "what's in it for your prospective partner?"

When Mark Cuban asked a contestant on *Shark Tank* what advantages her product had over a possible competitor's, she replied that she was extremely passionate about the product—not a good answer. Remember, your needs are not what matter to your prospective joint venture partner. It's all about *their* needs. Make it all about them. This is the essence of sales.

Your goal is to get them to agree to receive your proposal for the joint venture, which you've tailored to them based on your conversation with them. Here are some points to cover in your proposal:

◆ *The date*—when the joint venture will happen.

- *Length*—how long is the venture?
- *The product*—what do you plan to offer, and what are you asking your partner to offer?
- *Goal*—there may be more than one, such as list building and sales.
- *Benefits*—what everyone gets from participating.
- *Fine print*—what you're asking the partner to do and what you're providing.
- *Answers to all possible objections.*

You're looking to answer any questions they have and, ultimately, to acquire a signature from them. A written agreement is essential for spelling out all details and responsibilities in case there is a discrepancy or disagreement down the road.

Just keep in mind that a joint venture never goes entirely to plan. This is why it's important to have basic agreement about your venture's core values. The joint venture partners need to be in basic harmony about what everyone is trying to accomplish, what the responsibilities are, and perhaps most important, what ethical code will govern your operations. When things go wrong, you know each partner can rely on the other. Everyone is going to pitch in to make the joint venture work.

When getting started, keep things as simple and clear as possible. You can increase the complexity as you gain experience in joint ventures.

Affiliate Marketing

Entrepreneur.com defines affiliate marketing as: "A way for a company to sell its products by signing up individuals or companies ('affiliates') who market the company's products for a commission."

Affiliate marketing is a type of joint venture. You agree to promote someone's products or services (usually ebooks and other information products) in exchange for a commission on sales. Affiliate marketing is an excellent way to generate revenue for yourself and to meet customer needs outside what your business offers. You can even reach markets that would otherwise be inaccessible.

I offer an affiliate program via my website (you can also go here: www. BecomeAByAffiliate.com), in which I pay a substantial commission for every sale of my information products. Affiliates promote my products on their websites and through their email lists, and this lets me reach people I wouldn't reach otherwise. Meanwhile, the affiliate receives the commission for a product they didn't even create.

You can be either an *affiliate* selling someone else's product—or a *merchant* with affiliates selling your product. Keep in mind that some of what I write applies to affiliates and some to merchants.

Open and Closed Affiliate Arrangements

Affiliate programs can be either open or closed. Open affiliate arrangements allow anyone to become an affiliate for that product. Closed affiliate arrangements are restricted to those who apply and are accepted by the merchant. Merchants sometimes choose a closed program because they don't want just anyone promoting their product (and maybe giving them a bad name) or because the merchant wishes to limit the number of commissions for whatever reason. In most cases, I recommend an open affiliate structure.

Three Criteria for Choosing the Right Niche

Your success in affiliate marketing depends on choosing the right subject or niche. There are three criteria for choosing the right niche:

1. *Your knowledge.* What you know about the topic will govern how much value you can offer. It is always ideal to deal in affiliate marketing with topics that are related to your primary business. That way, there is little to no learning curve since you already have most or all of the knowledge you need.
2. *Your audience.* What is the size of the lists involved, and are these people proven to buy? What degree of traffic can you generate?
3. *Niche popularity.* Take a look at the keyword's search density as we've gone over before.

As you can see, the criteria for success in affiliate marketing are much the same as for success in a solo venture.

Increasing Affiliate Revenues

There are only two ways to increase revenue in affiliate marketing. You can send more people to the vendors you promote, or you can increase your conversion rate for the people you're sending.

Sending more people means increasing the amount of traffic. Increasing conversion rates means sending better traffic to your vendors—and writing better copy for your emails and conversion pages. So how do we get lots of traffic that's well-qualified to buy what we're promoting?

First, there's free traffic from blogging, article marketing, social media, SEO, and podcasts.

Second, there's paid traffic from pay-per-click (PPC) ads (such as Google AdWords and Facebook), sponsored links, and purchased ad space.

Paid traffic is the best way to quickly build an elist—if and only if the ads are written well and targeted effectively. You can easily lose thousands of dollars on AdWords, Facebook, and banner ads if you aren't careful. Always be aware of the economics of your situation, especially taking into account the fact that you're taking only a percentage of the total sale.

I'd start with free traffic sources. Here are two free things you can do right away to generate affiliate marketing traffic:

1. Add an affiliate URL to your email signature.
2. Add a button visitors on your landing page can click to become affiliates for the products advertising on those pages.
3. Add a resource page to your blog site and include the affiliate links or how to get them.

You can also approach someone and request that they promote your site to their list in exchange for something else, which is an example of a joint venture.

That said, don't expect a lot of traffic from affiliate marketing right away. It takes time to build a list through free traffic. Generating affiliate marketing traffic follows most of the same rules for generating traffic for any marketing initiative.

If you're looking to be an affiliate, you can do a Google search for affiliate marketing programs or start by becoming an affiliate of mine. Just visit www.BecomeABlyAffiliate.com.

Super Affiliates

Internet marketers know that 99 percent of their affiliate revenues will come from 1 percent of their affiliates. This 1 percent is often referred to as "super affiliates"—experienced, already successful marketers capable of selling a lot of your products.

Almost without exception, super affiliates are other large and midsize internet marketers with big lists and thorough knowledge of how to sell information products online.

The good thing about super affiliates is they will never ask you to teach them how to sell your products on the internet because they already know how. The bad thing about super affiliates is that every other marketer wants to sell his or her products to the super affiliate's list. Therefore, the super affiliate is slammed with marketers begging to do joint ventures with them, making it difficult for you to stand out from the crowd and make a deal with the super affiliate.

An effective strategy for forging a relationship with a super affiliate is to communicate with them on a person-to-person level—and the best way to do that is to meet them at an internet marketing conference they sponsor, speak at, or attend. I've also found you can stand out from the pack of wanna-be partners by following the super affiliate's writings and sending sincere emails of praise and appreciation when they write something that particularly speaks to you.

Another way to entice a super affiliate is with an oversize commission: offer them 70 percent of sales revenues instead of the usual 50 percent. The product price has to be at least $100 and preferably $300 or higher; they won't get excited about getting a cut of a $12 paperback book. Don't send review copies of your books or DVDs unsolicited.

Affiliate Commissions

Every affiliate is paid by check, direct deposit, or some online mechanism such as PayPal. The affiliate commissions differ depending on the program, but here are some general norms: information products generally have a 50 percent commission rate. If that seems high, remember that affiliates can often sell to people who would otherwise be inaccessible to you. 50 percent is obviously better than zero percent.

In some affiliate programs, merchants offer 100 percent affiliate commissions for a short time in order to encourage affiliates to drive traffic to the sales page. They also use affiliate contests and performance bonuses to reward high-performing affiliates.

One more important point about affiliate marketing: it uses a metric called earnings per click (EPC). It's an estimate of what affiliates earn for every 100 clicks generated. Here's how it works.

Say I'm the merchant, and I'm selling a $29 ebook. You're my affiliate. The ebook has a seven-day EPC of $11.20. During a typical week, every 100 clicks (on average) that go to my sales pages result in $11.20 in commissions. EPC is based on commissions *after* refunds. Always be sure the EPC includes refunds and is based on commissions paid rather than gross sales.

Licensing

Licenses enable you to legally participate in a particular activity. Your driver's license allows you to drive. A hunting license allows you to hunt. Licensing for our purposes allows you to re-label something as your own, use a piece of software, or resell something and keep all the money.

Here are the different kinds of licenses:

1. *Standard license.* You pay the publisher a one-time fee. This kind of license allows you to resell something at a price you've

set and keep the profits. What you cannot do is change the content in any way. You must sell it as is.

2. *Master license.* More expensive than the standard license, you get the same rights plus you can also sell standard licenses to others.

3. *Private label rights (PLR).* This kind of license lets you put your name on the product and sell it as your own. You can even change the content if you'd like. PLR is the license you can most readily use to grow your business because it allows you to produce content quickly and at a low cost.

4. *Access and use licensing.* This kind of license allows you to access information or use a product, and the only way to resell it is by becoming an affiliate. Creating membership sites is one of the best ways to create recurring monthly income.

Additionally, there are works in the public domain. Public domain isn't a license, but you can legally sell a work in the public domain because the copyright has expired. Selling e-versions of public domain works is a great way to quickly have a product of your own without needing to create one or pay someone to create one. Visit www.PublicDomainRichesOnline.com for more information.

Just keep in mind that you have to look at the licensing agreement carefully to determine exactly what you're allowed to do. Don't depend on terms. Whenever in doubt, ask the copyright owner.

License Pricing

There are two elements to pricing for licenses. One is the price you pay to obtain the license; the other is the price you charge when re-selling the product or service.

A vendor can set their price at any level they think appropriate for however long a term. You may create an online video course that offers a time-limited access license—say, for six months, for a flat fee of $300. Or you could make it a monthly rate or even charge a one-time license fee. WordPress theme vendors will typically offer a one-time license fee to use their WordPress theme but may offer theme updates and support for only a year so you'll purchase another license.

Resell licenses often come with suggestions for pricing the product when you resell it. PLR products always have a single price, and it's often quite low. Good PLR sites also tend to limit the number of copies being sold for any one PLR item. That way, you know that a set number of people have access to the same content you're getting.

Something further to consider in pricing your licenses is demonstrating the ROI. You want to show how you can save the person time, money, and energy—or how you can add something to their life (you want to do this for any offering whatsoever, in fact). Quantify this benefit as much as possible.

Let's say you own a membership site (a type of licensing product) that offers informative videos and a monthly one-hour consulting session. You've published the price of your consulting at $500 an hour. By offering an hour of consulting a month with the membership that costs $50 a month, you demonstrate that they're saving $450 on one consulting session alone—not to mention the other benefits of the membership.

Calculating ROI for yourself as the licensor is simple: just figure out the revenues you receive from the license, subtract the cost for acquiring licensees, and divide the remainder by the cost. Then multiply by 100. This is your ROI.

I sell licenses to a number of my audio products that retail for $47 to $97. A standard license is around $997, and a master license is $2,997.

How to Make More Money with Licensing

Here's a quick tip: always ask yourself, "What else can I sell?" When licensees sell your products to their lists, you can have back-end products lined up to sell. Make sure links to your site and other products are in your products. With a Master Resale Rights license, your licensee cannot alter the product in any way, so buyers will see and link to your other products as well. That's killing two birds with one stone.

Joint ventures, affiliate marketing, and licenses are not used enough by online marketers. The reality is that no marketing venture will succeed if you can't generate traffic. However, if there's one thing I'd like you to take away from this chapter, it's the power of the Mastermind to add to your store of knowledge and skills. Joint ventures in particular can take away many limitations involved in a solo venture. By teaming up with others in strategic alliances, you can rapidly make progress that would've taken many years on your own.

CHAPTER 15

MEMBERSHIP SITES

Imagine creating content one time and selling it over and over again, month after month. Imagine being able to help hundreds of people all at once improve their lives while making a steady, recurring income. Imagine having a resource where customers can learn more about technology, applications, and problems related to your product line.

That is what building a membership site as an adjunct to your main website can do for you.

Once strictly the province of information marketers, membership sites are now being launched by product and service firms of all types.

For example, say a career coach provides a coaching service to help people find new jobs and improve their job-hunting skills. Many job seekers ask him questions outside the consulting appointments, which they expect him to answer without charging them.

So he sets up a membership site where, for a small monthly fee, his clients and other job-seekers can access a huge library of content on resumes, LinkedIn profiles, networking, interviewing skills, job search, and related topics.

His membership site has two benefits. First, it gives clients the answers they need without the coach wasting his time giving away free advice. Second, it generates a five-figure annual passive income to supplement his active income from coaching.

Membership Site Pros and Cons

Is starting a membership site a good idea for adding a new profit center to your business or building customer loyalty? Let's look at the pros and cons of having a membership site. First, the pros:

- *Increased revenue.* Hosting your own membership site is like selling a product once and then getting paid over and over again each and every month without driving more traffic to your site.
- *Improved loyalty.* When you sell a typical product online, you never really get the chance to build a relationship with your customer. They get what they came for and leave. But if a customer becomes a member, you are providing a service and giving that member new information on a daily, weekly, or monthly basis. This builds respect and loyalty for both parties.
- *No physical product.* Most membership sites provide information in the form of PDF reports, ebooks, videos, and audio files, and these things have no physical production costs nor costs associated with warehousing or shipping. Whatever time and money you spent creating these products were all at the beginning.
- *Accountability.* Providing something of value on a regular basis keeps you accountable. Your members are relying on you to give them a big bang for their buck each and every month. You add structure to your day by not letting them down.
- *Unlimited cross-promotion opportunities.* Membership sites give you the leverage to recommend affiliate products to your paying customers, giving them even more value and making

more money. A career coach started a career-oriented membership site as a supplemental source of revenue for his active coaching practice. "I launched my membership site in fall 2014," he explains. "I never did a good job of marketing it as a standalone product but instead sold it as an enhancement to existing coaching services." He says it took some 500 hours to create the site content initially, and he puts in about five hours a month to maintain it. The site cost less than $1,000 to set up and costs approximately $300 a year to maintain. He says it generates around $25,000 a year in extra income.

Now let's consider the cons:

◆ *Constant marketing.* Running and maintaining a membership site means you have to constantly market it to potential new members. The more members you gain, the more money you make.

◆ *Commitment.* Membership sites take a significant commitment of time, money, and resources, especially in the beginning, and they are the same amount of work for three members as they are for 300. So until you scale up to a decent-size membership, at least 100 and preferably 1,000, your revenues are small.

◆ *Fresh content.* To retain members, you must continually provide fresh content on your membership site. Examples include new articles, white papers, special reports, ebooks, and webinars. So although membership sites look like pure passive income, there is still a considerable amount of work. And it never stops for as long as the site is open and has members paying a monthly fee to be on it.

◆ *Site maintenance.* Sometimes, things go wrong behind the scenes. Plug-ins get buggy, your system gets hacked, or you experience some other technical headache that requires your due diligence to correct.

◆ *Site attrition.* People drop out. It happens, and there's not much you can do about it. In fact, attrition—people leaving your site—is one of the greatest challenges that membership site owners face. According to internet marketing guru Yaro Starak, the typical lifetime of your average member is only three months. What this means for you is that you must strive extra hard to keep your content relevant and useful and always be marketing for that dropped-out member's replacement.

Weigh both sides of the issue, and make the decision that best fits your goals and needs.

Membership Site Structure and Functionality

The structure of your membership site, and how it functions, are important for attracting new members and keeping current members coming back month after month. You want a site with a simple, clean design—one that entices people to sign up. If there is one rule, it is this: keep it simple. The homepage of your membership site should give your visitors two choices: they can sign up for one of your three membership tiers, or they can leave. You should also have a clearly marked area where current members can log in and consume your content.

The following subsections talk about what else you need.

Your Pricing Tiers

I'll cover pricing in detail later, but you should have three levels of pricing for monthly membership: silver, gold, and platinum. The majority of people will take the middle level.

Your Guarantee

Your guarantee is one of the most important components of your membership site. It instills trust and entices people to become a member. For membership sites, I recommend a ten-day free trial offer. Why ten days? It gives people just enough time to sample your offerings without spending a whole month or more taking

Risk Free Guarantee!

If you are not 100% satisfied, just cancel within 10 days for a full and prompt refund. That way, you risk nothing. After that, you may cancel your Info Product Central membership at any time. Your membership access and billing will both stop at the end of the month during which you made your cancellation, with no further cost or commitment of any kind.

FIGURE 15–1. **Membership site ten-day trial offer.**

advantage of freebies before quitting and getting a refund. Figure 15–1 shows the wording I use on my site. Feel free to adapt it for your own use.

Content Offerings

Common content for membership sites include:

◆ Articles
◆ Audio (mp3 files)
◆ Video (streaming mp4 files)
◆ Ebooks
◆ Courses
◆ Private Mastermind Groups
◆ Coaching
◆ Live Webinars
◆ Q&A Calls
◆ Content Archives
◆ Community Forums
◆ Software Downloads
◆ Cheat Sheets
◆ Workbooks
◆ Action Plans
◆ Checklists
◆ Expert Interviews

As you can see, there are many ways to provide value to your members and vary your content; you're limited only by your imagination.

Private Groups

A private Facebook group is a great value add for your top membership tier. By hosting it on Facebook, you not only get it for free, but you can set the group to "secret" so that no one can find it in a Facebook search and only paying members can access it. Members like interacting with others who are on the same journey as they are, and it gives you additional opportunities to interact with them in meaningful ways, such as live videos and group coaching events.

To find the structure and functionality that works for you, check out other membership sites, especially those that cater to the same types of members you hope to attract. Studying your competition can not only help you decide on your membership site structure, but it can also give you ideas for how to improve on what they are doing and go them one better with your own site.

Membership Site Software

"This sounds great," you say. "But I'm not a programmer or web designer. How do I create my own member site?"

With today's software advances, putting up your own paid membership site is easier than ever. If you can run a regular website, you can create and run a membership site. There are many different software platforms to choose from. Let's look at a few.

MemberPress

For WordPress users, there's MemberPress (www.memberpress.com), an easy-to-use WordPress plug-in that lets you host a member site from your existing website. MemberPress lets you create unlimited amounts of product pages and membership levels and even has a coupon module. A powerful reports feature gives you detailed information about how your business is doing and how you can further optimize it.

Wild Apricot

Wild Apricot (www.wildapricot.com) allows you to create a mobile-friendly member application, automate renewals, and handle your members-only content and membership lists. And you can try it free for 30 days.

DigitalAccessPass (DAP)

DAP (www.digitalaccesspass.com) is another WordPress membership site management platform, but it can also be used by non-WordPress users. This is a robust program with dozens of features, including unlimited memberships and email autoresponders. It also integrates smoothly with popular services such as Paypal, AWeber, and 1ShoppingCart.

S2Member

S2Member (www.s2member.com) is a membership site plug-in for WordPress. Powered almost entirely by WordPress short codes, it makes complex integrations quick and easy. You can sell recurring subscriptions as well as access to file downloads. It also easily integrates with PayPal and ClickBank.

SubHub

SubHub (www.subhub.com) offers versatile features that have made it popular with sites and businesses that offer a wide range of content but understand that not everyone needs or wants a full subscription just to get the content they need. SubHub provides a directory of mobile- and desktop-friendly templates you can use to customize and create the kind of membership site that reflects your needs and the needs of your members.

WishList Member

WishList Member (http://member.wishlistproducts.com) is for those who want to create a membership site quickly instead of spending weeks getting it up and running. With WishList Member, you can create any number of subscription models and provide timely updates to your premium members. You can even integrate it with your existing WordPress site.

EasyMemberPro

EasyMemberPro (www.easymemberpro.com) has become a popular choice with marketing experts who sell marketing courses and video-related content. The basic features include content dripping, an affiliate program that allows you to promote your products and services through your own site members, set up multiple membership levels, set up special onetime offers, and easily integrate with payment processors like PayPal and ClickBank.

MemberGate

MemberGate (www.membergate.com) is a content management platform that allows you to create membership sites while also protecting your content from nonmembers. It has a fully integrated shopping cart, an affiliate program, sleek website templates, a discussion group feature, a built-in blog, and even a search engine.

aMember

aMember (www.amember.com) is arguably one of the oldest and most popular membership site platforms. It allows you to schedule content, encouraging your members to remain subscribed for longer to access content that you haven't yet released. Other powerful features include modules that extend your membership site beyond its normal functionality as well as an extensive affiliate program that encourages your members to sell your products for you.

Memberful

Memberful (www.memberful.com) is a fast, reliable, and easy-to-use membership site platform for WordPress users. Features include coupon codes, the ability to offer physical items and not just digital content, and email through integration with MailChimp.

MembersGear

MembersGear (www.membersgear.com) is easy to use but really delivers. They have an affordable pricing plan that makes their membership script available to those who don't have a huge budget, and MembersGear comes with an affiliate program you can use to promote your own courses and products with the help of your existing members.

MemberMouse

MemberMouse (www.membermouse.com) is a powerful WordPress turnkey membership platform that gets you up and running with your own membership site in minutes. With MemberMouse you can sell products, subscriptions, and memberships; set up a password-protected members-only area; offer one-click upsells and downsells; manage customers; automate your customer service; track critical metrics; and more.

This is by no means a full list, but it gives you a good idea of what is available. There are even free and open-source options, allowing you to customize your site and get exactly what you need and want.

Hiring a Programmer to Create Your Membership Site

Sometimes, you want something more robust or customizable than an out-of-the-box membership site solution, or maybe you need someone to create the special look you want your member site to have. That's where you need an experienced programmer who specializes in membership sites. But how do you find these people? A quick Google search can offer several helpful suggestions:

- ♦ Check out membership sites you like to find out who created them. Many sites give credit to the creator at the bottom of the main page. If not, you can ask the site's owner who built it for them.
- ♦ Put together a list of everything you want your membership site to do, and make sure the programmer can deliver on all of it or find out if they will need to farm some of it out. Can they install the membership site software you want to use?

Can they customize it for you? You need to know if they are capable of giving you the membership site you want.

◆ Ask around to get a range of prices you will be expected to pay. This ensures you have realistic expectations of what it will take.

◆ Once you think you have found the right person for the job, you now have to work with them to get your site up and running.

◆ Know exactly what you want. Nothing is more frustrating for a freelancer of any kind than a customer who keeps wanting to make changes midproject, adding and revising things that weren't part of the initial job. Knowing, and communicating, what you want to the programmer is key to getting the exact site you want on time and within your budget.

◆ Sign a contract or agreement letter that spells out exactly what is expected of you and the programmer as well as what to do in the case of a dispute.

◆ Your programmer is only writing code—not your site's marketing language or content. You will need to write the copy and content for your site yourself, or hire a copywriter.

Some membership site software companies hire out their own developers. WishList Member, for example, has a site where you can hire one of their developers to enhance the look and feel of your WishList Member site. Visit www.wishlistmemberdevelopers.com for more information. Other platforms, like WordPress, have an army of independent developers who create themes and plug-ins for the platform.

Don't Forget the Updates

You want a site you can do basic updates on yourself. You need to be able to add new content on the fly without having to wait for someone else to do it—and charge you for the privilege. With today's member software, this shouldn't be a problem, but if you're getting something fully custom, make sure you can upload content and make minor changes yourself.

Membership Levels

Most membership sites have three levels of membership with free or low, midrange, and higher price points. Here's why:

- *Increased membership.* Not all of your membership levels have to be paid options. By offering a free membership plan alongside your paid tiers, especially when your site is new and you don't have any member testimonials, you can help potential members overcome any misgivings they might have about registering.

- *Make more money.* You're never going to know exactly how much your target audience is willing to pay for your resources. By creating multiple membership tiers with their own prices and features, you have a greater opportunity to sell expensive plans alongside lower-priced options.

- *Perceived value.* Multiple membership levels give you control over how your potential members perceive your pricing. If you have just one pricing option, visitors can only either say yes or no with many choosing no if they perceive your one price as being too high. Creating more than one membership tier allows for a better, more nuanced conversion.

- *Eliminate the competition.* Potential new members want to make sure they're getting the best deal before signing up. Your multiple pricing plans enable your visitors to compare prices in one place without ever having to leave your site to check out your competitors.

- *Experimentation.* If you only have one membership tier, you could easily price yourself right out of existence by experimenting with price increases. But if you keep your lower- and midrange price plans static and increase your top-tier plan, you'll figure out how much your audience is willing to pay without missing out on entry and midlevel signups.

By following the simple tips in this chapter, you can find a solid membership site programmer and make working with them a headache-free experience.

Pricing the Memberships

A three-tier membership plan is certainly the way to go, but how do you go about structuring your pricing? Let's look at a few tips that will help you price your membership tiers effectively:

- *Give your plans descriptive names.* Don't name your tiers something boring like A, B, and C. Think of something aspirational, like silver, gold, and platinum. If you can, tie the names into what your member site is offering or what your members hope to gain from being a part of it. Also, make sure that your more expensive options are packaged in a way that helps your members justify the extra cost.
- *Don't go overboard.* Three tiers is plenty. The number three is hardwired into human culture and easy to remember. Think the three little pigs, three wise men, and so on. Offering three tiers gives you the flexibility to create a free or low-cost plan, a standard plan, and a premium plan, each with varying degrees of content.
- *Keep it simple.* Don't confuse potential members by listing every single benefit and feature of each tier of your membership site. Just list the core features in your pricing comparison table. You want your visitors to make an informed decision—not come down with a case of analysis paralysis.
- *Don't just set it and forget it.* Be sure to re-evaluate your pricing choices on a regular basis even if you are enjoying a constant flow of new members. Remember, there's always room for improvement, especially where pricing is concerned.

Figure 15–2 on page 289 shows the pricing tiers for my membership site, www.Infoproductcentral.com.

Now that you've got your three tiers, you still need to know what to charge for each level of membership. Price too low, and people will think your membership site doesn't have a lot of value and isn't worth joining. Price too high, and you will lose members. So how do you price your membership site effectively? Here are a few tips:

FIGURE 15–2. **Pricing tiers for my membership site, www. Infoproductcentral.com.**

◆ *Spy on your competitors.* What are they charging on their membership sites? How does your offering compare to theirs?

◆ *Think about value.* What value does the end result of joining your site have for the member? Will they be able to get a better job? Start a business? Launch a new, better-paying career? Members will pay higher fees for sites that have a higher perceived ROI. If you can show potential members that they will get back in return far more than they paid, they'll be more likely to sign up.

◆ *Survey your audience.* Sometimes, the best way to find out what your audience is willing to pay is to simply ask them. They'll tell you what price range they are comfortable with.

◆ *Think about your position in the marketplace.* Do you want to attract many people or be an exclusive high-end option?

◆ *Consider how much one-on-one or group support you want to offer.* You can typically charge more if your site includes a lot of hands-on coaching and support.

◆ *Calculate your fee based on the number of members you want and how much you want to earn.* If you want to make $1,000 per month and have 50 members, you will need to charge $20 a month. Just keep in mind your other membership tiers, as well as your overhead like hosting, site software, mailing list, and programming.

By following each of these tips, you'll be able to come up with pricing for your membership site that is competitive and keeps your list filled with new members.

Recruiting New Members to Your Site

Getting paying members for your site can be a real challenge, especially in the beginning when you're just getting started. But it is not impossible. By following the steps below, you'll have an army of paying members in no time:

◆ *Give it away.* To show people just how awesome and life-changing your content is, you're going to need to give some of it away—at least at first. Share your insights on a blog, driving traffic to it using social media and pay-per-click (PPC) advertising. Create a newsletter to offer additional information to a select group you can then upsell to the membership site. The key here is to make what you're giving away so good they'll wonder how much better the stuff they have to pay for must be.

◆ *Let some people in for free.* This sounds counterintuitive, but it works. Letting a few people in for free, especially in the beginning, lets them try out your site to work out any kinks and gives you some glowing testimonials you can use to attract other members. Consider it a gift or perk by giving away slots to people who leave lots of thoughtful comments on your blog posts or social media but who might not be able to afford any of your membership tiers. This generates goodwill and creates a few staunch advocates for your site that will help sell it for you.

◆ *Be a resource.* People join membership sites to learn how to do something that will improve their lives or solve a problem they have. They want an expert to guide them through this process. Be that expert for them.

◆ *Mix it up.* To make your membership site appealing to different kinds of people, vary the length and format of your content. Break up long blog posts with short-form content, and be sure to include video, infographics, and image-based pieces that add value and impact.

◆ *Get social.* Social media sites like Facebook, Twitter, Instagram, and Pinterest offer tremendous marketing opportunities if your target market hangs out there. The key here is to not just broadcast "Join my site" over and over but to really engage with your prospective members. By asking and answering questions and posting relevant content, you can build a large social media following that will carry over to your paid membership site. And don't forget, you can also place paid advertisements on social media sites like Facebook and Twitter.

◆ *Harness video.* I mentioned this briefly above, but it bears repeating. Video can be a valuable asset in not only attracting new visitors but also making your site more engaging. Not only that, but a good video encourages sharing, meaning your visitors will blast out your message to their followers and friends, giving you a much wider reach than you had before.

◆ *Make sure your site is mobile-friendly.* The days when web browsing was done entirely on a desktop computer are over. More people today access the internet on mobile devices such as cell phones and tablets. If your membership site doesn't look readable and navigable on those types of devices, your visitors are simply going to go elsewhere.

◆ *Email marketing.* So far, we've mostly been talking about content marketing, but good old-fashioned email marketing is still highly effective at attracting new customers no matter what you're offering. To get email subscribers, create a free report or other valuable freebie people can get in exchange for their email address. And once you have a list, don't bombard people with relentless emails asking them to sign up for your membership site. Again, be a resource, and get them to know, like, and trust you before trying to sell them on your site.

◆ *Host webinars.* Webinars are a great way to share your wisdom with your audience. Combined with an effective social media campaign, webinars can also increase your website traffic. Make sure to archive the presentation for later viewing, and promote your webinars through social media.

◆ *Join a membership site.* Yes, if you want people to sign up for your membership site, you need to do the same. It lets you get into the mindset of your potential members, gives you ideas for how to more effectively run your own site, and lets you spy on your competition.

◆ *Keep adding content.* A membership site is not a one-and-done thing. You need to constantly add new content—both for your existing members as well as new recruits. You should also jettison stale content to keep things fresh, especially if your membership site involves a subject of more technical nature.

Membership Retention

It's one thing to attract paying members to your site. It's quite another to keep them paying you for access month after month. As stated above, the average member leaves after three months. So how do you keep your paying members coming back? Here are a few strategies.

◆ *Provide the best content and website possible.* This should be obvious, but it bears stating. A lot of people focus on getting the most content they can in a hurry. But what you should focus on instead is quality—not quantity. Creating the highest quality membership site you can is the best way to keep your members coming back for more.

◆ *Reward and recognize your members.* Use discounts and special offers to reward your members for their loyalty.

Give perks to members who have been with you the longest. Recognize them on their birthdays. The reward doesn't have to be huge. Just recognizing your members can build loyalty and helps them see you as a person instead of a cold, faceless membership site that is only interested in dinging their credit card once a month.

◆ *Provide the best customer support.* A bad customer service experience can turn a paying customer into someone you'll never hear from again. You can't please everyone all the time, but you should always try. Make sure your site is giving your members the best support experience possible. When a member enters a support ticket and it is answered promptly and to their satisfaction, it creates a good feeling they will remember when it's time to decide whether or not to stick around.

◆ *Survey your members.* Reach out periodically to all your membership tiers, and ask them how you are doing. Are they getting the information and content they need? What else would they like to see on your site? What is their favorite feature? What type of content do they prefer the most? Doing so will help make your membership site the best it can be, and your members will thank you for it by remaining loyal.

◆ *Keep adding fresh content.* Your members are paying for access to high-quality content, so if you want them to stay, keep giving them what they came for. Replace outdated content with new material, especially in forms with higher perceived value such as videos, expert interviews, and webinars. Not everything will be evergreen; much of it will change as the industry you're talking about changes and your members advance to higher levels of success. Always be thinking of new ways you can present content and help your members.

◆ *Use a grandfather clause.* From time to time, it will be necessary for you to raise your prices. When this time comes, only raise prices for your new members, and give these new members a deadline to sign up before the new prices go into effect. Your old members are then grandfathered in at the old membership rates. This is not only a great promotion tactic for gaining new members, but also it keeps long-time members loyal because if they left and came back, they'd have to pay the higher price point. They'd rather stay in the program even if their participation in your site has waned.

Ancillary Services for Members

Offering your members other services beyond your basic member perks is a great way to increase retention and grow your profits. Here are a few ideas:

- *Coaching.* Coaching is a nice value add for almost any business and works especially well with membership sites. People like having one-on-one access to an expert—someone who can give individualized help for a specific problem they have. And coaching doesn't have to be one-on-one. You could also offer specialized group coaching either in person or virtually in a private forum—whatever you're most comfortable with.
- *Affiliate products.* Although not technically a service, recommending products you believe your members will benefit from is a great way to add extra value while putting a little extra money in your pocket. What are affiliate products? They are any products from other vendors that offer you a commission when someone clicks and buys from an individualized link you create. The world's largest example is, without a doubt, Amazon. Their affiliate program is easy to set up and use with one other great advantage. Say you recommend a book to your members though an affiliate link. Your members click on it, and without leaving Amazon's site, they buy something else like a TV or a laptop. You get commission on those, too! To find affiliate products of interest to your members, do a quick Google search as well as scouring Amazon. Every industry has affiliate products. Another popular source for affiliate products, especially information products, is ClickBank. When selecting products to show to your members, be authentic.

Don't pitch things just to earn a commission. Ideally, you should be able to personally vouch for the product you are recommending. A glowing endorsement from you regarding a product will go a long way with your members.

♦ *Affiliate program.* And while we're on the subject of affiliate programs, there's no reason why you can't create your own. If you sell books, ebooks, courses, or other content, why not create an affiliate program that encourages your members to do some of the selling for you in exchange for a cut of the profits? You could even add your membership tiers to your affiliate program, which will get your members to ask for more sign-ups for you.

♦ *Physical products.* I know I said that one of the pros of running a membership site is that there are no physical products involved, but that doesn't mean you can't offer them as a value-added bonus. Just because you're running an internet-based, information product–driven membership site doesn't mean you can't sell a physical product once in a while. Audio CDs or DVDs containing courses, along with print books, workbooks, and manuals, give your members something tangible to hold on to. These items have a higher perceived value than something that only exists as an mp3 file or electrons on a hard drive somewhere. There are several extremely popular membership sites based on offering physical products. Think Loot Crate and Dollar Shave Club. Following the Loot Crate model, the books and CDs you sell don't even have to be created by you but can be someone else's product you sell as an affiliate. Physical products could become a valuable, money-making component of your business.

There you have it. You can now build websites, microsites, squeeze pages, landing pages, and membership sites—creating a web empire that helps your business make more money. And the best time to start? Right now!

RECOMMENDED VENDORS

Audio Conferencing

Free Conference Call
www.freeconferencecall.com

OnStream Media
www.onstreammedia.com

ReadyTalk
www.readytalk.com

Audio Duplication

Chesney Communications
www.speakersdemos.com

Dove Multimedia
www.dovecds.com

Banner Advertising

Ad Designer
www.addesigner.com

BannersGoMLM.com
www.bannersgomlm.com

My Banner Maker
www.mybannermaker.com

Call Centers

Answer Connect
www.answerconnect.com

Global Sky U.S.
www.globalsky.com

Co-Registration

Lake Group
www.lakegroupmedia.com

Tiburon Media
www.tiburonmedia.com

Direct-Marketing Attorneys

Ballard Spahr
www.ballardspahr.com

Domain Names

DN88 Domain Brokers
www.dn88.com

Go Daddy
www.godaddy.com

Ebook Designers

Barb Willard
www.basicdezigns.com

Freelancer.com
www.freelancer.com

Leslie Murray Rollins
leslierollins@verizon.net

Email Services and Distribution

Bronto
www.bronto.com

Campaign Monitor
www.campaignmonitor.com

Constant Contact
www.constantcontact.com

Emma
www.myemma.com

MailChimp
www.mailchimp.com

Pardot
www.pardot.com

Pinpointe
www.pinpointe.com

Enewsletter Directories

The Ezine Directory
www.ezine-dir.com
Ezine Finder
www.ezinefinder.com

Jogena's Ezine Directory
www.jogena.com

Freelance Programmers

Freelance.com, formerly Rent-a-Coder
www.freelance.com

Phillip Theriault Spellweaver Inc.
www.spellweaver.com

Upwork
www.upwork.com

Fulfillment Houses

Speaker Fulfillment Services
http://speakerfulfillmentservices.com

Strategic Fulfillment Group
www.sfgnetwork.com

Graphic Design

Andre Paquin Associates
www.andrepaquin.com

Carrie Scherpelz
www.scherpelz.com

William Fridrich Design
www.fridrichdesign.com

Hosting Services

AMS Computer Services, Inc.
www.amscomputer.com

Host Gator
www.hostgator.com

Infographics

Infogram
www.infogram.com

Infomercial Producers

Direct Response TV Productions
www.directresponsetv production.com

Perlow Productions
www.perlowproductions.com

Internet Marketing Coaching

Dave Hamilton
www.WebMarketingMagician.com

Terry Dean
www.mymarketingcoach.com

IP-Targeted Advertising

El Toro
www.eltoro.com

Keyword Research

Trellian
www.keyworddiscovery.co.uk

Laurie Macomber
Blue Skies Marketing
www.blueskiesmktg.com

Mark Dommer & Associates
(707) 928-0400

Market Research

Pranses Research Services
www.pransesresearch.com

*The Livingston Group for
   Marketing, Inc.*
www.tlgonline.com

Media Buyers

Novus Media
www.novusmediainc.com

Medical Illustrators

Nixon Medical Media
www.nixonmedicalmedia.com

MedDraw Studio
http://meddrawstudio.com

Mobile App Designers

Joe Davison
www.joedavison.com

Online Researchers

Nurit Mittlefehldt
(281) 480-8258
nurit77@earthlink.net

Belinda Robinson-Jones
BRJ Research & Information
   Services
(773) 233-7385
brjones30@gmail.com

Photography

Kast Photographic
http://kastphoto3.
   businesscatalyst.com

FotoSearch Stock Photography
www.fotosearch.com

istock Photo
www.istockphoto.com

Podcasting

America Web Works
www.americawebworks.com

Cybernetic Media Inc.
www.SalesVideos.com

Postcards

AmazingMail
www.amazingmail.com

Modern Postcard
www.modernpostcard.com

Premiums and Incentives

4imprint
www.4imprint.com

Press Release Distribution

e-releases
www.ereleases.com

PRWeb
www.prweb.com

Printers

Unimac Graphics
www.unimacgraphics.com

VistaPrint
www.vistaprint.com

QR Codes

Kaywa QR Code
http://qrcode.kaywa.com

QR Stuff
www.qrstuff.com
Visual Lead
www.visualead.com/qurify2/en/

Radio Commercials

Marketing Architects
www.marketingarchitects.com

Remainder Book Sellers

American Book Company
www.americanbookcompany.
   com

Search Engine Optimization

Internet Marketing Group
www.internetmarketinggroup.
   com
Neotrope
www.neotrope.com

Site Security

DigiCert Online
www.digicert.com

GlobalSign
www.globalsign.com

Entrust Datacard
www.entrustdatacard.com

SSL Shopper
www.sslshopper.com

StartCom
www.startcomca.com

Visual Lead
Visual Lead

SwissSign
http://swisssign.com/en

VeriSign by Symantec
www.websecurity.symantec.
   com/ssl-certificate

Social Media

Hilary Sutton
www.hilarysutton.com

Inflexion Interactive
www.inflexioninteractive.com

Supplement Ingredients & Formulators

SourceOne Global Partners
www.source-1-global.com

Trademark Searches

CompuMark
www.compumark.com/

Transcription

Internet Transcribers
www.internettranscribers.com

Verbalink
www.verbalink.com

Translation

Auracom International, Inc.
www.auratrans.com

Virtual Words Translations
www.virtual-words.com

Video Producers

Primelight Productions
www.primelight.net

Upstage Media, Inc.
www.upstagemedia.com

Voiceover Talent

Bill DeWees Media, Inc.
www.voice-over-training.org

Mark Bashore
(517) 349-8226
Mark-Bashore@comcast.net

Webinars

GoToMeeting
www.gotomeeting.com

ON24
www.on24.com

WebEx Communications, Inc.
www.webex.com

Website Designers

Barbara Zaccone Associates
www.bza.com

Philadelphia Web Design
www.philadelphia-web-design.
    com

SOFTWARE AND SERVICES

Ad Trackers

AdMinder
www.adminder.com

AdTrackz
www.supertips.com/cl/
    adtrackz/index.html

Affiliate Marketing

Cake
http://getcake.com

HasOffers
www.hasoffers.com

Analytics

Looker
https://looker.com

Tableau Desktop
www.tableau.com

Anti-Virus

McAfee
www.mcafee.com

Norton
https://us.norton.com

Autoresponders

AWeber
www.aweber.com

Campaigner
www.campaigner.com

Constant Contact
www.constantcontact.com

1ShoppingCart.com
www.1shoppingcart.com

Interspire
www.interspire.com

Content Management

Quip
https://quip.com

Skyword
http://unbouncepages.com

Database

Airtable
https://try.airtable.com

Vividcortex
http://unbouncepages.com

Integrated Ecommerce Package

1ShoppingCart
www.1shoppingcart.com

Big Commerce
www.bigcommerce.com

iApps
www.bridgeline.com

Infusionsoft
www.infusionsoft.com

Miva
www.miva.com

Membership Website Software

Advanced Solutions International
www.advsol.com

Membergate Software
www.membergate.com

Merchant Accounts and Online Payment Processing

1st American Card Service
www.iacceptcreditcards.com

2Checkout.com
www.2checkout.com

ASecure Cart
www.asecurecart.net

CCBill
www.ccbill.com

ClickBank
www.clickbank.com

Creditcardprocessing.com
www.creditcardprocessing.com

Flagship Merchant Services
www.flagshipprocessing.com

Google Checkout
https://payments.google.com

PayPal
www.paypal.com

Online Surveys

Survey Monkey
www.surveymonkey.com

Sales Reports

Periscope
www.periscopedata.com

Sisense
www.sisense.com

Security Verification Services

DigiCert Online
www.digicert.com

Entrust
www.entrust.com

GlobalSign
www.globalsign.com

SSL Shopper
www.sslshopper.com

StartCom
www.startcomca.com

SwissSign
http://swisssign.com

VeriSign by Symantec
www.symantec.com

Slide-Making

NCH Software
www.nchsoftware.com

SmartSHOW
http://smartshow-software.com/order.php

Spreadsheets

Domo
www.domo.com

OfficeX
http://officex.org

Video Software

Avangate
www.avangate.com

Camtasia
www.techsmith.com/video-editor.html

Nero
www.nero.com

SAMPLE INFOGRAPHIC

Infographics convey key facts, ideas, and data about a subject in a graphical format.

MARKETING RULES of THUMB

The 10-80-10 Rule of You and the Marketplace
- 10% of people won't like you no matter what you do.
- 80% will swim with the tide - they can take you or leave you.
- 10% will follow you devotedly even if you don't deserve it.

The 99:1 Rule of Affiliate Marketing
- 99% of your affiliate sales will come from 1% of your affiliates - the "Super Affiliates".
- The other 99% of your affiliates will sell virtually nothing and are not worth your time and attention.

The 90/90 Rule of Free-to-Paid Conversion
- Of the prospects who will join your e-list for the free content, 90% of those who buy something will do so within the first 90 days of being on the list.
- Therefore it behooves you to induce new subscribers to buy something now.

The 50/50 Content/ Sale Ratio

- 50% or more of your e-mail marketing messages should be pure content.
- 50% or less of your e-mails should be sales messages.

The 0.1% Opt-Out Threshold
- Each time you e-mail your list your opt-out rate should be no greater than 0.1%.

4 Steps to a Happy and Successful Life
1 - Money.   2 - Enjoyable, meaningful work.
3 - Love and friendship.   4 - Good health.

The 25-50-25 Rule of Time Management
- 25% of your time should be spent studying your business or profession.
- 50% of your time should be spent rendering your services or selling your products.
- 25% of your time should be spent managing and administering your business.

Fred Gleeck's Rule of 10X Price
- All products you sell should be worth at least 10 times the price you charge for them.

Jeffrey Lant's Rule of 7
- To succeed in any market you must contact the prospects a minimum of 7 times within 18 months.

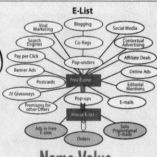

Name Value
In online information marketing, your list will generate average revenues of a dime to a dollar per name per month.

Doubling Day Doubling Day for Direct Mail
- From experience you will learn how long it takes your mailings to produce half the orders they are going to get - that day is "doubling day".
- On doubling day, count orders received to date and multiply by 2 to predict total response to the DM campaign.

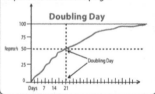

The Agora Model for Online Marketing
- Your initial marketing should focus on getting subscribers, not selling products.
- Reason: People already on your e-list are much more likely than strangers to buy products you offer.

SCHEDULE FOR PRODUCING A DIRECT-MAIL PROMOTION

The table on page 310 shows the steps required to implement a direct mail campaign and the approximate timeframe each takes.

Direct Mail Schedule and Checklist
4 Week Leadtime

☐	Write Sales Copy for Your Offer	Must Be Done Prior To Scheduling Out Direct Mail Campaign	Date: _____
☐	Sales Copy Design - Lay Out the Sales Piece in the Format You Want to Mail		Date: _____
☐	Give List Broker the Mail Schedule & Ask For List Recommendations	32 Days Prior To Mail Date	Date: _____
☐	Request Printing Quote for Sales Piece	32 Days Prior To Mail Date	Date: _____
☐	Place List Orders with List Broker	28 Days Prior To Mail Date	Date: _____
☐	Give Mailing Schedule to Data Processing Company	25 Days Prior To Mail Date	Date: _____
☐	Artwork Due at Printer	25 Days Prior To Mail Date	Date: _____
☐	Approve Bluelines and Color Proof From Printer	22 Days Prior To Mail Date	Date: _____
☐	Send Data Processor Suppression Files and Seed List	15 Days Prior To Mail Date	Date: _____
☐	List Due Date	14 Days Prior To Mail Date	Date: _____
☐	Issue Merge Purge Instructions	14 Days Prior To Mail Date	Date: _____
☐	Approve Merge Purge	11 Days Prior To Mail Date	Date: _____
☐	Issue Key Codes and Splits	11 Days Prior To Mail Date	Date: _____
☐	Issue Lettershop Instructions	11 Days Prior To Mail Date	Date: _____
☐	Approve Key Codes and Splits	10 Days Prior To Mail Date	Date: _____
☐	Mail File Due at Lettershop	7 Days Prior To Mail Date	Date: _____
☐	Printing Due at Lettershop	7 Days Prior To Mail Date	Date: _____
☐	Postage Request from Lettershop	3 Days Prior To Mail Date	Date: _____
☐	Approve Address Panel(s)	3 Days Prior To Mail Date	Date: _____
☐	Special Reports Due From Data Processor (Broker Report, Net Name Report, Interaction Report)	2 Days Prior To Mail Date	Date: _____
☐	Postage Due	1 Day Prior To Mail Date	Date: _____

Mail Date:

ABOUT
THE AUTHOR

Bob Bly is an independent copywriter and consultant with nearly four decades of experience in B2B, online, and direct marketing. McGraw-Hill calls Bob Bly "America's top copywriter." Clients include IBM, the Conference Board, PSE&G, AT&T, Ott-Lite Technology, Intuit, ExecuNet, Boardroom, Medical Economics, Grumman, RCA, ITT Fluid Technology, and Praxair.

Bob has given presentations to numerous organizations including: Social Media Marketing World, National Speakers Association, American Seminar Leaders Association, American Society for Training and Development, U.S. Army, American Society of Journalists and Authors, Society for Technical Communications, Discover Card, Learning Annex, and New York University School of Continuing Education.

He is the author of over 90 books, including *The Copywriter's Handbook* (Henry Holt 2006) and *The Elements of Business Writing*

(Pearson 1992). Bob's articles have appeared in *Cosmopolitan, Writer's Digest, Successful Meetings, Amtrak Express, Direct,* and many other publications.

Bob writes a monthly column for *Target Marketing* magazine. *The Direct Response Letter,* Bob's monthly enewsletter, has 65,000 subscribers.

Awards include a Gold Echo from the Direct Marketing Association, an IMMY from the Information Industry Association, two Southstar Awards, an American Corporate Identity Award of Excellence, the Standard of Excellence award from the Web Marketing Association, Marketer of the Year from Early to Rise, Honorable Mention at the New York Book Festival, and Copywriter of the Year from AWAI.

Bob is a member of the Specialized Information Publishers Association (SIPA) and the Business Marketing Association (BMA). He can be reached at:

Bob Bly
Copywriter/Consultant
31 Cheyenne Drive
Montville, NJ 07045
Phone: (973) 263-0562
Fax: (973) 263-0613
Email: rwbly@bly.com
www.bly.com

INDEX